An Unsuitable Boy

A Life in Scripts

Andrew Davies

ALMA BOOKS

ALMA BOOKS LTD
60 High Street
Wimbledon Village
London SW19 5EE
United Kingdom
www.almaclassics.com

Represented by:
Authorised Rep Compliance Ltd
Ground Floor
71 Lower Baggot Street
Dublin, D02 P593
Ireland
www.arccompliance.com

An Unsuitable Boy first published by Alma Books in 2026

Cover: Nathan Burton

Printed in Great Britain by CPI Group (UK) Ltd, Croydon CR0 4YY

FSC www.fsc.org MIX Paper | Supporting responsible forestry FSC® C013604

ISBN: 978-1-84688-476-4

An Unsuitable Boy is a memoir based on the author's best recollections of various events and dialogues. Some names and identifying characteristics of individuals have been changed to respect their privacy.

Contents

TO

MY CHILDREN AND GRANDCHILDREN

An Unsuitable Boy

Foreword

This memoir started as a bunch of stories about things that have happened to me over a long life and writing career. Various people (thank you, Jenny Hewson – thank you, Ed Docx) had encouraged me to write them down, but, when I started, I found I much preferred telling them to writing them. So I asked Fiona Lindsay if she would listen, ask questions, record the conversation and write it all up. In the process I found that the book was turning into the story of a Welsh boyhood, a problematic mother and a long marriage, threaded through with tales of lengthy lunches, unexpected encounters and friendship.

The sensible thing now would be to wander back to the beginning and see how it all started. But life is not a straight line, and perhaps that is why this memoir refuses to arrange itself chronologically – which, now that I think about it, is not so very different from how I've always approached writing, letting one moment illuminate another, even if they are years apart. And so this is also a book about how to write for the screen, or at least how I do it, and all the stories have some sort of lesson that aspiring writers might find useful. But mostly they are there because they have to be told.

To give you a flavour, let's start with one from quite early on in my career, before we wade into all the love and death stuff.

The Heimlich Manoeuvre

It was nineteen seventy-something and we were eating in this genteel country place on the Welsh border. I was having steak. Rosie Hill had told me to take our director Mike Vardy out for dinner and... well, basically, tell him he was being too timid, and he needed to sex things up a bit. A lot, actually. Not the sort of thing a director likes to hear, but I had been saying this for a while to Rosie, and Rosie agreed with me, and she felt the brutal instruction would come better from the man who had written the script.

Rosie Hill was the producer, and the film – or "play", as we called it in those days – was *Heartattack Hotel*, about a gloomy and neurotic doctor and his uninhibited girlfriend, who go to stay in an isolated country-house hotel with a genial but sinister owner called Mr Todd. The guests are encouraged to eat and drink deliciously unhealthy meals, while pursuing all sorts of violent and unaccustomed exercise, from squash to hang-gliding. And, of course, the guests succumb one by one, in various expected and unexpected ways, more or less at the whim of Mr Todd.

Naturally, I had had a drink or two to prepare myself for what was bound to be a tricky conversation. I can't remember exactly how I expressed myself to Mike, but I was getting pretty animated and already attracting the attention of other diners when I realized I had inhaled a fair-sized chunk of steak and was choking to death. What a way to go. Tragic early death, promising career cut short, and so on.

But Mr Todd must have decided to spare me. Just the day before, when I was driving down the motorway, I had heard someone on the radio talking about the Heimlich manoeuvre, where you get behind the choking person and jerk your clasped fists sharply upwards into his solar plexus. And if there's no one there to do it, you can do it for yourself. So I stood up abruptly, clasped my fists together tightly and smashed them into my abdomen, while uttering the loudest roaring sound I could manage, as recommended by the man on the radio. Mike was staring up at me, ashen-faced, as well he might be. The piece of steak flew out of my mouth and landed on the next table. They weren't best pleased. I sat down, feeling fine now, and went on telling Mike how to do his job. Perhaps unsurprisingly, he quickly conceded all my points without a fight.

Job done.

Jessie, Diana, Jake and Me

It was Jessie and Diana who were friends. Back then.

I had Jake, our big cinnamon-coloured working cocker. He would lie by my feet, or on them, at one end of the sofa while Jessie and Diana had the other end. Jake loved Diana, but not as much as he loved me, and she minded that, but accepted it. Then Jake died of leukaemia, aged fourteen, in the first lockdown. He was fine on a massive dose of steroids, until he wasn't. We sat holding him while the vet gave him the injection and watched the life slip out of him. We were both grief-stricken. Diana made a big collage of Jake photos, which is still up there in the kitchen, and I still love to look at it. Now there are photos of Diana among the Jake ones.

Jessie and I tended to ignore each other. I was not a cat person. As Diana's mother, also not a cat person, would frequently say: "I wouldn't *harm* a cat, but I don't really like them." That always made me laugh. So, different ends of the sofa. Separate lives, for much of the time. She had painting and gardening. I had my writing. She had her friends. I had mine, mostly script editors and producers who liked to come to Kenilworth for meetings and lunch, and Diana would usually come to the lunches, and I was always happy and proud that my brilliant young work friends liked her and welcomed her company.

But we always had lunch together on Saturdays. Just her and me. Always at one of two or three local places we could walk to, Ego, Poms or Zizzi, because we both liked to drink wine with lunch. And we'd talk about her painting, and what I was writing or thinking of writing, and the books we'd both been reading, and our children and grandchildren, and we'd make each other laugh. The first time I made her laugh was over *Henry V*. We were both nineteen, both doing English at University College London. I annotated her copy of the play by inserting a stage direction.

MONTJOY (picking his nose): You know me by my habit.

It made her laugh then, and it still raised a smile when she was eighty-seven.

We would sometimes talk about shared experiences that went back as far as the 1950s: hitch-hiking all over Italy, the lion dog who lived in the youth hostel at Lerici and the strange green drink you could buy halfway up the steps to the castle.

We'd speculate about the other diners. There was a guy who always sat on his own in Ego and got through a whole bottle of wine at lunch, and we would wonder how many bottles he drank in the evening, and what he thought about while he was drinking. And then he wasn't there any more, and we sadly concluded the wine had done for him, "there but for the grace of God" sort of thing. He reappeared quite recently, looking absolutely fine, drank a bottle of wine with his lunch. I was so pleased to see him back at his usual table – I wanted urgently to tell Diana "He's back!", but not only could I not tell Diana, there was nobody who I could tell, no one who would find it interesting, or funny, or life-enhancing.

Sixty-eight years of us.

She was the sensible one and I was the silly one, in general. She'd been a deputy head, and she was good at managing disputes in her surprisingly volatile friendship group of elderly painters. Calm. Tactful. So it felt uproariously funny when she (very rarely) said or did something silly.

Sixty-eight years of knowing each other.

I could talk to Jessie, I suppose. I do sometimes. "I do have a life, you know, Jessie, apart from looking after you." I never used to talk to Jessie. Now we're closer than I could ever have imagined. Now she follows me upstairs. No announcement, no declaration. She didn't ask for permission. She didn't need to. She just took me over, took her place on the other side of the bed. She tells me when it's time to stop work for the day by coming to sit on the computer keyboard and shoving her pretty little face into mine. Why was I never a cat person before? Cats are wonderful. My love affair with Jessie started just after that Saturday.

We'd walked to lunch. It was warm for mid-October. The sort of day that tricks you into thinking life might be endless. Diana was buoyant. Her painting class had praised her recent work, rightly so, and I was in a good mood too. Lunch was particularly pleasant. We ate. We laughed. Keira, the manager, came and talked to us. She was expecting a baby and promised she'd bring it to show us when it arrived. And then we parted ways. Diana had some bits of shopping to do. I had a meeting at the Talisman Theatre – the local amateur theatre. They wanted me to write them a play. I said I'd think about it. Ninety minutes later I returned, breezing through the door with my usual "hello".

But something was off.

Her reply came from the living room, and her voice sounded wrong. I found her collapsed on the sofa, pale and listless. She'd been sick. I assumed it was just a violent stomach upset. Diana had a delicate stomach, and I assumed that she was going to be all right by the next day. She was dizzy. Couldn't stand. The next twenty-four hours were a blur of worry and waiting. Ringing 111. No, it didn't look like a stroke, but she kept getting worse. A doctor came. "Ears," he said. Something about balance, fluid, benign vertigo. We nodded. It sounded plausible. There had been trouble with plane travel in the past, and so it sort of made sense. For a while.

She was dizzy most of the time. Something wasn't right. Her face looked the same, and she could lift both her hands in the air. None of the classic stroke symptoms.

She tried to get up. Fell.

It was a stroke after all, as it turned out. A massive one.

She was getting worse all the time, more confused – she kept trying to get out of bed, but was too weak to stand. She wanted to drink, but she couldn't swallow. And all the time, she was trying to smile, trying to talk. Eventually the ambulance came, and they took her to the local hospital, where they diagnosed the stroke, then transferred her to the specialist unit at the big University Hospital in Coventry.

Missed by the first doctor. Caught too late. The bleed was deep and devastating, flooding her clever, kind, inquisitive brain.

"There's no point operating," the specialist said, with the sort of clarity that leaves no room for bargaining. She was moved to a side room.

And that was more or less that. Diana died.

Not that Saturday, but five days later, 19th October 2023. Time for Bill and Anna to come from Manchester and Shipley to say goodbye.

And now...

Now it's me and Jessie. We sit together in the evenings, the telly on, the wine open. She lets me rest my hand on her furry belly. It's comforting.

Me: "What does a gorgeous girl like you see in an old man like me?"

Her: "Shut up and get me some Cheese Dreamies."

We hadn't expected this ending. I was supposed to go first. I'd even had a rehearsal of sorts. 2009. Bowel cancer. Terrible stomach pain. A&E sent me home. Never go to hospital at the weekend, it's mostly locums and fill-ins and stand-bys. Constipation, the guy said, and sent me home with a stool softener. Luckily, my gut feeling was right – so to speak – and I went back and was saved, in the end, by a sharp-eyed trainee doctor called Miss Murphy, who was wearing a rather smart little cross-body bag, which I thought very stylish, though my pain level was now up to 9. They told me that I could have died. Diana joked that I was too bloody-minded to die. I don't even remember being scared. I still thought I was indestructible.

Recently I came across our Kitchen Diary for 2009. I hadn't realized that we'd kept it. Why would we? Diana kept things. "You never know when we might need it," she'd say, filing away receipts, old diaries, calendars. It was her way of preserving the past. We argued about it, mildly but regularly. My instinct is to discard what's no longer useful and move on. Hers was to store almost everything in two fireproof boxes the size of large briefcases – car repair bills, insurance papers, vet records – until the lids barely shut. I'd quietly remove the more irrelevant documents when she wasn't looking. It was an ongoing domestic equipoise. The calendar was full of appointments, then nothing for the second half of October and the first half of November. The illness month. And then, at the end of the month: Writers' Guild Awards. They were going to give me a Lifetime Award, otherwise known as a "fuck off and die" award.

But I refused to accept that, having just survived. I felt frail, thinner than I'd been since my twenties, suit hanging off me. I must have looked as though I'd been through something. I had. When I stood up to speak, I made a point of reassuring them. I said that I'd no intention of "fucking off and dying" – that I intended to carry on writing. There was laughter, of course. But I knew quite a few of them thought I looked ready for the knacker's yard. Seventeen years later, I'm still here, very much to my surprise.

We started planning after that. Putting our affairs in order, as they say. But we both assumed it would be me who'd go first. I certainly did. In my forties I used to think I'd be ready to die by fifty. But then you hit eighty-nine and realize you've become a walking paradox, ancient in age, but somehow still startled by it. Diana and I used to say, "I can't believe I'm eighty." Her mother would kick her legs in the air saying, "Look at that: not bad for eighty-four!" Age is a peculiar condition. I walk up a hill and feel a hundred. I write lines for Lydia Bennet or Louisa Musgrove and I feel like a nineteen-year-old girl. *Catch me, Captain Wentworth!* I look in the mirror and see… well, it depends on the angle. The older I get, the closer I feel to all my younger selves, including the ones that I don't particularly like.

Is there a name for that peculiar period between someone dying and their funeral? There should be. It's a strange, suspended zone, full of phone calls and paperwork, undertakers and arrangements, as if bureaucracy might shield us from grief, if we just fill in the right form. Registering a death is a curious business. Because Diana had died in hospital in Coventry, I had to register her death there.

I went in on the little train from Kenilworth. The Register Office was surprisingly difficult to find, in a little tangle of medieval streets that had escaped the bombing during the Second World War. The registrar had a wary look – was I going to fall on her shoulder in floods of tears, or rage at her incoherently? I guess she must get a lot of that, hence the thick Plexiglas screen between us. But I wanted to be a good boy and do it right, and I thought I saw relief flooding her features – "Good, this one's an easy one." I felt an urge to tell her about that Saturday, but I guessed she would get a lot of that too, so I didn't. I'll tell you, though.

We didn't know that Saturday would be our last lunch. Just two people sharing a meal in a place we'd been to dozens of times before. What would we have done differently if we'd known? Probably nothing. In that in-between time, I wrote a poem. And I read it at her funeral, without choking up, just about.

Last Lunch

She had the fish cakes and the skinny fries,
Ketchup and mayonnaise,
Large glass of Chardonnay:
She knew what she liked.
I ordered pepperoni pizza for a change.
Both of us happy with our choices
And happy with each other too.
I thought how pretty she still was.
But didn't say so. We were happy.
Neither of us had the least idea
It was our last lunch together.

Lots of people came back to the house, and we drank a lot of wine, and people chose paintings to take away as keepsakes. And quite a few people stayed the night, and there was a lot more drinking and some improvised meals. And then, all of a sudden, I was on my own with Jessie and a lot of admin to do.

*

I've started sketching myself – charcoal, mostly. I try to capture what's really there. Some days I get the lines right. Other days I give up and start again with my left hand. The lack of control makes it strangely more honest. Something about surrendering precision allows the truth to seep through.

Drawing has been with me for as long as writing has. It's not something I feel I have to be good at. I *have* to be good at writing. Drawing can be more like playing, and I try to keep it like that, resist being too self-critical. When I draw with my left hand, things appear on the page that feel raw and unguarded. It's a bit like dreaming on paper.

I had a painter friend in Bristol, years ago. Actually, it was John (Sukey) Phillips, my friend since primary school. And I envied him. Diana and I would visit his studio, full of canvases and turpentine and half-finished sculptures. Physical, permanent things. He'd ask what I was writing, and all I had to show him was words on paper. Made me feel a bit insubstantial.

Diana and I used to go to life-drawing classes together in the early days in London, at Saint Martin's on the Charing Cross Road, then spend an hour at the cartoon cinema (Bugs Bunny, Mr Magoo) and then a meal at the Athenian restaurant. Spaghetti, rissoles, rice and chips for two and sixpence. There was a crazy old man who would sit on his own with a big book on the table, having a furious argument with his imaginary friend. We would spend happy hours drawing each other in the nude in our ramshackle flat in Holloway. When we were older, but not yet antique, we took to walking holidays. The arrangement was satisfyingly simple: a comfortable hotel, breakfast fortified with Italian coffee, then the walk. Downhill to start – Italy is full of hill towns – walking for four hours or so, then a van would meet us at lunchtime with a picnic lunch and as much wine as you wanted. If you were knackered, or just feeling lazy, you could take the van in the afternoon. Otherwise, the day finished with a steep climb to the next hill town. Diana and me and a group of strangers. At the beginning we always wondered how we were going to survive a week with this lot – by the end, we were comrades. Or survivors.

I would sketch every time we stopped – quick pen sketches on an A6 pad, small enough to go in the pocket of a pair of shorts. A row of shuttered windows, a vineyard stretching away into the distance. And Diana. I would draw her ahead of me on the path, or sitting at a café table, or studying the map. I always drew her younger than she was. Not deliberately. That was simply how she existed in my mind. Some part of her had never left her twenties. She used to tease me about the colouring. I'd do the drawing on the walk, then wait until evening to add the watercolour, back at the hotel. "If you're going to use colour," she'd say, "you should do it properly, outdoors." *En plein air*. "You're just like a kid colouring in."

Drawing and painting were something we shared without rivalry, which may be why it worked. Our work was entirely different. When Diana began painting in earnest, she was almost stubbornly naturalistic. Then gradually things loosened. She would start with an accurate depiction of the view, then it would get more and more abstract – you could see the progression through three or four versions. Every so often she would hit on something that really sang to her. When that happened, I would suggest she push it. Do more in that vein. Do twenty. Do thirty. Diana never agreed. Once she'd done a thing well, she had no interest in repeating herself. I admired that about her.

*

Now at home I draw Jessie, or my own reflected image. We have a hand mirror and a full-length mirror. (I still say "we" – maybe I always will.) And sometimes, when I position each just so, I can catch both profiles. One side is firm, defiant. "Don't mess with that old man," it says. The other side looks cautious. Slightly apologetic. As if it's not quite sure life was the right decision. Someone once said to me, with a sort of fond contempt, "You're just a timid venturer, aren't you?" She was someone who was reckless with herself and suffered for it. I was never that reckless with myself. I hedged my bets. Now I'm an old man, my parents long dead, my wife recently dead, I feel an urge to be bolder, to go all the way.

Neil, who teaches our life-drawing class, is obsessed with realism, working slowly and meticulously. I'm faster. Looser. Happiest when I scrawl something in sixty seconds that tells the truth the longer drawing missed. I like the surprise. And I've started writing more like that. No plan, just let it happen. I can do it the other way, make a meticulous plan, know in advance what will go on every page, but it's more exciting to launch into the unknown, try to surprise myself. And sometimes, if I'm lucky, it takes shape. The thing you didn't know you needed to say. So here I am. Trying to turn the lens inwards for once. Trying to make sense of being human, of being near the end, surrounded by the remnants of a lifetime, and still feeling remarkably frisky.

*

We've been in the same house since 1970. A big Edwardian 1902 semi. It was only ever the second house we lived in together, and then we bought the house next door in 2000 on a slightly mad whim and knocked through, creating far more space than we really needed. But Diana wanted a studio to paint in, and I fancied a proper office, something like the one Michael Wearing had when he was Head of Drama at the BBC in the Nineties. I had this vision: a large desk at one end, where the actual writing happened, and then a comfy bit with sofas and chairs at the other end, for meetings, or simply relaxing. I made it happen, and it was my writing base for a couple of decades. Now I write in the front room downstairs, where I started. It's the one with the best light and the right kind of distraction from the street outside, and it's near the kitchen, where the drinks and the cheese lurk temptingly. I call it "the front room". It's the *dining room*, Diana would say. It was a long-running dispute, but we struck a deal: if more than one guest was expected, I had to clear away my papers and restore it to its former life as a dining room. She would walk in, inspect the table like a headmistress checking for graffiti, and nod, sometimes even smile, when it passed muster.

These days, there's no more wrangling about rooms. And the dining room remains my preferred battlefield, where I sit, as I'm doing now, wondering whether today is a writing day or one of those oddly seductive days when *not* writing feels almost like part of the process.

Jessie has just walked in.

Me: "What do you think, Jess? Should I write the story of my life?"

I feel Diana's presence. Hear her voice, dry, amused, affectionate: "Isn't that what you've always done?"

Hilda, Wynford and Me

My parents, Hilda and Wynford, owned one of those rather grandiose maple-wood dressing tables, an Art Deco thing, with a three-way mirror that could either reflect your best angle or reduce you to a fragmented patchwork of limbs, depending on how you positioned the wings. And there, as a child, I would often find myself, on the dressing-table stool, the big double bed behind me, watching the mirrored world unfold, fascinated by the multiplied images of my parents and me. Hundreds of images, getting smaller and smaller until they shrank into tiny dots. It is, curiously, one of the very few memories I retain of them in the same bed. What was their sex life like? I didn't like to think about it. But there was a book in the glass-fronted bookshelf downstairs, *Ideal Marriage: Its Physiology and Technique* by Doctor Theodoor Hendrik van de Velde – Dutch, obviously, and relentlessly informative.

Doctor van de Velde thought that the aim of marriage consisted in sexual gratification shared by husband and wife. There were diagrams, descriptions, helpful hints. Very idealistic. It would have been my father who bought it. He was always teaching himself stuff. He taught himself Russian in the war, just in case. He was also inclined to try to please and satisfy my mother. But she was not easy to please, and became less and less so. As to sex, who knows? Not me, for sure. But there was something wrong, I think.

My mother, Hilda. Glamorous in her youth, all smouldering Celtic beauty with dark hair and eyes the colour of sea glass. In early photographs she looks like trouble. You can see why my father fell for her.

When I was born in September 1936, I was just what my mother wanted: blue-eyed like her, curly-haired, eager to please. I was a performer. She liked that. So long as I remained an extension of her, singing solos at Sunday school, topping the class, she was delighted.

But her adoration was conditional. She had been a much-indulged youngest child, and she didn't play nicely.

Maybe she adored my father once, too. He was handsome, in a wiry sort of way, big brown eyes like Rudolph Valentino, lean verging on skinny. "Steel and whipcord," he'd say, flexing his biceps. "Steel and whipcord." And very clever. My mother, who had many admirers, chose him at university. She studied History. He read Modern Languages. After university they followed the usual pattern of their era: courtship, engagement, teaching jobs (his in London, hers in Presteigne, a Welsh border town where her pupils still rode ponies to school) and then marriage. He secured his dream post at Cardiff High School for Boys, "the best school in Wales, bar none", he would say to anyone who hadn't asked. She gave up teaching, as all married women had to in the Thirties. He was fulfilled. She was frustrated.

Her family were comfortably middle class, grocers, though of the upwardly mobile variety. My grandfather famously declined a merger with a fellow called Thomas. Had he agreed, the business would have been named Thomas and Jones. Instead, Thomas found an Evans, and Thomas & Evans went on to become the largest grocery firm in Wales. My maternal grandmother, Elizabeth Rudd, was half Scottish and half Middlesbrough, not posh at all. She told me I was part of the Murray clan, which thrilled me until I discovered the tartan was mostly sludge-green and depression-blue. She liked to recite Scots rhymes – I remember one fragment that went:

> As I gi'd by my granny's house,
> I smelt the smell of bun;
> I gi'd in and soughed a bit;
> She widnae gie us a crumb;
> She took up the butter plate
> And broke it o'er me bum,
> So I took up the bellowses
> An' blew her up the lum!

She laughed a lot, and once, with a wink, pointed out the middle one in an old photograph of three grinning sailors, and said, "That one could give you a good squeeze." I didn't fully grasp the implications at the time, but I knew this: she had none of my mother's tight-lipped fury. Looking back, I don't think she started life as middle class, but when I knew her, she had a fur muff and a fox fur with sharp eyes and sharper teeth she used to waggle at me. I was a bit scared of that fox. And she had a Pekinese called Roger who was a bit irritable. He used to get carried a lot, and I think as a consequence he would quarrel with dogs who walked on their feet: "Come and have a go if you think you're hard enough!" – but he knew he was safe, and Grandma would tuck him into her muff. She died when I was eight and was laid out on the dining-room table – I think they put the extra leaf in to accommodate the coffin. The adults suggested that I might want to go in and "say goodbye". I said, "No, thank you." The truth was, I liked her alive. I was frightened of her dead.

*

Dib, my mother's eldest sibling, was very pretty and had been brought up as a young lady. She did voluntary work for St John Ambulance, lunched with friends, wore gloves. She was a wonderfully affectionate aunt, and she was also my champion. Unlike my mother, Dib loved me unconditionally. Time with Dib was always an occasion. If I was drying the dishes or trudging beside her on a long walk, she'd pass the time by recounting the films she'd watched at the picture house. She went twice a week. Her storytelling was sublime. Better than the films themselves, I suspect. She could make even a limp B-movie sound like *Casablanca*. I fretted for the heroines. I admired the villains. I learnt more about narrative arc from Dib's retellings than I ever did in English lessons. And probably more about people too, about longing and folly and why adults so often make a mess of everything.

Walter, my uncle, was another vivid presence. He taught History at Cardiff High School for Boys and directed the school play. He smoked a pipe, and had a leather tobacco pouch, which smelt wonderfully fragrant. He called me "Andrew Wynford Billy-Buster Davies". I liked that. It made me feel important. Walter, like Dib, lived at home with Grandma, and it looked for a while as if he was destined for lifelong bachelorhood, until scandal struck. He fell in love with a schoolgirl.

Now, I must clarify: he was a teacher, she was of age (eventually), and this was an era when such things were whispered about but not automatically criminalized. Her name was Jean, and she was a beauty. I remember her decades later, when she was an old lady, telling me wide-eyed, as if shocked by her younger self: "We'd catch the train together from Heath Halt to Queen Street and, if no one was looking, we'd kiss on the platform. And me in my school hat!" My mother, who had been Walter's pet, resented Jean from the start. Jean was ravishingly pretty and fond of getting her own way, like most of us, and Walter was crazy about her. They were forty-two and twenty-one when they married.

Compared to Dib and Walter, my mother seemed tightly coiled. Why she was so bound up, so resistant to pleasure or abandon, remains an ongoing mystery. She was happiest, oddly, at the seaside: she would let herself go then, allowing the waves to slap her around while she bobbed like a cork. Always cheerful even when it was raining. It's great to be in the sea when it's raining. Not so much fun getting dressed afterwards. Perhaps the water reminded her of a freer time, of a self she'd long since hidden away. The odd thing was, she couldn't swim.

My father's childhood was altogether different. He was the youngest of eight, born into a working-class Welsh family who'd left farm labouring for the mines. All his brothers went down the mine by fourteen and emerged, miraculously, as union men, businessmen and even a mayor of Porthcawl. Their father, my grandfather, was a coalface contractor – which meant he was the man who negotiated a deal with the bosses to open up new seams, basically to hack through mountains for a living. Piecework. He had a small team of terrifying men who worked with him. Difficult and dangerous work, and my grandad was the brains of it. Some of his gang were Irish. One of them had no teeth, and one of them spat into the fire when he was waiting for his share of the wages, which my grandad doled out on a Friday night from the front room of the family house. My dad remembered being terrified by these underworld monsters, having himself been brought up with good manners. Wynford was lucky enough to escape the mines entirely. By the time his turn came, the family had money, enough so he could stay on at school. And he ran with it. He won a scholarship to Cardiff University and got a First.

And so these two wildly different people collided. Perhaps she was drawn to the faint air of danger that clung to his rough Valley roots. And perhaps he was captivated by her polish and pedigree. A bit like *Lady Chatterley*, with significantly fewer orgasms (though how would I know?). Two people looking for something in each other that neither of them possessed. There's something tragic about an intelligent woman thwarted by the very domesticity she was trained to long for. It's not that she wanted more, necessarily. It's more, I think, that she didn't know what she wanted, except to be the object of everyone's attention. I wonder whether she resented him, or the situation?

*

For the first eight years of my life, it was just the three of us: Andrew, Hilda and Wynford. Then my brother Peter was born, a late addition. He arrived like a conker dropped from a tree: a round-faced, brown-eyed boy. I liked him well enough, but the age gap meant we were slightly out of step. I was conquering imaginary kingdoms; he was barely managing stairs – though by the time he was four or five he was showing signs of being a mathematical prodigy with a photographic memory. If you told him your birth date, he could tell you the day, and all the days up to your hundredth birthday. And he taught himself to read from the names of the local cinemas in the *South Wales Echo* – the Monico, the Plaza, the Regent, the Ninian, and so on. He was clearly on the spectrum, years before anyone had heard of it. An infant prodigy.

Once he could walk without toppling, I allowed him into my private adventures. It was very much of a country childhood: bows and arrows, butterfly-hunting, bird-nesting, catapults. No TV, of course. Then came the incident on the Wenallt. The Wenallt was, still is, a big hill to the north of Cardiff, between Rhiwbina and Caerphilly. One day I marched him up it and we both ran down, which was enormously exhilarating up to the moment when he tripped and snapped his wrist. I took him into the house of some friends, who called a doctor. I was, of course, entirely to blame, but no one asked, and I wasn't volunteering. That feeling of being guilty but having got away with it is a familiar one, and still comes back to poke at me in dreams.

An example: when I was about nine, an annoying kid kept hanging around me and my friends, and he wouldn't go away, so I beat him up. He was bigger than me, but he was a soft kid, and I knew I could beat him up, so I did, and he ran home crying. His father came round to our house to complain, and my father called me to the front door. My victim's dad gaped and said: "What, this little chap?" I did look very sweet with my curls and everything, but I knew I was to blame. The kid was asking for it, but even so, I didn't have to hurt him that much, or at all. My dad seemed quite proud of me. He'd have been in fights as a kid – the Rhondda Valley was a tough place. Steel and whipcord. But I wouldn't, couldn't tell him the truth: that I was the villain of the story.

*

Another soft boy called Eryl Basset lived over the road, and his indulgent dad bought him a real bow with a quiver of real steel-tipped arrows, which was a bit silly of him, come to think of it. Now I thought of myself as king of the home-made bows and arrows – I used to shoot the goldenrod arrows right over the roof.

I demanded a go with Eryl's brand-new bow. I must have had a gleam in my eye or something, because he panicked and ran back over the road. I got him in the bum just as he was going through the gate. It was like *Seven Samurai*, or something, though Kurosawa had not made his masterpiece yet. Anyway, another dad at the front door. I said it was an accident and got away with it again. I was not nearly as nice as I looked.

A few years earlier, I was four or five. I had a friend called Jennifer. Her parents, Uncle Ron and Auntie Kay, were close friends of my parents, and I have lots of photos of us having picnics or playing in their big garden. Ron was an expert photographer with a proper professional camera, and he took lots of lovely photos of Jennifer and me in our Red Indian suits. Their house was larger than ours, painted white, with green shutters. It wasn't part of Rhiwbina Garden Village, where we lived: it stood out architecturally and socially. I think I had a sense even then that Uncle Ron and Auntie Kay came from a posher and more moneyed class.

One afternoon we were in the garden and Jennifer said:

"Let's make poisons."

"Erm… OK," I said, not yet sensing where this might lead.

"We'll make them out of rosehips and things like that."

"Who are we going to poison?" I asked, already uneasy.

"Our mummies and daddies."

I was deeply troubled by this proposal. At that point in my life, I was very fond of both my mummy and my daddy and had no wish to see them slipping quietly away after ingesting crushed rosehips. Jennifer, however, was quite emphatic. I learnt much later that her mother was in the process of leaving her father for another woman. In the early 1940s that was not merely private upheaval: it was scandal. My mother found it incomprehensible that a woman might prioritize her own longings over the supposed stability of her family. It seemed to her an act of betrayal. But my father was shocked too, he told me much later. They'd been very close with Ron and Kay, and this marriage breakup made him feel that nothing was secure and anything could happen. But Ron, he said, seemed to take it in his stride. Perhaps he had seen it coming for a long time. Jennifer's poison plot now strikes me as less theatrical and more remedial. Something was breaking at home. She wanted to retaliate or perhaps restore order by drastic means. Poison felt decisive.

We met for lunch a few years ago, me and Jennifer, at the National Gallery in London. Two octogenarians discussing childhood over lunch. We talked about her parents' separation, about that period of whispered conversations and adult tension. And then, quite calmly, she said, "Erm... and we looked at each other's private parts."

I hadn't expected that to surface. It was an oddly spicy memory to dust off in a gallery café, surrounded by tourists and Renaissance madonnas. But there it was. We'd been curious. That was all. There's something deeply comic about discussing childhood misdemeanours when you're in your mid-eighties. And also, not comic at all. As children our friendship had been intense, and eighty-year-old Jennifer had wanted to remind me of it. That time of innocence and transgression when anything seemed possible. However placid Jennifer looked now, she wasn't placid inside. She wanted to remind me of how close, how intimate we had been. We finished our lunch like civilized people and went our separate ways, carrying with us the awkward brilliance of having been children amid adult chaos.

We lived in Rhiwbina Garden Village, which sounds like something out of a pamphlet promoting utopian living – and, in a way, it was. Even now, if you tell anyone from South Wales that you come from Rhiwbina, they'll say "There's posh!" – even though it wasn't, not really. But it was a nice place to grow up in. Every house was built to look identical, a sort of egalitarian Lego set, and the idea was that the mix of large and small houses on the same street would create a socially harmonious blend. All the gardens were neatly trimmed, nobody owned anything outright, and everyone rented. The effect was equality, or at least the illusion of it. Our road, which was called Lon-y-dail, had wide grass verges on which we played cricket. Idyllic, really. My school, Rhiwbina Junior, was just at the top of the road. Those early years, in that village, felt so safe. Even the war didn't darken the tone too much.

Cardiff was a port city, blackened by industry, strategically useful and therefore vulnerable. The docks at Tiger Bay and Splott suffered bombing raids during the war. German aircraft targeted the coal exports, the shipping, the industrial infrastructure that made Cardiff matter. Incendiaries fell. Warehouses burned. Windows shattered. People died. Stories reached us in fragments. Adults spoke in lowered tones about nights when the eastern sky glowed red. About explosions near Bute Street. About roofs gone and families relocated. Names of streets would circulate like cautionary tales. The war did not feel abstract, nor did it feel close. In Rhiwbina the destruction seemed to subside before it reached us. It was as if some invisible dome had been placed over our tidy semi-detached world. Bombs had fallen elsewhere in Cardiff. But, to a child, familiarity and safety become synonymous. If your house still stands, the universe appears reliable. Blackout curtains were part of a nightly ritual. Street lamps dimmed. Occasionally the siren would start – that long, mechanical wail slicing through conversation – and there would be brisk instructions. Indoors. Quickly now. No fuss. Some families had underground shelters in the back garden. We had a vast thing in the dining room called the Morrison Table. It was made of sheet steel, like a tank. When there was an air raid, we all got underneath it. I was forever getting egg-shaped bruises on my forehead from walking into it.

We were lucky enough to have an extra bit of land at the side of our house. It was called "the spare bit". There was a cherry tree on the front part of it that grew huge. Behind that was a twisted tangle of scrub, like a Japanese jungle, good for imaginative games. One time, one of my little girl friends – was it Alison? – wanted to do a number two, and I persuaded her it was perfectly OK to do it in the spare-bit jungle, where there were convenient dock leaves to wipe herself with. So she did, and I watched the surprisingly large bright-brown turd emerge from her bottom.

At the side of the spare bit was the lane that led to the shops. Before you got to the proper ones, there was Mrs Jones's shop, a tiny hole-in-the-wall place I was allowed to go to when I was very small because no proper roads were involved. It was more of a gossip hub than an actual shop, and one day I was in there and people were talking, and I got the impression that they thought we were not winning the war. I was scared, and went home and told my parents, who said of course we were going to win the war. I got a feeling that they weren't so sure. It would have been 1940 or 1941 then, before the Americans got into it.

We still ate well, by our standards. One of our staples was Woolton pie, a celebration of root vegetables named after the Minister of Food, Lord Woolton. Whether he invented it or not, we blamed him entirely. Mum would serve it with a grand flourish, and we'd chant: "The Woolton pie, the Woolton pie, Willie Willie Woolton, the Woolton pie!"

She wasn't a great cook. Her heart wasn't in it. My dad would grow huge marrows, like Zeppelins full of watery green juice, and my mother would cook them in more water. But food was fuel, and not supposed to taste nice. I was amazed when I got Elizabeth David's *Book of Mediterranean Food* and followed her instructions. Something as simple as an omelette could be a delicate delight. I was twenty then, cooking for the first time, and living in a top-floor flat at 20 Buckingham Street, WC2, the poshest address I've ever had – I will tell you later how I came to be there.

Hilda did love words, though. I remember the teacher asking us to make up a nursery rhyme, and my mother entered one of her own. It went:

> Mousy, Mousy Mumper,
> Can you knit a jumper?
> One pearl, two chain,
> Get to the end, and begin it again.
>
> Bunny knit a sweater.
> She could do it better.
> One pearl. Two plain.
> Get to the end and begin again.

My father loved music. We didn't have a piano or a gramophone, but he listened to music on the wireless all the time.

When I was very little, he would carry me in his arms and sing to me. He sang a lot of the songs from *The Beggar's Opera*, which had had a popular revival in the 1920s, 'Pretty Polly' or 'Over the Hills and Far Away' – and, if not those, the grand strains of Beethoven's symphonies, into which he wove lyrics of his own invention. There was a peculiar magic to it, a kind of enchantment wrought from music and warmth, the steady rise and fall of his breath beneath my cheek. I sometimes wish someone could arrange for me to be carried like that again, carried about and sung to. I would do it myself as a young married man, carrying my baby boy Bill in his Babygro suit, singing "Hey, Mr Tambourine Man, sing a song for Suit… He's not sleepy and there ain't no place he's going to…" I sort of long for those days too.

My dad told stories.

"One day, Andrew went walking in the forest, all by himself. And there, in a little clearing, was a big stag… and the big stag came right up to Andrew… and what did Andrew say?"

"Boo!" I'd shout.

"And away bounded the big stag!"

*

After he died, I found the beginnings of a novel about a teacher who seemed very much like him, in a school very much like Cardiff High School. Abandoned after a few pages. Maybe he felt that he didn't need to be a writer. He was a teacher, the best teacher I ever had.

He had a party piece, a mock sermon, 'The *Ship of Cardiff*', which he would do in the vein of an old-style preacher.

"And so the *Ship of Cardiff* sailed out from Cardiff Bay that Sunday, and all the people were happy and gay, all of them in their best Sunday suits, just as you are now, and they couldn't have been happier, and they couldn't have been jollier… but oh, my friends, a terrible thing – I can hardly bring myself to tell you – the *Ship of Cardiff* sank. It sank to the bottom of the sea, and every one of those people was drowned. But why did it sink? Why did it sink? Because it had a hole in its bottom. Yes. It had a hole in its bottom. (Sudden fortissimo roar) AND ALL OF YOU HAVE GOT HOLES IN YOUR BOTTOMS!"

I remember once, when I was about fourteen, I said, "I think I have a natural flair for modern languages."

My father, unmoved: "That may or may not be the case. But if you don't learn your irregular verbs, your natural flair will be neither here nor there."

Not long after, I told him I wanted to be a writer.

"Only a handful of writers make any money," he said. "You'd be better off getting a job that doesn't demand too much of your time. Then you can write what you like."

"What about teaching?" I asked.

"No," he said. "Do something more interesting than that." Why would he say that? I knew he thought there was no better job than teaching. Nevertheless, I became a writer. And my day job? Teaching. I enjoyed both, and in time I found some early success with the writing, though never anywhere near enough to live on. When I was twenty, he told me, "If you haven't published a novel by the time you're thirty, you might as well pack it in."

I turned thirty. Still no novel. I asked him if he thought I should give up.

"Why?"

"You told me I should pack it in."

"Did I?" He looked bewildered, then shook his head. "Silly thing to say. I mean, you've had a Wednesday Play on, and all sorts."

"But I've been carrying what you said around for ten years."

He laughed. "You shouldn't take so much notice of me. What do I know about anything?"

*

Years later, I found myself in Los Angeles, in the sleek, air-conditioned hush of Sam Goldwyn Jr's office. My son, Bill, had just earned a First in Electroacoustics. I asked Sam whether he minded if I made a quick call to my father to share the news. "Not at all," Sam said. "Put him on speaker."

I told my father, the pride swelling in my voice.

"Well," my father said, "I'm not surprised at all. Talent often skips a generation."

Sam Goldwyn Jr looked appalled. "A father would say that to his son?"

"It's all right, Sam," I said. "It's a joke. South Wales humour."

Another bit of South Wales humour, not my dad's, but in the same vein: the Welsh have their own version of the BAFTAs, sometimes rudely called "the Tafftas", which they take very seriously. I had adapted Kingsley Amis's novel *The Old Devils*, set in South Wales, and we had been nominated in every category. We were up against three other shows, all in the Welsh language, and as every category came up, one of the Welsh-language shows would be announced as the winner. Tristram Powell (the director) and I went for a consolatory piss. And as we were standing at the urinal, we heard this lugubrious Swanseaish voice: "Look at them. In their dinner jackets. All the way from bloody London. Nominated in every category. Haven't won a bloody thing. I mean, you have to pity them, don't you?" And this other voice said: "No, you don't." We never saw who they were. Hard to turn round when you're peeing.

My parents encouraged my individuality in different ways. Mum insisted I shine, and I was happy to. At Sunday school, I was selected to sing solos. The woman in charge, Mrs Oldfield-Davies, was married to someone important at the BBC. She favoured me, and Mum glowed. I'd coop in the huge pulpit, hiding until it was my moment to rise. My companion in this ritual was Pat Thomas, whose voice was angelic. We'd wait together, crouching like conspirators, and then rise up and mesmerize the congregation. Me and Pat Thomas. She was pretty too.

School Days

Before I went to Rhiwbina Junior, I went to a little private school called, rather pretentiously, Greenways Preparatory School. It was a dame school, really, run by two ladies who were both called Miss Emery. They seemed old to me, and, though kind, they could be very firm indeed. If you said swear-words, they would wash your mouth out with soap and water, it was said, though I never knew that to happen, even to Vivian Fox, who knew lot of naughty words. Did I have a blazer? Probably, though I can't remember it. I certainly had a cap, quartered into red and green segments. We walked to the school up Beulah Road, named after the chapel at the crossroads – which was pretty much the village hub, and still is. Of the four corners the chapel had one, its hall the one opposite, and the other two were the newsagent's (from whom I would later steal pens and notebooks) and the library. The first shop up from the chapel hall was Lewis the butcher's, which usually had a couple of dogs outside, hanging about hopefully. Mr Lewis had only two fingers on his left hand: he had chopped the others off.

It always seemed a long walk up Beulah Road, less so on the way back. I can remember (this is probably when I was just a toddler) walking behind my parents up that road and getting left behind, and thinking I would never catch up to them, they seemed so impossibly far ahead. I remember wailing "Wait for meeeeeee!" I recently wrote that memory into my Charles Dickens biopic: little Charles toiling up Gad's Hill behind his father: "Wait for meeeeeee!" The Misses Emery taught us the old-fashioned way, pot-hooks and hard sums. There were only about ten pupils altogether. You could stay for lunch, but I went home for mine. The only time I did stay they gave me slices of liver sausage, which seemed very exotic to me, and I formed a lifetime fondness for it. In fact, I wouldn't mind a bit now.

*

When I was nearly seven, I started at Rhiwbina Junior School, which was just at the top of Lon-y-dail, where we lived at No. 10. But when I got there, I was directed to the Infants, which alarmed me. I was not an infant any more, I was a big boy now, I felt. But I was too shaken to assert myself. It turned out that they were making a ceremony of the transition. We would spend the first half of the morning in the Infants and then process to the Juniors. In the mean time, the teacher gave us some writing to do. I had been taught copperplate handwriting at the Misses Emery's, and I set about it. The kids around me started giggling and pointing: "Look! He can only do scribble!" The teacher came to see. "No!" she said. "What he is doing is *real writing*, which you will start to learn in the Juniors. What you have been doing is *printing*." I felt vindicated, but it didn't make me immediately popular. Then it was playtime.

My mother had unwisely sent me to school in my Greenways cap, and as soon as we were in the playground someone snatched it off my head and they all started playing catch with it. I tried and tried to get it back, and I was close to tears. Then a boy took pity on me and got my cap back. "Put it away now and don't bring it tomorrow," he said. He was called Graham Leonard, and he became my first good friend at school. He wasn't very big, but he never had to fight, because everybody knew how tough he was and would avoid confrontation with him. Having Graham for a friend gave me a good start in playground life: if Graham liked me, I must be all right, despite my posh kid's cap and my funny handwriting.

*

Tom Sawyer was my hero, and I had a romantic streak largely because of Becky Thatcher. I had my own Becky, of course. Sheila Bateman. Jet-black hair, olive skin, sharp nose and, crucially, intellectually superior. She once asked me, "What's the adjective from *bugger*?" She thought it might be "buggerish", or "bugarish" as she spelt it. I was enchanted. I knew she was wrong, but it was charming. I was smitten and determined to make her mine. It was on Good Friday when I decided that I'd call on her and see if she wanted to come on a walk with me. I went round to her house and stood on the doorstep waiting anxiously for someone to open it and hoping that it wouldn't be her mum. It was, and clearly very amused by this small curly-haired boy saying, "Can Sheila come out?"

"Well, you need to tell me what you want to do first."

"Just go for a walk."

"Well, she'll have to wear her wellies."

Sheila emerged, in her wellies, and we walked. It was an ordinary moment that has lingered for decades. So much so that years later I even wrote a poem about it.

First Date

Sheila her name was. Sheila Bateman.
We sat together at the back.
Her thin brown face,
Eyes almost black.
She had the sharpest nose I'd ever seen.
Listen – we had this caterpillar in a matchbox,
And he was ours, not mine or hers,
And he was green. We had
Ambitions for him.
We had this argument about an adjective:
I said it was "buggering", but she took
Her Conway Stewart fountain pen
And wrote down "bugarish"!
I admired her handwriting
And didn't tell her she was wrong because I loved her.
On Good Friday, I went round her house and rang the bell.
Her mother came. She said yes, Sheila could come out,

But she would have to wear her wellies.
We walked for miles. Bright grass, black hedges.
No one but her and me. We were so
Quiet and slow together.
Listen – it felt so strange
Just walking. Holding her hand,
Walking this slow quiet walk,
Looking down at our wet black wellies
Pacing together. Hers skinnier than mine,
Their dark firm imprint on the bright wet grass,
Each step unique and irrecoverable.
I don't remember walking back. It was our first and only date.
I think I must have felt it was enough.

Across the road from our house lay a vast, communal field, our own Arcadia, ideal for cricket, camping and a burgeoning curiosity about the world. It was where we had bonfires for VE Day and VJ Day. The big boys let me join in their games, as long as I wasn't a liability. A dropped catch or a misfield would earn you a swift rebuke: "You silly cow!" or "You silly cunt!" I knew that "cow" was rude, so I assumed "cunt" was simply a milder version of "cow". I returned home and, watching my mother spill some milk, declared helpfully, "You silly cunt!" The look on her face! The explosion of outrage!

"Where did you learn a word like that?"

"Over the field," I said cheerily. "The big boys say it all the time."

"Well, you must never go there again!"

I did, of course. Every chance I got.

*

The field became our kingdom – a muddy, sunlit laboratory of juvenile misrule. We built dens, invented secret societies, fought battles and tested boundaries. One hot summer afternoon, a mixed crowd of boys and girls began peeing on each other for no particular reason – it just seemed like a good idea at the time. We were all laughing fit to burst. Our arcing piss caught the light like fountains in Versailles. It was the kind of thing you only do once – or so it seemed to me – though I guess it can be the hobby of a lifetime for some people. We dabbled in camping, too, hauling canvas tents into the field and pretending we were intrepid scouts. Most of us sloped off home to sleep in proper beds after dusk. I did once brave the night, only to be caught in a thunderstorm, drenched to the skin. One day, we received a visit from a figure of legend. He was a barrel-shaped boy with a genial, piggy face – Spud Murphy, he was called. The rumour, probably unfounded, was that he regularly buggered his brother. I wasn't even sure what it meant, but at that age this made him both taboo and oddly glamorous. He arrived, accepted our invitation to come in our tent. He showed us his prodigious todger, and invited ours to be displayed in return, but was unimpressed.

"Can you get stuff to come out of it?" he asked.

"You mean piss?" someone ventured.

"No. Spunk."

He demonstrated. We were astonished.

"Never mind," he said magnanimously. "You'll all be spunking away in a little while."

He was wrong in my case. It took me longer than predicted. When it did arrive, it came in the form of a catastrophic wet dream in which I was trapped in bed with my mother, trying to get out but being suffocated by the bedclothes and her hot, hairy body, culminating in an explosion that felt as if all my insides were coming out of me. Not a propitious start. Nor the last time that my mother haunted my dreams.

*

Rhiwbina Junior School was strange, sometimes reassuring, sometimes alarming. I was good at pretty much everything, so that meant I had an easy time in the classroom, rarely getting into trouble. The headmaster was called Mr Pugsley, and he did have a face like a dog. He was short and squat, wore a black suit and carried a cane. I did get caned once by Mr Pugsley, on the hand, and it hurt. There was a very fierce teacher called Mr Green, whose shout made you jump. He had a very hairy green jacket that felt all prickly when he called you out to the front to inspect your work. And then in the top class we had Miss Foster, who wore a curious leather flying helmet sort of thing, and was a fiend for mental arithmetic. The playground was a different world, more brutal and anarchic. We would play rough games like Bomberino. One team would line up, bent over, each with his head between the legs of the boy in front, with the front boy right up against the wall. Then the other team would take a long run-up and leap-frog onto the crouching team and try to collapse them. And on the school field, as well as the usual games, we would play War, with sides of as many as fifty or sixty. I learnt the pleasures of getting wounded, which meant you got to be nursed in the long grass by the girls. That was my favourite bit of War. The toilets were outside, and they were horrible. There was a brick wall between the boys and the girls, and we used to pee over it, I am sorry to say. I once needed to do a number two, and I ran all the way home rather than go in the noxious cubicles. I once looked in one of the bogs and saw what looked like a skinned rabbit, a sight that I remember from time to time. I suppose some poor girl had given birth there.

*

The transition from junior to secondary school was dramatic. It was heavenly to me. I still had a lovely treble voice, and people noticed. I remember one time very early on, when I was standing on the school stage rehearsing my song for the Eisteddfod competition, and two big girls stopped to listen. I think the song was Purcell's 'Fairest Isle', which had a tricky bit on "Jealousie, that poysons passion", where you had to go really low (for a treble voice), but I was acing it. The two big girls were both lovely, and they gave a beautiful performance of "two lovely girls on the brink of womanhood moved by the sound of a boy treble, singing about a love and passion he is obviously far too young to comprehend". Meanwhile, I performed my role of "cute boy singing who doesn't even realize how beautiful his song is, and how the two girls will remember this moment all their lives". I was fully aware of all this at the time, and I'm pretty sure they were.

*

During my first year at secondary school, there was a dog I encountered every morning on the walk in. I began persuading him to accompany me all the way to school. He took to it readily. I then trained him, and I use the term generously, to respond to the name "Bugger". The appeal was obvious. One could stand in the crowded playground, adopt an expression of innocence and shout "Bugger!" at full volume. Moments later, this cheerful creature would bound towards me, tail wagging, delighted to be addressed. The teachers were less delighted. At roughly the same time, we acquired a dog of our own, Sam – who was handsome, loyal and slightly judgemental. I can only describe his politics as conservative in temperament. He disapproved of scruffiness. If a passer-by looked unkempt, Sam stiffened. He was deeply suspicious of dirt. Most embarrassingly of all, he harboured an inexplicable aversion to people who limped. But he had one great love: the milkman's horse. Every morning the milkman would halt his cart outside our house and feed the horse. Sam positioned himself strategically beneath the nosebag, waiting for any spillage. If, on any given morning, Sam failed to appear, the horse would drag the cart a little closer to our gate and stand there, looking expectant. A small alliance built around routine and carrot peelings. It was a beautiful friendship.

*

In our first year at Whitchurch Grammar, we dined in our own special room, under the supervision of sixth-form girl prefects who appeared impossibly sophisticated and, in some cases, bewilderingly well developed. Our prefect was called Thesca. She was gentle, kind and liberal-minded, and clearly thought that we were cute as buttons.

"This term, you'll get to go to the Christmas party, and you can ask someone you like to be your partner. If you walk them home afterwards, you can kiss them, if you want to."

This struck me as astonishing and thrilling. I knew immediately that I wanted to ask Hilary Taylor. The other boys were puzzled by the notion. Girls? Feelings? Kissing? But I was bewitched. Hilary was small, sparkly-eyed and crackling with an energy I now recognize as charisma. Objectively, she wasn't beautiful, but she lit up a room the way some actresses can light up a screen. I told her I loved her. She said she loved me too. We held hands and chased each other around the chemistry-lab benches. Kiss chase.

Mr Morgan, our chemistry teacher, either didn't notice or had long since given up caring. His *laissez-faire* approach allowed romance to blossom. I remained in love with Hilary for years, but her unique charm had started to attract older boys who smoked, even had cars. She was still my friend, however, and my partner at ballroom dancing, though even there, after a while, the dancing school said that with her talent she needed a taller partner. "Never mind, boy," said Phil Williams, our dancing teacher. "I had the same problem. Could have been a world champion, I had all the talent, but I didn't have the bloody inches."

But it was good growing up with girls and being friends with them. Squibby Davis had permissive parents, and I remember a party at Squibby's when we were twelve, where we played all those games like Winking and Hyde Park Corner, and Squibby's big sister and her boyfriend, who were at least fifteen, taught us all how to do proper French kissing. They were kind and patient, like sex therapists. I think we all appreciated it at the time, and indeed later.

Decades later, when we were all sixty-one, John Gerrish organized a fifty-year reunion of the 1947 intake at Whitchurch Grammar.

He chose a private room in an upmarket country pub – exposed beams, discreet staff, good wine. It was the sort of venue that suggested a man satisfied with the direction his life had taken. You could see why John wanted the reunion. He looked handsome and prosperous. He was the headmaster of a private school, plus he had a new, younger wife to introduce to us all. Fair play, we said. Good for him. I was desperate to see what Hilary Taylor looked like. Would she break my heart all over again? It seemed unlikely at our age, but one never knows. Certain people retain a peculiar power over one's nervous system. I didn't even recognize her at first. Small, plump, cheerful. Entirely at ease. She had achieved the air hostess's dream: married the captain and lived happily ever after – or as close as anyone does. Squibby was different. Still skinny. Still sharp. Now divorced, still nursing, still with that quick intelligence and faintly dangerous edge. It was touching that they were still friends with each other. And still, somehow, my friends too. Conversation flowed as if only a weekend had passed since we'd last seen one another. That ease was a gift. Then, without preamble, Squibby said, "God, Dai, but your mother was terrible!"

Hilary nodded. "Yeah, she scared the pants off us!"

I felt something loosen inside me. A curious relief. It wasn't just childhood exaggeration after all. It hadn't simply been me.

John Gerrish, the event organizer, had been in my friendship group too, along with Brian and Rose, childhood sweethearts and, remarkably, still together. My best friend and best man, Polly, was in Tasmania, so he couldn't attend. I missed him. But David Croot was there. I remembered him as a short, pugnacious boy, permanently bristling, as though life had already offended him in some fundamental way. And he hadn't changed. He was a short, pugnacious sixty-one-year-old man. He came straight up to me.

"I never liked you," he said. "And when we was in school, I used to give you hell."

"Did you?" I said. "I don't remember that. Actually, I barely remember you."

"Yes, you bloody do," he said. "Gave you bloody hell, I did. And I still could."

And, with that, he walked off. He remembered something entirely different from what I remembered. I don't recall being bullied at Whitchurch. I don't remember fear. But he clearly carried a grievance I had long ago discarded or perhaps never properly registered. Baffling. Memory is not a communal enterprise. We each walk away from the same building with entirely different films playing in our heads. Looking at Hilary across the room that evening, I found myself wondering something else. I think now that maybe what I saw in her at eleven – that look which so completely undid me – was not entirely about her. When I look at photographs of my mother as a very young woman, there is a similar expression – something of the small wild animal about both of them. Unaware of the effect she might have. Or maybe she was very aware. Hilary was an indulged youngest child too. Hilary broke my heart, but neither of us could disappear into the sunset. There were years of school corridors and classrooms still ahead. And because she was really a very nice person, we became friends.

Various people, W.B. Yeats, Kingsley Amis, have likened male sexuality to being chained to a madman. There's some truth in that. But it alters. It settles. It becomes something else. Now I have very good friends who are women, and I like to think I am a good friend. Hilary and Squibby, without any intention of doing so, taught me that at Whitchurch Grammar.

*

I started being "Dai" early on in secondary school. Dai is usually short for David or Dafydd, but it can also be short for Davies. In my case it was economical. A neat trimming of identity to suit the climate. I liked being Dai, because in that very Welsh milieu Andrew seemed a bit alien, a bit posh. Andrew sounded like someone who might correct your grammar. And Wynford, my middle name, was even worse, too easily shortened to Winnie, which would never do. I had no intention of beginning my adult life explaining that, yes, I was a boy. That particular bullet was dodged early. Though Polly never minded being Polly, and no one ever thought of him as girly. Dai sounded like someone who could take a knock. So I was Dai. It felt right. Hilary and Squibby still know me as Dai. There is something about being called Dai that instantly takes me back to corridors smelling faintly of polish and ink, to adolescence and its uncertainties. Diana first knew me as Dai too. There is a version of me preserved inside that name – thinner, perhaps, anxious to please, not yet sure where he was heading. When did I start being Andrew? It happened gradually, but I can date the official transition to my first teaching job at St Clement Danes. I didn't want to be pigeon-holed as some sort of professional Welshman. I guess I felt ready to be Andrew Davies, not Dai Davies. And Andrew Davies sounded like a good name for a writer. So now virtually everyone knows me as Andrew. Though I'm still a bit Dai, deep inside.

*

After our magical first year, many of the best teachers who had been there at the birth of the school left, most of them for greater things: Miss Thomas, whose English lessons felt wonderfully playful as well as instructive; Leslie Moore, the Head of the Art Department, who couldn't resist taking over and improving your painting with bold, colourful strokes. I never resented it, because he was so talented. He was replaced by an irritable man we called Bag Rees, which probably says it all about him. A joyless prat. One of the originals who stayed on was Leonard Manaton, Head of Music. Uncle Len, we called him. He was gay, of course, but nobody minded that. We had two music lessons a week, one singing, the other musical appreciation, and I loved both of them. We had a book called *The New National Song Book*, full of these great melodies, mostly traditional folk songs. I've tried to track it down, but it seems to have disappeared off the face of the earth. John Stuart Williams rose to become Head of English. He was clever, had been to Cambridge, and wrote and published poetry, but he never seemed to enjoy teaching. We called him Slug, though not to his face. He had a furious temper. When we were in the sixth form, he once seized Terry Darlington by the throat in an argument over what Eliot meant by the "objective correlative". Terry Darlington stood up abruptly. He was very tall, and as Slug was very short, he dangled off Darlington with his feet off the ground. "I think we had better go to the Head's room to sort this out," said Terry, with immense dignity, I thought. And they did.

*

But sixth form was a long way off. I had to go through years of bad behaviour first.

Puberty arrived, accompanied by lust, when I was twelve. I found myself with an erection nearly all the time, which is very embarrassing, especially in gym shorts. And our school was full of pretty girls, some of them in gym knickers. Mrs Urwin, our French teacher, was distractingly beautiful. When she bent over to check our work, her perfume swirled around us like a spell. She was married to a French professor and said to be entangled with someone at the BBC. The grown-up world, we were beginning to realize, was awash with intrigue. Mr Reed, our rather fearsome Head of German, nicknamed "Moses", clearly fancied Mrs Urwin, or so we thought. I was moved to write a doggerel poem about them. It was quite long, but the only stanza I remember goes like this:

He kissed her
She kissed him back.
He took her knickers off
And put them in a sack.
She took his underpants
And put them in her bag.
He said, "*Excusez-moi*, but could I have a shag?"

This poem circulated in samizdat and went all around the school. I had enjoyed official praise for my writing since junior school, but this was different. Crude as it was, it was an important moment in my development as a writer. You could write beautiful things to please the teacher, but you could also write transgressive things that revealed the truth behind the façade. After my "Moses and Mrs Urwin" poem, I remember a big boy coming up to me in the schoolyard.

"Hey. You the one that wrote that poem?"

"Er… yes?"

"Bloody good, mun! Bloody good!"

Of course it found its way to the authorities, and my parents were summoned. Not good. My mother was very shocked, and my father pretended to be. I began to have a reputation to live up to. I wasn't the biggest or strongest – far from it – but I was witty, sharp and popular enough to straddle the dual roles of class clown and top of the class. At home, the atmosphere chilled. The dining room was cold in more ways than one. We'd sit in glacial silence, waiting to discover who had caused my mother's latest mood. She disapproved of most of my friends. She particularly loathed Donald Spry, who once had the audacity to go upstairs without being invited. "The boy who goes upstairs," she called him, as if he were a ghost in a Henry James novella. The exception was Sukey Phillips, real name John, a self-taught fire-eater and occasional sword-swallower who later became the painter and sculptor of some note mentioned earlier. Mum had a lot of sympathy for him, as he had a horrid dad, a bully, who was always shouting at him, so loud you could hear him from streets away.

"John! John! What do you mean by leaving these wet marks on the lavatory seat?"

When Sukey was sixteen, he knocked his dad down the stairs, and no one blamed him for it. Well, I suppose his dad did.

I got a sense that my mother was jealous of most of my friends. As for girlfriends, I knew it would be best not to tell her anything about anything – and so began my secret life. Secret crushes. Secret fantasies. Graham Leonard, who had been my friend since primary school, had an older brother in the army in Germany, and he had some dirty pictures that I bought from him. I was curious about it all. Black-and-white images of middle-aged people having sex. I mostly remember the men with huge moustaches. And the women had black beards *down there*. I must have looked on edge when I brought them into the house, and my mum searched through all my things hoping to find incriminating evidence that I wasn't her darling boy any more. Graham, who had big sisters too, was always ahead of me in the (still theoretical) carnal-knowledge department. I remember saying to him: "I know all about sex now."

And he said: "No, you don't, because you don't know about women's periods."

"That's not sex," I said.

Around that time, I began to think of myself as quite bad. It made me feel brave. I even dipped a toe into very petty crime, stealing pens and notebooks from the tobacconist. I wasn't very good at it, and I got caught. The shopkeeper threatened to tell my father. He may have done, but nothing was said. The shame was enough. But "nothing ventured, nothing gained" was my motto, and my career as a solo bandit continued. My father, ever virtuous, loomed large in my psyche during that time. I kind of conflated him with the minister at chapel, a model of holiness, and Jesus Christ himself. I thought he was no good as a role model for me, because he was too good. But paradoxically I had dreams of him standing with me at a cliff's edge, his hand on my back. I feared he might push me. He never did, of course. Not in dreams, and certainly not in life. As I grew up, I grew closer to my dad and further from my mother. I couldn't cope with her fierce neediness, her resentment, her sulks.

"You never listen to anything I say!"

"I do listen. I just don't agree with it."

I had to make choices – between living my life and being the sort of son that she wanted. And so my secret life continued. Rich in contradiction, bristling with tension, occasionally ablaze with awkward triumph. It was, in short, a very good rehearsal for adulthood. And the engine that would power my writing.

Escape to London

It was 1954. I was nearly eighteen and desperate to get out. I was ready to flee. Flee my mother, chiefly, but also Beulah Chapel, Rhiwbina, all that small-town bunkum. I longed for London, specifically Soho, where my hero Dylan Thomas had strutted his stuff. The school wanted me to try for an Oxford scholarship, to get another name on the honours board, which looked a bit empty. But that would involve having to do National Service, as well as staying at school another term, and I was desperate to get away from Whitchurch too. University College London struck me as far more enticing. At the time, I thought it was the only university in the city. The notion that there might be more didn't occur to me. It was also within walking distance of Soho. The interview was surprisingly enjoyable. As I stood to leave, the interviewer said, "What are you doing for the rest of the day?"

"I thought I'd walk down to the West End," I said.

"Get yourself some more flashy ties?"

I looked down at the tie in question. I hadn't thought of it as flashy. But apparently it was memorable. I got in. English at UCL. Three years in London. Freedom. Escape. Sending my trunk ahead felt momentous. It was the prelude to the film of my life, the opening shot.

> Trunk rolls away.
> Fade in. me.
> London-bound. No mother. No bedtime. No scrutiny.

A room of my own awaited me in Bentham Hall, a men's residence within strolling distance of the university. My only previous bedroom had been in our house in Rhiwbina Garden Village. Now I had my own key. My own door. Bentham Hall was a curved row of Georgian townhouses stitched together with staircases and unexpected landings. My room was L-shaped, with a single bed and a desk that seemed to know it would never be overworked. I still dream about that place, wandering its winding corridors, looking for someone I once knew. Or maybe for a version of myself that still haunts the stairwells. What's that all about? Being stuck? Lost? Trapped?

Freedom came written within Bentham Hall's small print. We could come and go as we pleased, but technically we had to be in by 11 p.m. A late key gave you until midnight. And then there was a late, late key, for which you had to undergo an interrogation. These keys weren't tracked with much rigour. After my first term, I accidentally-on-purpose took one home to Cardiff. My uncle David, married to Aunt Dib, had a hardware shop. He could cut keys. I returned with six duplicates. Kept one. Sold the rest. Just about the only successful business venture of my life.

If I was to be a character in my own London film, I needed the costume. My trousers were tapered until they could barely accommodate ankles. I sported a duffel coat, all the rage, and a thick seaman's roll-neck jumper. I eschewed my perfectly good briefcase and instead, for reasons still unclear to me, began carrying my books in a brown paper bag which I inscribed with my initials. Poverty chic. It was all rather performative. But then, so was I.

The Marlborough Arms in Bloomsbury became the place to be on Friday nights, if you felt up to it. It was conveniently close to Foster Court, where the English Department resided, which meant it became an extension of academic life lubricated with beer. Professor Smith, an Old Norse specialist, presided over things like a chieftain in Beowulf's mead hall. He would empty his pockets of notes and coins onto the long wooden table in a rustling, clattering heap, and no one would pay for their own drink until the hoard was consumed. Dodgson – surnames only in those days – who was the most junior member of staff, would be dispatched to the bar. Smith, always at the head of the table, would hold forth about the Order of the Elephant, about sagas, about himself. Arguments about literature slid into debates about politics, then into controversies about the proper translation of an Old Norse obscenity – the air thick with tobacco and opinion. But that was only half the department, the language lot, the "Anglo-Saxon attitudes" lot, the burly archaeologists who despised the notion of studying any literature after Beowulf. What would be the point? A gentleman can read the books in his library, no need for some preening booby to tell him what they mean: he can see that for himself. The literature lot tended not to go to the Marlborough. The literature prof, an ascetic Scotsman called Sutherland, tended not to go out at all. And there were others who would sip sherry in their rooms, shunning the company of the burly diggers, whom they regarded as uncivilized oafs. The literature guys – and they were mostly guys – were not clubbable, though one or two of them were quite nice when you got to know them.

For us, the students, there was the College Union with its cheap beer, coffee bars and other pubs less intimidating than the Marlborough. For a boy from a Welsh village, it was a paradise. The recently opened Bunjies Coffee House & Folk Cellar in Seven Dials was a good place to be – bohemian, smoky and teeming with nurses. I liked nurses. They knew things, and they were warm and friendly. There was Acapulco, with flamenco dancing, and the Macabre, decorated with skulls. Pubs were pricier, and I was skint, so I'd sip at a coffee for hours, talking revolution, literature and other things I barely understood. My cohort consisted of thirty students, mostly women. I bonded with two of the men. John Reardon, working class, steady and freshly demobbed from Malta, where he'd had a Maltese girlfriend. Exotic! I'd barely kissed anyone, and here was John, casually recalling assignations beneath Mediterranean stars. Another friend called John Cumming, a Catholic, claimed an expertise on nuns. The peculiar thing was that wherever you walked with John, nuns would appear. Down Charing Cross Road one day he said, "Watch this. You can't walk between two nuns. They always close up." Two were approaching about fifty yards away. John aimed himself directly for the gap between them. As he reached them, they silently adjusted formation and he bounced off. It was as if they'd rehearsed defensive manoeuvres.

"Do you know them?" I asked.

"Only in the sense that I know nuns," he said. "They're all the same, man."

He then advanced the theory that nuns, despite appearances, disregard minor rules with cheerful indifference – littering, ignoring signs, signalling right and turning left. I began observing. There was evidence. Later, as a lecturer, I noticed that whenever I was about to embark on a particularly delicate or sexually explicit topic, two nuns would mysteriously appear in the front row, smiling benignly. Naturally, I put two nuns into every episode of *A Very Peculiar Practice* and created Sister Conception and Sister Purification for the Marmalade Atkins TV series – formidable creatures both. If you doubt any of this, try walking between two nuns. They will close up!

My other friend was Paul Vernon – fat, brilliant, Marxist. Raised in a communist household, he considered most of our lecturers to be closet or indeed open fascists. One in Anglo-Saxon particularly loathed him, likely because Paul had taught himself to speak the language fluently. Paul fancied pretty, delicate boys who were always straight. Or claimed to be. Sadly, Paul resembled a rotund owl and rarely inspired mutual longing. While others were losing their virginity, I was still sending my dirty laundry home in brown-paper parcels. (Didn't I ever think about my poor mother? Was it for this that she had endured the pains of childbirth? No, I didn't, sorry to say. I had other things on my mind). Change was coming.

Enter Babbie.

Seventeen. Irish. A maid at the Men's Hall. Big blue eyes. She was the sort of girl that shouldn't have been let out on her own. We kissed against the walls of dark cobbled alleyways. A couple of gauche waifs. She talked continuously and told stories about her seven sisters and their dalliances and how her father would kill her if he knew what she was up to with me – which, in fairness, wasn't much. I had gone much further with Pamela Biggs at school. With Babbie, almost everything was either a *venial sin*, or worse, a *mortal sin*, and she would give me a running commentary which was quite erotic in itself. But I did love her. Her breath on my cheek, the smell of her skin. We were both too shy to explore any further. I longed for her, but was content with what I had, her closeness, her trust, her confidence. She loved me and I loved her, and she gave me a photograph the size of a tea tray to take home at Christmas. I'd hoped for a smaller one that could fit in my wallet and that I could easily look at whenever I felt the need. Instead, I had to wait until I was home from my holiday job to sneak up to my room and let her slide out of my folder and stare up at me. Babbie wrote to me every couple of days – tender love letters riddled with spelling mistakes. I didn't care. She was my girlfriend. She was my own. My mother, who never recognized the rights of privacy and would always find time to poke around in other people's things, found the letters. And the photo. Ever articulate, she had a great deal to say on the matter.

"A cleaner? And Irish?" she gasped.

She assumed we'd been having sex. We hadn't. But she launched into a tirade about responsibility, class, power, sex and, possibly, sin. My father sat mute. I tried to explain. I got as far as "Look, you don't..." – and then my chest caved in. I sobbed. Convulsively. Threw myself onto the cushions. My mother stood still. Possibly stunned at being upstaged. Dad said, after a long silence: "Cheer up. I'm going to a wine-tasting. Want to come?" I couldn't think of a reason not to. My relationship with Babbie fizzled out in a pleasant way without drama. Over the Christmas break she found somebody else that she felt very serious about, and by then there was someone else that I had my eye on.

*

Elizabeth Savage was part of a little group of posh girls in the first year, and I had a fondness for her and she for me. With auburn hair, green eyes and small, neat features, she looked like a very cute rat, and I thought that she was lovely. We'd walk hand in hand through Heal's on Tottenham Court Road and choose a nice sofa to sit on and just talk and talk. I don't remember us kissing, though we must have. I just remember us talking and listening to each other, and that felt like enough. I was in love with her, but it was very, very chaste. I gathered that she was engaged to someone else, and that he was a brewer. I thought that this was a bit odd, as I'd been on one or two brewery visits, and this didn't look like a job with prospects to me. Then one of the other posh girls explained that being a brewer didn't mean that you had to stir the mash yourself, it just meant that your name was Watney or Charrington and you'd been to Eton and had been a Guards officer – it meant that you were very wealthy and set to inherit a great deal.

*

When I was eighteen, I wanted to be an actor as much as (or even more than) I wanted to be a writer. At school I had been Jaques in *As You Like It* to great acclaim, and in my first term at UCL I auditioned for, and got, a leading part in *Venus Observed*, a verse play by Christopher Fry, who was highly regarded in the Fifties, but is only remembered now for *The Lady's Not for Burning* – and that only because Margaret Thatcher's speechwriter borrowed the title for one of her boastful speeches. Christopher Fry went in for long, mellifluous speeches in *vers libre* about sod all. That was one of the problems with *Venus Observed*. Another was that I was not great as an actor, which was a very good thing to find out at an early age. It wasn't just that I was giving a weak performance in a dud play. There was more humiliation in store for me. My character, who was called Edgar, I think, son of the duke of somewhere, has a scene in which he has to shoot an arrow offstage. There's a cry of rage and pain offstage, and on comes the duke, in a beautiful double-breasted suit, with an arrow stuck in his arse. It's one of the few real bits of action in the play, perhaps the only one, and it should get a big laugh. We didn't have a bow to practise with in rehearsal. That didn't bother me, because, as you know, I had been a whizz with home-made bows and arrows. The real bow only turned up on the morning of the first night. I don't remember even trying it out, I was that confident. But when the moment came for me to shoot the arrow offstage, I couldn't do it. My hand had frozen solid with tension – the arrow was squeezed between my knuckles, and I couldn't release it. After two or three failed attempts, I let the arrow fall to the floor and kicked it offstage, feigning nonchalance.

Big laugh from the audience.

Then we had to endure another exchange of vapid versifying, knowing that seconds later the poor bastard playing the duke was going to come on with another arrow protruding from his rear. This he did, to the delight of the audience. Then I had to get to the end of the play, which was a good hour away. The rest of the cast were very nice to me about it. So was the director, a charmingly affected third-year called Marcus Félix Toulmin-Rothe. And I managed to get through two more performances in a state of numb misery. My friends were commendably frank. They told me I was fucking terrible, and I should never go on a stage again. I agreed with them, and I never have, from that day to this. So big thanks to Christopher Fry and his bow and arrow. Without him, I might have spent my life as a fucking terrible actor.

*

The only one who didn't join in the chorus of condemnation was Elizabeth Savage. She said, "I liked it because you were just like yourself" – which is one of the nicest things anyone's ever said to me. She invited me to her birthday party, which was full of very tall posh men with lovely manners, who were all quite nice to me. I expect one of them was her brewer, but they all looked the same. I was dimly aware that they were nice to me because I wasn't a serious contender, being small and Welsh and seriously unposh.

That didn't seem to put Jill off, though. Jill was a third-year who smoked like a chimney, wore a bright-orange mac and walked into lectures like a catwalk model. She had a proper boyfriend who was tall, athletic and everything that I wasn't. But she liked me too. We played tennis. Went to the cinema. Snogged while she smoked. It felt sensual and sophisticated. Her bed was very bouncy, and we nearly had sex on it. It was all very educational. But she wasn't "the one".

*

Academically, I nearly derailed during my first year due to too much emotional distraction, so much so that I almost didn't get back in for the second year. One of the entry requirements was that you had to have Latin A-level, which I didn't, but the university ran a bridging course whose attendance was mandatory. At the end of each term there was an exam. I got 34% after the first term and thought, "All I have to do is get to 50%. That's not too bad. I'll get it up easily." Then at the end of the second term I got 17%, and so I was quaking in my boots as I awaited results after the third term. The woman who ran the Latin course said slowly and very deliberately, "Well, since you did a rather charming essay about Horace, you've scraped by."

*

It had been a year of living dangerously, not just because of my three love affairs, but also because of the snooker table in the basement of Bentham Hall. I loved snooker. The quietness of it and the theatrical atmosphere, the light over the pool table surrounded by darkness, the stillness, the concentration... I spent hours in the basement playing on my own and thinking, "You should be working on your Latin. Just one more frame. One more."

*

The very first UCL lecture that I ever attended was the best of my three years. "Where is 'Ode to a Nightingale'?" the professor asked. It was Socratic. Provocative. We were led gently to the idea that a literary work lives in the space between the writer, their history, the world and us. That became the foundation of my later teaching, and, without realizing it, my adaptation work. Tutors varied. Emslie was my first, a bad-tempered Scotsman. He threw books at me. It is safe to say we didn't get on. Turner followed in second year – vague, gentle, rather like a forgetful uncle. And then Charles Peake in third year – engaged, thoughtful, generous – someone who treated us as real people and took an interest in us. He'd done his own degree as a mature student at Birkbeck. Crazy about Joyce. He paid attention to detail and loved his job. A proper teacher who became a good friend. Most of the others were either dull, lazy and couldn't teach, or desperate to show how clever they were in some pathetic display of superiority. However, despite this, UCL was a life-changing experience.

I met Diana.

It was 1955, and, having just scraped my way, by charm, luck and a Horatian essay, into my second year at UCL, I was still nursing a slightly bruised ego from the Latin debacle. But academically shaky foundations didn't stop me from attending lectures open to the whole English department. These grand gatherings were fertile ground for distraction, and in among the sea of cardigans and earnest faces, one person stood out like a flame in a blackout: Diana.

Diana was in the first year. She had a cool, interesting manner about her, half Parisian existentialist, half Hepburn (Katharine, not Audrey). Apparently, she'd had her eye on me from the start. I looked a bit different, and with pock-marked cheeks like Richard Burton (chicken pox, I hasten to add: I got all the childhood diseases late, in my fifth year at Whitchurch, plus appendicitis, a broken collarbone and a kettle of scalding water poured over myself).

We began bumping into each other more – lectures, the jive class we both attended. We danced together, first tentatively, then with growing confidence. And we became rather good, not just at the dancing, but at getting to know each other. She wore capri pants, which back then was a bold move. Her ability to raise one eyebrow quizzically was honed, I later discovered, through hours of adolescent mirror practice. And while she had an innocence that was genuine, it coexisted with a shrewdness that made her utterly compelling. Boys had hovered around her before, she told me, but she fended them off like an elegant goalie. Diana was from York, and her dad was an engine driver and racing cyclist. She was the first person from her family to go to university. She was sort of going out with Tom Courtenay and was sitting on his bony lap in the Union bar when I made my move. Tom quickly faded out of the picture. He'd never been that keen, to be honest. It was always more about his latest performance at that time than it was about Diana. He had a thing where he'd roll a bottle across his fevered brow, just like James Dean in *Rebel without a Cause*. It didn't look quite so cool with a milk bottle. None of us had the smallest idea that before very long he would be world-famous.

A lifetime later, at least fifty years, Jo Willett sent me a book by Angela Lambert called *A Rather English Marriage*. It was about two elderly men whose wives die in hospital on the same day. Reggie is posh, cultivated, comfortably off and hopeless even at boiling an egg. Roy has spent years nursing his sick wife, and knows how to run a house, stretch a pension and make a decent stew, but hasn't a penny to rub against another. An imaginative social worker decides the answer is obvious and installs them together, creating an unlikely companionship. The novel ends on a sombre note. I rather wanted to tilt it towards something warmer – not sentimentality, but the possibility that life, even at seventy-five, might still contain surprise and a kind of grace. Clever Jo somehow assembled a dream cast: Albert Finney as Reggie, Tom Courtenay as Roy and Joanna Lumley as the woman who complicates matters. Paul Seed, who had directed both *House of Cards* and *Inappropriate Behaviour* with subtlety and panache, was in charge for this one too, which made me feel comfortable. We filmed in Tunbridge Wells. There was a dinner before filming began. Albert sat at the head of the table – expansive, theatrical, telling stories about filming with Kris Kristofferson and others of that vintage. He held the floor beautifully. Tom was beside me, listening, then murmured under his breath: "Don't you think he's looking awfully old? Honestly, some people think I'm his son." I choked, rather inelegantly. Albert clocked us at once. "What's he saying now?" he boomed. "It's all lies, whatever it is!"

Diana came down for part of the shoot, and one evening we had dinner with Tom and his wife. There was something faintly surreal about it. Diana and Tom had been together when they were eighteen. There had been dancing, earnestness, possibility. Now here we were: middle-aged, ordering wine and talking about cholesterol. Tom wasn't very good at the practical details of life, being wholly dependent on his very nice wife for all that sort of thing. Afterwards, back at the hotel, Diana delivered her verdict.

"I definitely made the right decision," she said.

*

Courting, in the Fifties, tended to be an affectionate struggle, controlled by the girl. No did not always mean precisely "no" – sometimes it meant: "No, not yet". Diana had been used to that with her Yorkshire lovers, none of whom had been allowed to go "all the way". It was clear that we would go all the way – just not quite yet. And Diana lived with Janet, which made things tricky.

Janet was shy and unworldly, but razor-sharp. Diana, though still innocent, had more experience with men. She understood the dance of it all. She knew when to tease, when to listen, when to hold a gaze an extra second. Janet did not. This didn't make her less attractive – in fact, quite the opposite. There was something disarming about her reserve. One particular lecturer, cadaverous Paul Turner, special subject Classical Background, adored her. She was original without trying to be, and never seemed to notice the effect she had. Diana, meanwhile, moved through rooms more easily. They balanced one another beautifully, shared jokes, exasperations, hardship.

Janet was also eccentric in practical matters and quite wilful. Diana told me they were returning from the shops one afternoon, arms laden with groceries, faced with the steep hill home. Halfway up, Janet had simply stopped. She put the bag down.

"I'm not carrying this any longer."

And that was that. She meant it. Underneath that delicate shyness, Janet was one tough cookie. But she had to go away sometimes, and one night she did. She went home to Sleaford to visit her parents, and I was coyly invited to stay the night.

I still thought of Diana as quite a cool customer, and in a way she was. But at the same time, she was this shy, dreamy Yorkshire girl who loved me and had decided to trust me with herself. That night she hadn't bought anything special to wear. She wore her old blue nightie, washed so many times it was virtually colourless, and she looked so nice, and so vulnerable, that I felt a sudden rush of tenderness that made me dizzy, but fortunately did not unman me. It was a huge step forward, but at the same time not. We'd gone so close quite a few times before, but it felt like a big change. And we both loved it, and we both wanted lots more of it. And we wanted to know each other better than anyone had ever known anyone else. I guess most people feel like this at least once in their lives, but there's nothing to beat it, is there?

After our rather tentative beginning, we grew bold. We had sex in the library during opening hours. The Egyptology section was blissfully quiet, and its mummies proved remarkably non-judgemental. If a Tube carriage was empty, we'd risk that too. You had to move fast between stations, but we were young, flexible and faintly deranged with desire. People often paint the 1950s as a repressed decade, all twinsets and church fêtes, but under the surface there was a powerful craving for something freer, something real. We were that craving, embodied in skinny trousers and roll-necks, armed with condoms and Keats. David Lodge, who was also at UCL in the Fifties, describes a very different world – very earnest and anxious and Catholic. It seems odd that there were two different UCLs existing at the same time.

We had no secrets from each other. Diana, however, was my secret. There was no way I was offering her up to my mother's critique. When we went hitch-hiking together that first summer, I concocted some fictitious male companion. But, of course, my mother found out. She always did. This time it was letters, Diana's, complete with lovingly drawn illustrations down the margins of us having sex in multiple positions. Diana had a knack for figure drawing. My mother was appalled.

"This is disgusting," she declared, clutching the pages as if they'd been dipped in sin. And with that, Diana's relationship with my mother began. It remained chilly for some years. Happily, fate intervened in the form of my younger brother, who got his girlfriend Anne pregnant. My mother believed he'd been "trapped", and that his girlfriend was a seductress with an agenda. In truth, they adored each other and remain happily married to this day. But the scandal redefined Diana in my mother's eyes. Suddenly, Diana was the good girl. The girl who would *never* do such a thing. Perspective is everything.

*

For my third year I had to move out of Bentham Hall. I was too idle and feckless to fix up a place to live, and when I was away in the summer (Italy again, Diana again) my mother arranged a room for me with a family in Golders Green. I had nothing against moving so far out, but it was worse than living at home with my own parents. There were a couple of other lodgers, and you had to eat with the family. I remember roast ox heart, among other delights. One other thing I couldn't bear was that although you could use the toilet after 11 p.m., you were not allowed to flush it. I went to the UCL lodgings office and said: "Please, please, you have to find me something – I will kill myself if I have to stay here another minute." (I know, this is not like me, or even me as I was then, but I was desperate.) And they said, "Well, you could try this very difficult, bad-tempered man – he's turned everybody down so far, but it's a very good address."

So I went round to 20 Buckingham Street, WC2, and met Cedric Enna. He was twenty-six, but carried on as if he was at least fifty. He had a beautiful grand piano in his living room. He started off by complaining about the lodgings office: "Apparently there was one madman who was threatening to kill himself, and I said: don't bother to send *him* round, he can kill himself somewhere else, not here, ha ha!" I realized he was talking about me. Perhaps they had twigged what I failed to at that first meeting. (I *was* very cute at twenty.) I admired his piano and promised I'd be very quiet, as I was working for finals, and he said OK, let's give it a go. Luckily, I didn't mention Diana or say we would be quietly shagging in my bed a lot of the time. I moved in, and it was wonderful. I had a comfy sitting room and a bedroom, and I shared a kitchen with Enna. He told me a lot about basic chap's cooking, steaks and sausages, then I got Elizabeth David and blossomed.

He was very disappointed about my having a girlfriend and being straight, but took it on the chin like a man. And when he met Diana, he was impressed to find her dad drove express trains on the East Coast Main Line. Enna worked in the City doing the same job that T.S. Eliot had done, so he was quite helpful with *The Waste Land*. Before, he had taught in prep schools, which he loved, probably too much. Gradually we became quite fond of each other. He had got himself into a bit of a situation. He was giving piano lessons to a boy of about twelve, for whom he had a tendresse – then the boy's mother developed a similar feeling for Enna. Two sad people frustrated to the point of frenzy, and the boy blissfully unaware – or was he? I was sorry to leave that place. Diana would come round and we would have baths together – I remember teaching her to blow smoke rings in the bath. And when it was hot, we'd go up on the roof. Bliss.

*

As the end of my time at UCL loomed, I began pondering the future. It was the tail-end of the 1950s, and there was a heady sense of optimism. We all believed we could walk into any job.

My parents Wynford and Hilda on their wedding day in 1930.
On the left, my mother's older sister Dib.

Myself as a toddler, probably sulking.

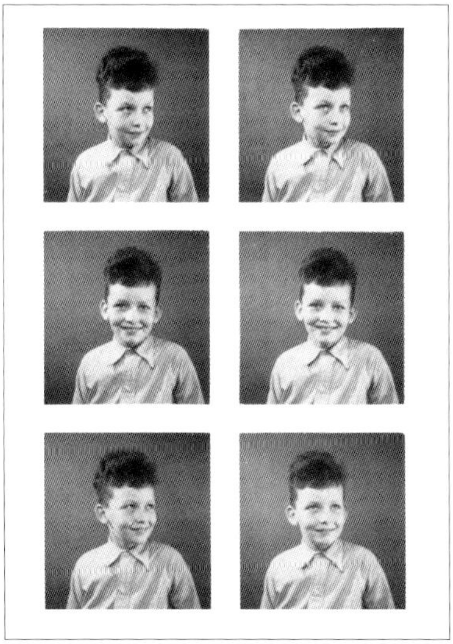

Six versions of my six-year-old self.

Playing with my best friend Jennifer in her big garden.

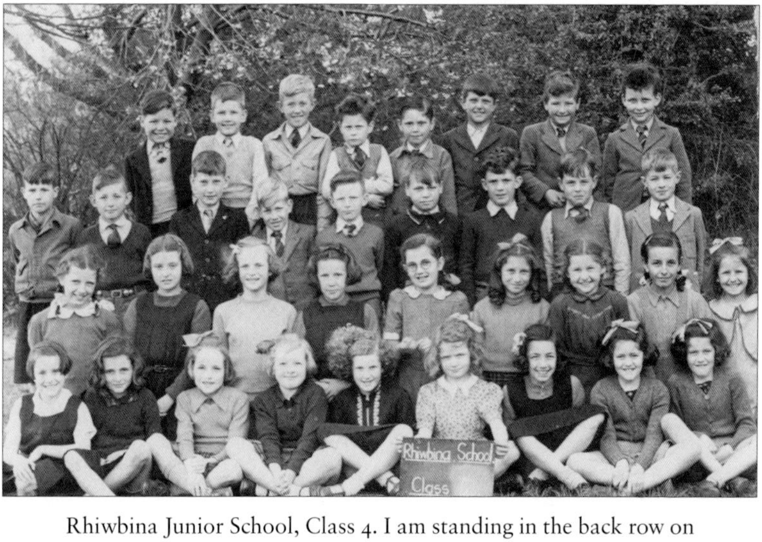

Rhiwbina Junior School, Class 4. I am standing in the back row on the far right, next to Graham Leonard, my first good friend at school.

Myself as a member of the junior cricket team, aged thirteen (front row, far left) – the only one in the photo clearly not paying attention.

Myself as a fifteen-year-old (left) and as a carefree eighteen-year-old, smoking a cigarette (right).

My life companion, Diana, at around the time when we first met.

A photo of myself and Diana with with my mother,
brother Peter and dog Sam.

With Diana on our wedding day, 9th April 1960.

The bridesmaids – Diana's cousins Vivien and Elaine.

Diana at the seaside with Bill and Anna.

Diana holding baby William (Bill) and me holding Chowder outside our first house in Bertie Road.

Enjoying a cup of tea during a break from work in the early Seventies.

Myself as a dapper, bearded teacher trying (in vain) to inculcate T.S. Eliot's poetry into the minds of my students.

Myself at fifty, finally a full-time writer.

For a moment, I toyed with the idea of going into advertising, but it felt too like *Mad Men* before *Mad Men*. National Service, meanwhile, still hovered like a bad smell. I wanted out, and took the Civil Service administrative exam as my means of doing so. Hans Eysenck, the famed psychologist, had devised a battery of tests said to be the gold standard in intellectual and psychological analysis. I couldn't resist. It sounded like a great way to prove something, although I wasn't sure what. We did group debates, partnered exercises, logic tests, psychometric wizardry. I got as far as the final interview, but I sensed I wasn't doing that well. My results were as follows: 150/300 for intelligence; 100/300 for character and background. Averagely intelligent, morally suspect. They offered me a consolation prize: troubleshooter in the Post Office. Was that a career for the morally suspect as far back as 1957? The prospect of National Service loomed again. A possible posting in Hong Kong, silk shirts, Chinese women. It might not be too bad. But reality beckoned in the form of Catterick, North Yorkshire. I panicked.

*

I discovered that training to be a teacher would get me a deferment. The course was in Cardiff. Uncle Walter, by now a college principal, could pull strings, which meant leaving Diana in London and returning to the parental minefield. We agreed to keep things open – not exactly a "hall pass", but more a mutual understanding. During that year, we both had affairs. I remember attending a college debate titled "Should You Have Sex before Marriage?" It seemed to me an absurdly rhetorical question. A girl named Hilary sat beside me, nodding along to my arguments with increasing warmth. We left together and started a relationship. Possibly that same evening. I remember us going round to Hilary's family house in Penarth with bags of chips. She had a brother and a big black Labrador. Her brother's favourite trick was convincing the dog that Hilary had got his dinner. "Look at that, boy! She's eating it all up! I wouldn't stand for that! Get it off her, quick!" – and the dog would leap on Hilary, and the chair would go over backwards, with her brother laughing fit to burst.

Many years later, one of the young actresses in *Mr Selfridge* came up to me saying, "I think you knew my grandma once upon a time? Hilary Phillips?"

"Gosh, yes," I said. "At one time I knew her very well."

"I know," she said. "She told me all about it."

I introduced Hilary to my fire-eating, sword-swallowing painter friend, Sukey Phillips. They clicked, got married, had children. That match felt more like fate than anything Hilary and I shared. I felt oddly proud.

*

Back in Cardiff, I kept a low profile. The key to familial peace was avoiding my mother's attention. We didn't argue, and that felt like a success. The teacher-training course, meanwhile, was pleasantly undemanding. I spent a lot of time in the old Cardiff public library just opposite the market, reading a lot of philosophy and anthropology, with a break for cockles or faggots at lunchtime. I was also writing short stories, and one or two of them were quite good. And it turned out I enjoyed teaching and was good at it. I did one teaching practice at Rhiwbina Junior, where I had been a pupil, and another at Lewis School, Pengam, where Neil Kinnock was still the ginger schoolboy, not "the Welsh Windbag" or "the greatest Prime Minister never to be elected". I wrote half of a radio play about Lewis School, Pengam, and left it unfinished.

*

Diana and I, when reunited, confessed our transgressions – not immediately, but eventually. And far from driving a wedge between us, it strengthened our bond. She'd been having it off with an older Egyptian man, which impressed me. And she said the sex wasn't nearly so good as with me, which made me feel proud and happy. We hadn't gone looking for other people. It had just happened, as things do when you're young and horny and trying to figure out who you are. And it felt good, and right, to come together again. By the end of that year, one thing was clear: we wanted to be together.

The Proposal

Was there a special dinner? No, there wasn't. A sunset? A ring? Did I go down on one knee? None of these. This was how it happened.

We'd been having sex in my lumpy, uncomfortable bed in the flat over the greengrocer's in Marchmont Street, which I shared with Paul Vernon, and where Diana was a frequent visitor. I'd drifted off to sleep, and I think she had too. I was awoken by a shriek from her. The condom had come off inside her. She dashed up to the bathroom, stark naked – it was daytime, and everyone else was out. The bathroom wasn't in the actual flat: it was a shared one, up a flight of stairs, and it was pretty primitive, even for 1959. The water was heated by a gas geyser, which was supposed to come on with a comforting roar as soon as you turned the hot tap on. But sometimes the pilot light went out, and Diana wasn't familiar with this geyser's ways. I was just drifting off again when there was a loud explosion and another shriek. I came out onto the landing to see Diana one flight above, still naked, unhurt, but shaking like a leaf.

"It exploded!" she said, meaning the geyser.

"It's all right," I heard myself say in my state of drowsiness, referring to the condom. "We'll get married."

And, you know, that felt OK. It was time for the next stage of our lives.

*

We married in 1960, and my mother doesn't appear in a single one of our wedding photographs, because she'd flung herself off a train and landed on her head to sabotage the wedding. Well, not *literally*. But that's how it felt. She wanted me for herself, even though we didn't really get on. The truth is, she'd had a minor mishap getting off a train – not on my wedding day, though. And at another time, she'd tripped on the garden path and bashed her head. These falls may have been the start of what went wrong with her, what she eventually died of. We'll never know. What I do know is that she didn't come to the wedding, and I sometimes wonder if she did it all on purpose. I know how that sounds. If I were reading this, I'd probably think, "This chap's got issues, he should talk to someone." And maybe I should. But honestly, writers need this sort of thing. It's what keeps you churning out pages at eighty-nine, long after anyone's asked you to. Dickens had mother issues too, which fuelled a disastrous marriage, traumatized his children, made him fairly appalling all round… and gave us some cracking books. My mother missed both the ceremony and the reception, and we never spoke about it.

*

Everyone else turned up on 9th April 1960, though. My dad was there, the rest of the family, and Diana's whole clan: her mum, six aunts and one uncle.

Dorothy was the youngest of Diana's many aunts. Being the youngest, she was, like my father, able to stay on at school and go to teacher-training college. She did more: she did a Froebel course, which made her a very superior, arty sort of teacher, not a million miles from Miss Jean Brodie. She drew, she painted, she did expressive dance. I've still got one of her paintings, a crowded cubist canvas of couples dancing. It would make good cover art for *Vile Bodies*. There was no one like her in the family, and she was a big influence on Diana growing up, taking her to the ballet and to art galleries. She had a little dog called Pierrot, whom I never met, but heard a lot of stories about. Dorothy fell in love with Douglas Andrews, who was a bit of a cad, serving in the RAF and married to someone else. He was good-looking though, and had a lovely 'tache. Dorothy secured him by befriending his wife and then gradually easing her out.

By the time I met Dorothy and Douglas, they were married and living in a flat on the Chelsea Embankment. That's where we had our reception. It was compact, stylish and classy. They would drink with a fast crowd at the Surprise, a chic little pub tucked away by Christ Church. I once got talking to one of their friends, an architect called Ray. He asked me what I did, and I said I was a teacher, which I was by then. "How much money do they give you for that?" he asked. I said six hundred and eighty pounds a year. "Good God," he said. "I spend more than that on gin."

There was a period when Dorothy became convinced that Douglas was having an affair. Rather than confront the fact head-on, she devised an immensely ambitious roundabout strategy: remove him from temptation altogether. The plan involved relocating not just themselves but virtually the entire extended family from London to a large house in Suffolk. Her sisters were installed as a discreet surveillance patrol. It was all done with good intentions and a great deal of shared furniture. Dorothy continued teaching in London during the week and went down at weekends. Douglas, who did not take kindly to being on a leash, carried out small, passive-aggressive acts of rebellions. He would disappear to the pub and return late for Sunday lunch, by which point all would be overcooked and tense. He could be charming, though. As an uncle he was generous, taking Diana and her cousins to smart restaurants and treating them to glamorous outings. He had a lovely white Armstrong Siddeley convertible, and he would pick her up from college and take her to Simpson's-in-the-Strand (of course he was being kind to himself as well, but why not?). He was nice to me too, although I was Welsh and not posh. He didn't mind us coming round to the flat and drinking his gin, even when we did it in the bath. He did have one significant character flaw though, and that was a compulsion to expose himself to his wife's nieces.

The first time it happened with Diana was when we were at university. She was very short-sighted and reluctant to wear her glasses. Vanity trumped practicality, so she often had to peer across rooms to make sense of what she was seeing. On one visit to Dorothy and Douglas's house, she noticed something odd. He was standing on the far side of the room, and she found herself squinting, trying to focus, not quite sure of what she was looking at. Then the penny dropped.

Oh.

She said nothing – simply stood up, composed herself and left the room as calmly as possible. She never made a scene. Nothing further occurred for a while, until Diana's cousin Vivien, one of our bridesmaids, announced one afternoon, "Do you know what Douglas did? He exposed himself to me."

"What did you do?" Diana asked.

"I told him to put it away," Vivien replied, with considerable indignation, "and asked him why on earth he thought I'd be interested in a thing like that." Vivien was formidable. When Diana admitted he had done the same with her, Vivien said, "Well, I hope he doesn't try that with Elaine. She'll tell her mother, and there'll be war."

Of course he did try that with Elaine – and of course she did tell her mother, and there was war.

Douglas attempted to dress it up by claiming to be in love with Elaine, who was fifteen at the time. No one believed him. It was shortly afterwards that Dorothy accelerated her Suffolk relocation scheme. Families have odd ways of patching over cracks.

Diana and I were twenty-three. Getting married felt slightly absurd, but nice. We honeymooned in Bath for a week. We'd bought brand-new clothes, because that's what newly-weds did. I happened to be teaching *Northanger Abbey* at the time, so naturally we traipsed around the city retracing Catherine Morland's footsteps. Later, we took a trip to Seville, where Diana fell quite ill. I tried to cheer her up by reading her bits from *Emma* and *Pride and Prejudice*. Our shared love of literature and art was one of our earliest bonds, and remained so throughout our lives – Jane Austen, Alison Lurie, Amanda Craig, Ivon Hitchens, Howard Hodgkin, Gwen John.

Back in London, we lived in that same flat I'd nudged Janet out of. It was... well, it was crappy – but the nice kind of crappy.

Bohemian. When it rained, the water ran down the walls, but it had a great view of Holloway Prison from the kitchen window. We were broke, but happy. We haunted the galleries, little theatres, the cinema – anything cheap or, better still, free. Long walks round the Docklands. Charles Marowitz had an experimental theatre group we loved: it was free and full of strange, exciting energy. I found him an inspiration for my writing.

I remember seeing *Psycho* at the local cinema when it came out in 1960. I went to a matinée alone. It terrified me. Our flat was at the top of a big, gloomy Victorian house, close enough to the one in the film to give me the creeps. When I got home, it was dark and Diana wasn't back yet. She worked late in a publisher's office. I sat listening for her footsteps on the stairs. When I finally heard them, I was whispering to myself, "It's only Diana. It's only Diana." I couldn't go near the bathroom until she was back. I was grey-faced and shaking by the time she walked in.

*

My first teaching post was at St Clement Danes Grammar, which was then on Du Cane Road, next to Wormwood Scrubs. It was boys only, and second in the West London pecking order (Latymer Upper was top). The place was gloriously wasteful of talent. After the first year, they streamed the students into four tiers. The bottom two were labelled "the Dregs" – and, surprise surprise, those boys became thoroughly disaffected. Some of them went on to be distinguished gangsters, holding court in local pubs. But there were some lovely kids too, real joys to teach.

The headmaster was a mad old relic named Clouston, who fancied himself head of some grand public school. He gave baffling talks about "service" and "playing the game", and he was prone to verbal gaffes. "Every time I pass the lavatories," he would say, "I find the odd boy floating about in there." Or: "Mr Dean, I want you to look into the boys' trousers and see what makes them tick." One day I was on the football field, and the school secretary came running out and told me Mr Clouston wanted to see me urgently. I ran full pelt to his study, and when I got there he shouted: "No! Not you! I want the other Jones!" The staff were called "masters", and we wore gowns, except for the Art and PE teachers. But they treated me like a grown-up, and I suppose I became one there.

One of the English masters was Michael Baldwin – a real published writer: three poetry collections, two novels and a book of short stories at only twenty-eight. He treated me as an equal, a fellow writer, even though I'd published nothing. He introduced me to a writers' group called "the Makers", who accepted me too. Mike had a forceful presence and heaps of conviction. His belief in me made a difference I can still feel. It's an enormous boost for a young writer to be taken seriously by someone already inside the gates. Later he did more for me: got me onto the *Daily Mirror* Young Writers' Competition, judging children's writing, which was later taken over by WH Smith. It was quite well rewarded – but, even better, you got to meet and argue with such illustrious figures as Laurie Lee, Ted Hughes and Angela Carter. Ted was just as impressive in the flesh as he was on the page: a craggy man with a gentle Yorkshire accent. And a huge whisky drinker too, as was Mike Baldwin. I was strictly junior league in those days, booze-wise. Mike made some bad mistakes, left his very nice wife and sons for a destructive affair, drank too much, so that his fine writing talent got a bit blurred. He went out of fashion too, and was often short of money, but he could not have been nicer to me.

I wasn't just teaching English. I taught Art, first-year French and games. That sounds more impressive than it was: I was mostly running around with a whistle, trying to keep up with the game. I loved teaching Art, though, and ran art-appreciation sessions for sixth-formers. Every other week, we'd head into the West End to visit galleries. We'd set off and I wouldn't look back. Twenty boys would start out, but only three or four actually cared about where we were headed. I didn't take a register. The keen ones made it to the gallery; the rest peeled off to I didn't know where – and I didn't ask. I still have dreams where I get found out for that.

*

At Woodberry Down in Hackney, the second school I taught at, there was a colleague who belonged to a slightly grander world than the rest of us. She was well spoken, wore good coats and had married a man who worked in the City. They had all the trappings of a life less suburban: Scotland, sea air, a boat. The boat was not one of those gleaming white things: it was old, wooden and faintly heroic-looking – the sort of vessel that inspires confidence in some and vivid fantasies of catastrophe in others. They spent long weekends aboard it, pottering along the coast, drinking wine in harbours, discussing literature and weather systems. And then came the invitation.

"Why don't you both come up? A few days on the boat. It'll be wonderful."

Diana's eyes lit up instantly. Mine did not. Outwardly, I was calm and polite. "How lovely… Let me have a think." Inwardly, it was havoc: "No way. I don't want to go on your boat. I'll be sick. I'll fall off."

Most of all, I didn't want my lovely colleague to see me as a seasick moron. And I was daunted by her very manly husband, who was going to renovate a cottage on Mull.

"Perfectly straightforward if you understand the principles of rough carpentry."

So I turned it down. Diana was disappointed, and cross. She would have loved it. Wind in her hair, tin mugs of tea, eccentric conversations in distant ports. She got on extremely well with this colleague and admired her appetite for life. I've thought about that refusal more than once over the years.

*

All the while, I was desperate to write. A BBC radio variety programme called *Monday Night at Home* ran short sketches and monologues. Harold Pinter contributed to it, as did Ivor Cutler.

I thought, "I could do that." I submitted a few pieces, and two or three were accepted. One night, I was invited to a recording. The regular producer was away, and a young BBC trainee stepped in. He looked like a lower-sixth student, all earnest and bespectacled. Afterwards, we had a drink at the Langham and shared our hopes and dreams. In the mirror behind the bar, I admired my sharp jacket, slim tie, crew cut and winkle-pickers. I felt sorry for him, thinking, "You're sweet, but going nowhere." It was Melvyn Bragg.

I found my old radio play about Lewis School, Pengam. It still seemed good to me, so I completed it and sent it off to BBC Wales. It caught the fancy of John Griffiths, a senior Drama producer, who was just about to retire. "I want to make this my farewell production," he told me. "And I want to record on location: I am going to go back to my old school, where I haven't been for over forty years, and capture the essence of it. I'll give you the echoing screams of the boys as they get shoved head first into the toilets. I'll capture the sickening tone of hypocrisy of that slimy headmaster. Don't you worry, Mr Davies, I will do you proud."

You probably won't believe this, but the school he had not been back to for forty years was Lewis School, Pengam. The headmaster got very excited about the BBC's visit. He asked if he might read the script. He did and recognized himself immediately.

"This is me! I will sue!"

The play was withdrawn. They even had one of those announcements that begins: "In place of the advertised programme…" And my career looked like being over before it had begun. The moral of that story is: be authentic, but not to the point of libel.

PS: The play was eventually produced, in 1960.

A New Life

Diana and I had dreams of a house, not a flat, with three bedrooms and a garden. We wanted children and a dog, and this wasn't going to happen in London. And so, in 1963, I applied for a job at Coventry College in the Midlands. I'd applied to various places, and this was my third interview. It was an afternoon occasion, and so I decided to stay the night in Cov and have a look at the city. The Belgrade Theatre immediately drew me in, as there was a production of *The Caucasian Chalk Circle* on that evening, directed by an up-and-coming chap called Trevor Nunn. It was brilliant. Much more like Joan Littlewood's Theatre Workshop than any of the shows in the West End. The theatre was packed, three deep at the bar during the interval, swilling pints, and full of all sorts of people, all classes. "This is my sort of place," I thought. The show was very rambunctious, with lots of pissing and farting, and I thought, "Bloody hell, Coventry's a good place." The college must have quite liked me too, as they offered me a full-time position, and so it was that a few months later Diana and I moved our worldly goods out of London and into our first-ever owned home on Bertie Road in Kenilworth. We arrived there in late 1963, and I can remember running through the house thinking, "What a lot of rooms we've got!" We'd come from a one-bedroom flat, and to have an actual house with three bedrooms, a living room, a dining room, a kitchen and a garden – well, that was just wonderful.

*

Coventry College turned out to be a great place to work. It had been a women's college, only admitting men three years earlier. There were a lot of very well-fed female staff who lived in college accommodation and enjoyed three substantial meals a day, cooked by the college chef. These ladies tended to live in couples, and there was much speculation about the details of their relationships. Miss Browne, the principal, was a real old-fashioned bluestocking – very clever, no small talk and surprisingly liberal and left-wing in her views. She had a soft spot for bright delinquents, both students and staff. She had a first name, Joan, but I never dared to use it, I was so much in awe of her. And then there were Miss Ibbotson (Ibby), the vice-principal, who lived with Miss Browne, and Miss Shilitoe (Shilly), the head of the history department, who was sharp as a tack. I once had the job of interviewing prospective students with Miss Ibbotson. She said of one nice but dim girl: "She'll never set the world on fire, but I think we should take her – she's one of those deep-bosomed girls who are always good with children." Miss Ibbotson also confided that when she was a schoolteacher she had had Mandy Rice-Davies in her class – "and she was a little madam even then!" (Mandy Rice-Davies was a good-time girl in the Sixties and a star witness in the Profumo Affair – if it's before your time, it's worth looking her up.)

*

I loved the students, the teaching, the sense of possibility. I even had a car, my first, a Triumph Herald convertible, light green, and I drove all over the Warwickshire countryside visiting students on teaching practice. It mattered to me that I was helping create good teachers. Maybe because I'd had so many terrible ones. Besides teaching, I ran a creative-writing group for the rebels and the romantics, the ones who didn't quite fit the mould. We held poetry and jazz evenings. My friend George Moore and I would mix it up – the writing, the music, the mayhem. We both became hooked on doing the daily crossword, and would put ourselves under the pressure of solving it in the fifteen-minute break we had before heading back to our students. George was my first writing partner. We were very close for a while. It was a real bromance, before that word even existed. We could each tell what the other was thinking or was going to say. We wrote jokes and posted them off optimistically to various shows. They weren't used. Then, some weeks or months later, versions of our jokes began surfacing elsewhere on different shows from the ones we had submitted to. The common denominator was a script editor called Dick Vosburgh, who worked across a number of them. Harvey, my then agent, made a formal complaint. The response was terse and bland:

"There is no copyright in a joke."

We also wrote comedy material for a children's show called *Little Big Time*, starring Freddie and the Dreamers. It was Southern TV, based in Southampton, and we had jolly trips to Southampton to work with Freddie, who was a ball of energy and positively priapic. He had a bright-red Alfa Romeo sports car. "Lovely car, Freddie," I said. "Aye, you'd be surprised – you can have a bloody good fook in the front seat! Zip zip zip! I could go all night tonight!" He was having a thing with one of the waitresses in the Polynesian Roof Room. ("Hey! What d'you say to a hula-hula girl? Gracias! Geddit? *Grassy-arse!* Zip zip zip!")

Little Big Time was the ingenious notion of producer Angus Wright, who noticed that with the death of the music hall and the decline of working men's clubs, a lot of speciality acts were going cheap – performing seals, ventriloquists, comedy vocal quartets, contortionists, and so on. Children loved that sort of thing, hence a variety show compèred by Freddie – genius, right? And it was very popular. Angus made us swear not to reveal that a very distinguished Dutch sea lion was actually getting more money than Freddie was. This sea lion had two caravans, one half full of water for him to splash about in when he was off duty. *Little Big Time* led to more kids' shows, then schools programmes for ATV in Birmingham. We wrote a little educational soap that was supposed to appeal to apprentices, featuring a couple of likely lads. In fact it attracted mostly pubescent girls. And we did two or three other things, all fun to do.

*

At that time, we spent a lot of time in and out of each other's houses too and holidayed together in Swaledale, surrounded by small children. And yes, we had affairs. Me first with Barbara, George's wife, then Diana with George, a liaison that lasted over twenty years and severely tested our conjugal bonds. But both marriages survived, and so did our friendship, though George's and mine became less of a bromance, to put it mildly. George died a couple of years ago. He'd gone downstairs to make a cup of tea and died sitting up at the kitchen table. Barbara remained a close friend. We had lunch together in Poms a few weeks ago and talked about old times. Shortly after this, she was admitted to hospital with breathing difficulties. It turned out she had stage-4 lung cancer, though she had never smoked, and she died within days of the diagnosis. There's no denying that the death of one's oldest friends is one of the bleaker aspects of old age.

*

Diana and I didn't have a telly at first, so we'd go round to friends when we wanted to watch something. Before George and Barbara, we were friends with a very intense couple called Brian and Margaret. Brian was a colleague at the college, and a passionate D.H. Lawrence fan. We would turn up at their house, ring the bell and wait till eventually Brian would come to the door, all pink-faced and sweaty. "Sorry! We've been making love!" Margaret was a bad cook and wrote awful novels, but Brian was convinced she was a genius. He published them privately and bullied his friends into writing endorsements for the jacket. Margaret kept a journal, which was also to be regarded as a work of genius. That was a load of nonsense too. She wrote in it that I was consumed with lust for her, but nothing could be further from the truth. (I am afraid I was a bit uncompromising when it came to figure and fashion: Margaret was much too portly for my taste and wore sandals with socks.) They were both intellectual snobs too, and talked about people having second-rate minds. They had a sex-mad dachshund called Putzel who would hump your leg with fierce determination. But it was good knowing Brian and Margaret. When you are new to a place, you have to make the best of it in terms of friendships, until you find the friends who are most like you, and the differences can be very stimulating and enlightening. We used to read Shakespeare aloud together (how's that for a fun night out?). Actually, it *was* fun, and I sort of long for those days. Margaret, in particular, read brilliantly.

One day I was walking with Brian in some woods near the college, and I happened to be making the case for dogs as being better than human beings. Brian was a bit shocked by this, and refused to believe I was being serious. I said yes, I was. At that moment, three Dalmatians ran out of the wood, two with muzzles, one without. The one without a muzzle ran straight up to me and bit me in the leg, as if trained to act in support of Brian's argument. A tweedy woman appeared, with dog leads.

"Your dog just bit me," I said.

"Which one?"

"The one without the muzzle."

"Oh," she said. "That one doesn't usually bite."

And she walked on.

*

Eventually we got our own TV. I remember watching *Top of the Pops* for the first time and seeing Sandie Shaw sing '(There's) Always Something There to Remind Me'. I was mesmerized. She wasn't a brilliant singer – Dionne Warwick did it better – but Sandie had cheekbones and bare feet. Then came the Wednesday Play. I watched it and thought, "I could do that." So I did. I wrote one – sent it in. It felt a bit like doing the Littlewoods pools. To my astonishment, they accepted it. The play was called *Who's Going to Take Me On?* and was about a young woman called Steph Smith, a typist in a knicker factory, who wants to be a rep. She had read *Death of a Salesman* at school and got hold of the wrong end of the stick – she thought that working as a sales rep was a wonderful job. She gets teased, tricked and exploited, but remains resolute and defiant till the end. I was invited to the Television Centre in Wood Lane for an interview with Lionel Harris, executive producer of the Wednesday Play. Lionel Harris was plump and sweaty, and in a hurry. He wanted to get to the Harrods sale, he said. He excused himself, and left me with Kenith Trodd, the script editor.

"This is a fucking good play," said Ken. "And we are going to give it a fucking good production." It was the first time I had ever heard anyone swear in a posh accent. (Ken Tynan was later the first to use the F word on British TV. Sweary buggers, those Kens.)

Anyway.

After the success of my first Wednesday Play in 1967, I assumed that I'd made it. I didn't leap about, but inwardly I thought: "Well, then, this is it: I'm thirty-one – life now changes. I may have to give up teaching. I've arrived." I was going to be the next Dennis Potter, already a rising star. I had joined the ranks. Surely more would follow. Nothing did. I didn't sell another television play for five years. People would say, "Your scripts are great, but just not quite what we're looking for right now." So that was that. But I had a day job that I loved. And I still had *Little Big Time* and Freddie. Zip zip zip! What was not to like?

*

Around this time, I wrote a play called *Is That Your Body, Boy?*, about a PE teacher we'd had at school in Wales. The teacher was old-fashioned, rigid in his notions of discipline and service, and unintentionally comic. He belonged entirely to a world that was disappearing. The 1960s were on the march – he was still standing firmly in a pre-war moral landscape. The play keeps him in detention with a group of boys while he tells them the story of his life. It was a good, meaty part, a role you could get your teeth into. Innes Lloyd, the producer, and Louis Marks, then a script editor, saw that at once. They thought Ron Moody might play "Cracker", as the teacher was nicknamed. A lunch was arranged at the BBC to introduce us. The Beeb in those days had tiers of lunch. There was the ordinary canteen, thrilling because you might bump into a Dalek while queuing; there was the restaurant, undeniably grander and a sign that things were going well; and then there were private dining rooms. These were the summit, though in practice the menu tended towards cold cuts. We were in one of these private rooms.

A large plate of ham was placed before us. Ron Moody surveyed it and said:

"I can't eat this. And I can't eat any of the other meat that's on the plate with it."

The implication that someone should have noticed that he was an observant Jew hovered in the air. It had not occurred to Innes, who was mortified.

"Oh, my dear chap, I'm so dreadfully sorry..."

The lunch wobbled slightly at the outset, but Ron loved the play. He wanted the part. There wasn't a great deal for us to discuss. I'd put it on the page. He understood it instantly. For him, Cracker wasn't merely comic: he was tragic, a man whose values no longer fitted the age. Ron spoke about lost virtues: service, endeavour, bravery, duty. He recognized something in that character. Perhaps something of himself. The play was directed on film by Claude Whatham, a hot director of the time. Ron was magnificent. The mixture of stubbornness and vulnerability was exactly right. It was well received. And, for once, something did follow it. Louis Marks, who had backed the script early on, became something of a patron to me. We did an Edgar Allan Poe story, 'The Imp of the Perverse', with a young Michael Kitchen. And Louis, so unselfish, introduced me to another producer, Rosemary Hill. It was the beginning of another chapter, though of course I didn't know that at the time. I was simply relieved that the silence after the first success had finally been broken. Which is to say: in television, as in most things, you are never as established or as finished as you think you are.

*

Fortunately, my life didn't depend on it. I had a job I loved. I had friends. And then our children arrived. Arrived? No, someone gave birth to them. Bill was born in 1965. I was twenty-eight. I felt secure and settled in my job and in my marriage to Diana. He was born at home, in Bertie Road in Kenilworth. It was thrilling and terrifying. I remember thinking how strong Diana looked, her veins strained like a weightlifter's, no howling like they always do childbirth on the telly, just determination and the will to get it right. As she gave her final push, he practically launched himself into the world. He wasn't the easiest baby. Diana had a tough time with him: sleepless nights, endless crying. During the day, I could escape to work and have a jolly time teaching my students. She couldn't. It felt like we were leading two very different lives at that time. Diana was always very good at just getting on with things.

Bill was a terrible sleeper, and I remember lying on the floor, holding his finger until he slept. The thing was, I fell asleep too, and I'd wake up cold and cramped. There were nights when it was impossible, and I'd put him into his carrycot and drive down the M1 to Milton Keynes just to get him to sleep in the car, which he did as soon as the engine got going. Diana lost a lot of weight, and the doctor prescribed Mackeson Stout to build her up. She hated it, and I drank it, as I didn't want to waste it. I even bought a fatherhood suit, a traditional three-piece number that made me look like a Victorian patriarch. Waistcoat, tight trousers – the lot. All that was missing was a watch chain draped across my Mackeson-enhanced belly.

When Bill was a few weeks old, we visited my parents in Cardiff – me, Diana, the baby and our beagle puppy, Chowder, acquired during Diana's pre-birth broody phase. Dad, who was a late starter to driving and not natural with it, picked us up in his jalopy, which had been bumped along the way. The radiator was damaged and leaking, and the car was reluctant to start. In the end we got a taxi. Mum was livid. "Poor Wynford! You left him there with the car!" She didn't waste a moment thinking about the fact that we had a young baby, all the paraphernalia required, plus a puppy. Rather than being happy to see us, she fretted about having the dog in the house and was insistent that he needed to remain outside. My father had to trap him in the garden with wire netting, which nearly strangled him – the dog, not my dad. It wasn't the warmest of visits, and threw me back to the household tension of my younger years. But this was our family now. Ours to make as we wished. Me, Diana, Bill and, a couple of years later, our daughter Anna.

*

Diana's second pregnancy was, from where I was standing, entirely different from the first. Memory is a treacherous thing, but I don't recall the nausea, the fatigue or the anxiety that had accompanied Bill's arrival. This time she seemed to carry Anna as if it were the most natural extension of herself. She looked healthy, beautiful, amused by the whole process. In the later months she wore a red dress that suited her so well it became like her late-pregnancy signature. It lit her up and did something to the room when she walked in. The day before Anna was born, Diana was driving about as usual in our bright-red Sunbeam Alpine, which at the time felt almost indecently showy. There she was: red dress, red car with fins and the top down, Bill in the back – a handsome pregnant woman conducting her life without drama. Anna arrived the next day.

She was born at home, with Bill and me present. It looked effortless. I am quite certain it wasn't. But Diana had a way of making the difficult appear entirely manageable. And I felt proud, relieved, excited for everything that lay ahead. Once Anna was born and the dress was no longer required, it began circulating among pregnant friends, each of them glowing in it in turn. It became, in its way, a shared talisman. I liked being a family man, especially in the company of other families going through the same stage of life. There was a sense of shared experiment about it. None of us quite knew what we were doing, but we were doing it together. We made friends with other young parents; the children became friends too, and our lives overlapped in a cheerful, slightly chaotic way.

The college had a swimming pool, and, as staff, George and I enjoyed certain privileges. On Sunday mornings we'd march our entire double brood down there, fling them into the water and then repair to the bar afterwards while they ran riot. It felt perfectly normal at the time: children playing, adults nursing pints, chlorine still in our hair. Nobody worried too much. We weren't strict parents – and, in truth, we didn't need to be. Bill and Anna were both good kids, though very different. Bill was quiet, introvert, prone to long periods of imaginative absorption, and with a quirky sense of humour, even as a toddler. ("What d'you think I've got in my pocket? Blue Bear's nose!") Anna was affectionate, even passionate. Once, as a baby, she wrapped one of her feet up and gave it to me as a present. Perhaps the best present I ever had. She would occasionally stomp upstairs in righteous fury, only to reappear ten minutes later, sunny and affectionate again. At weekends they'd climb into our bed, bringing with them an assortment of toys. Chowder, our dog at the time, would leap up too. Bill adored him and saw no reason why he should not be encouraged to burrow under the covers. Diana took a firmer view on dogs and hygiene. We'd drink tea and juice, invent stories and linger there for far too long. That's really how I began writing for children: out of those times of closeness and our shared sense of humour came stories better than anything you could find in most kids' books.

Bill had an imaginary friend called Dr Boox. He would hold elaborate conversations on the telephone with him. Diana and I would ask: "Where is he now? What's he drinking?" It turned out that he was usually in the pub, "drinking beer and wine". Over time a fully formed figure emerged: an eccentric, slightly grumpy vet who lived in a house overrun with animals and who absolutely allowed them into bed with him. Bill approved of that detail. Eventually that became my first book for children, *The Fantastic Feats of Doctor Boox*.

Long before I'd left teaching – back in the days when I was supplementing my income by taking on whatever small writing jobs came my way – I was asked to contribute to a series of reading books designed for what were then called "slow learners". The brief was straightforward: stories written with a very limited vocabulary, carefully controlled so that young readers encountering words for the first time would not be overwhelmed. It turned out to be quite a creative challenge. You cannot rely on complexity of language, so you must rely on rhythm, repetition and a sense of adventure. The story has to move. The sentences have to carry the reader forwards without drawing attention to their own simplicity. It becomes a kind of verbal engineering. I had a vivid memory of learning to read myself, which helped. There was a small book I had before I went to school that was very phonetic, very determinedly simple, but full, to my mind, of tremendous drama. I can still recall the lines:

> Ben was in the fen.
> A mad ox is in the fen and ran up to Ben.
> Ten men ran to get Ben in the fen.

Magnificent stuff – danger, rescue, community action. All in about twenty words.

There is real pleasure in making up stories that delight children in that way. The language must be spare, but the situation must feel alive. And I was always aware that these books would not only be read by children, but read aloud to them by parents, teachers, older siblings, which means the rhythm matters enormously. A sentence must sound good in the mouth as well as on the page. (That's why I can't read *Harry Potter* – but millions can, so what do I know?)

When *Doctor Boox* was published, it felt thrilling. Then, at seven, Bill became obsessed with war. He read war comics and concluded that I was a disappointing father, largely because I was useless at DIY – although I did once plumb in a bath with the aid of the *Reader's Digest* manual. But Bill wanted me to make a tank-shaped go-kart so he could hurtle down the hill in the Abbey Fields, firing imaginary ammunition at passers-by, and I was not up to it – or inclined to try.

"You wouldn't really like to shoot people, would you?" we'd venture cautiously.

"Yes, I would," he'd reply. "And I'll tell you who I'd like to shoot."

I remembered Jennifer and the poison, and was grateful that he didn't nominate Diana and me as his targets. Out of this ferment – my supposed inadequacy and Bill's martial fantasies – came *Conrad's War*. It follows a boy who begins by trying to build a tank because his father is useless, and then slips into a blend of wartime reality, comic-book logic and dream. Bill loved it. Diana declared it the best thing I'd ever written, perhaps because it caught something true about our household at that time. It went on to win the Guardian Fiction Prize, and for a few years I was known as a children's author. I wasn't particularly enamoured of most children's books at the time. I wanted to write about real life – about sons shouting, "Dad, why are you so useless?" When *Conrad's War* was published, Anna, who must have been about seven, demanded equal treatment. She wanted a book about a bad girl. She was a very good girl with a robust fantasy life (though she did once push a boy down the stairs and got away with it because everyone thought her incapable of such a crime. She confessed years after, quite unrepentant).

So we began *Marmalade Atkins*. Anna dictated, I took notes. She was ruthless. Marmalade would lie, cheat and cause havoc in a way that Anna never did – at least not on a comparable scale.

Around that time, I had a student who was resistant to my authority and unimpressed by my teaching. "Come to my place," she said one day, "and I'll show you how it feels." She offered to teach the children to ride, if I would join in. It seemed a reasonable exchange. Anna took to horses instantly. Bill was less convinced. My student put me on a horse called Gypsy, a Welsh cob who was as sweet as pie until you got on his back. Then he was a very naughty horse indeed. Once I was in the saddle, he concluded that he could dislodge me by scraping me against walls and charging hedges before halting abruptly. At the end of the lesson, we would turn and trot back to the gate for some carrots. That was the idea, but Gypsy didn't trot back: he galloped – actually, "bolted" would be a fairer way of putting it. Sitting on a horse when it's bolting at full gallop is a bit like being on the roof of an express train. You are utterly powerless, and that is how my student wanted me to feel. There was also a donkey named Rufus, indisputably in charge of the entire establishment. In later years he was employed to keep a highly strung racehorse calm, which tells you everything you need to know about Rufus and his kind. Living next door to my student was a couple who seemed determined to own one of every possible species. I thought Marmalade's parents could be like them. All of it went into the book: the donkey, the horses, the dreams of anarchy, terrible parents and one very bolshy girl, the stubborn pride of children, the unspoken negotiations of adulthood. When Sue Birtwistle, one of my former students who was now a producer, asked me to write a kids' drama for TV, I wrote a show called *Educating Marmalade*, based on the books, and it starred twelve-year-old Charlotte Coleman, who had herself been expelled from school, and would go on to star in *Oranges Are Not the Only Fruit*, *Four Weddings and a Funeral* and a film of mine called *Inappropriate Behaviour*, about a delinquent country girl who falls in love with her behaviour specialist. Everyday life observed and slightly rearranged. It was rich material – it always is.

Tough Times

Looking back, I can see what shaped the marriage that Diana and I would go on to have. The physical move to Coventry was one factor; my close friendship with my colleague George was another.

Diana and I had a long marriage: sixty-three years wed and sixty-eight together in total. And it was a good one. It wasn't standard-issue – but whose is? We lived several marriages within one. Different chapters, different selves, as we grew and changed. What matters is we remained kind and close to each other, all the way to the end.

Well, most of the time.

Round about 1973, we were having problems due to our blurring the lines of our friendship with George and Barbara. Affairs have a way of expanding beyond the neat private compartment one imagines for them. There were painful conversations and a good deal of wounded trust. What remains slightly surprising to me is that the friendships themselves didn't collapse. In fact, they endured. Our lives continued to intersect – socially, professionally, domestically. We worked together, our children grew up alongside one another, and the complicated history simply became part of the background. But these things never truly go away if left untreated, and I spiralled into sexual jealousy.

I spent a lot of time looking for things I didn't want to find or didn't like when found. It didn't occur to me at the time that I was turning into a version of what my mother had been, a mad sleuth hurting no one but myself. Diana and I were not getting on, though we still liked and respected each other as parents. Why didn't we split up? That's what people do these days. But we still loved each other, even though we weren't getting on. And we each loved the way we were with the kids. They still came in our bed every morning, we still had our stories and our jokes. I don't think Diana ever seriously considered leaving me or asking me to leave. Nor did I want to. She wanted to stay married and be in love with me and another person too, and somehow I had to come to terms with that.

But I couldn't.

People were beginning to notice. Then a friend told me about an encounter group he'd been to, role-play therapy to exorcize emotional demons. "There's quite a bit of casual sex going on, too," he said. And he was not wrong. But something quite extraordinary happened to me there, in a psychodrama workshop. The idea was, you tell your story as clearly and honestly as you can, then choose someone to play the other person in your story. I chose a woman who looked vaguely like Diana, a woman who had been rather boring me with her "daddy" problems. She looked me in the eyes and said, as Diana: "I'm not trying to hurt you. I still love you. I'm just trying to be happy." I thought, "Fuck, I'm going to cry." I was so moved. Why had I been putting her and myself through it? Of course she has a right to be happy. And I can be happy too. I went home, and when Diana asked how it had gone, I said, "I'm going to be different now. I'm not going to be jealous any more." She didn't believe me. But I had changed. I had been giving out the wrong vibes for a while, being quite spiky and aggressive to people in general, not just Diana. But now I was a changed man, and almost immediately Pat came into my life.

*

Pat was a PE and dance student. We met in a very odd way. One of the tutors and I had set up a joint poetry and dance workshop, exploring how they might inspire each other, how poems could come out of dance and vice versa. Look, it was the Seventies – we used to do all sorts of things in those days. So there I was in a circle of people, and this girl jumped into the centre and lunged at me. Not just once. It went on and on. It felt like a challenge. I had to do something. I tackled her to the ground, and we wrestled. Not my finest moment, but emblematic of something between us: combativeness, curiosity, chemistry.

After the class, I asked her what it was all about.

"You don't remember me, do you? I was on your Children's Literature course, and you were rubbishing Paddington Bear! It's wrong!"

I said that I'd nothing against the bear himself. I just felt Michael Bond's prose was dated and dull. I felt a bit of an idiot saying that.

"You want to come for a swim with me?" she said. "I'll teach you life-saving. Got an advanced certificate."

I said all right, and we went straight to the pool.

"Get in the deep end and pretend you're drowning," she said. I did as I was told and thrashed around in the deep end. She dived in, grabbed my chin, yanked it back and towed me to safety. I felt helpless like a baby.

"Relax. I've got you," she said.

And I did. She was twenty and I was thirty-five, and she was in control from the start. For the first time in ages, I let go. She was strong, wise – and exactly what I needed. Pat entered my life and the family's just when we needed it. Diana accepted her immediately. She could see that I was different – that the obsessive rage had vanished. And Pat? She wasn't a secret. She became part of our family landscape. She was great with the kids, lively and boisterous, swinging them round, a leg and a wing. They loved her, and still do. Pat and I were lovers for about twelve years. She had her own life. She wasn't mine. It wasn't exclusive, yet I loved her dearly for her strength, her friendship and her ways. When we first met, she basically lived on steak and ice cream (her dad was a butcher). Over time, she moved from straight teaching to being an expert in rejects, rebels and school refusers, and an adviser on alternatives to custody. She ran a unit for her baddies, and they loved her and she loved them. And over time she slowly transitioned from straight to gay. She broke it to me very gently.

"Time to renegotiate our relationship," she said one morning, serving me eggs in bed.

"Does that mean I am still in it?"

She looked at my directly.

"As a friend."

And she's still my friend, and so is Chez, her partner.

From Kenilworth to Broadway and Back

The move to Coventry was important in terms of my writing life too. I had the time to write, and I was in a new, exciting environment. I started off writing radio plays and developed a wonderfully productive relationship with Anthony Cornish, a BBC producer based in Birmingham. Tony had what seemed like an enviable amount of freedom and independence, much more than producers seem to have nowadays. He taught me how to write more economically, to cut to the chase, get into a scene late, get out early. No dithering.

As I mentioned before, the heroine of my Wednesday Play was Steph Smith, a typist in a knicker factory who dreams of becoming a rep and driving up and down the motorways in a Ford Escort. I adapted the play for radio, then used the character of Steph Smith to explore further narrative opportunities. We follow her as she becomes a young mature student at university and has various problematic relationships, observed in a wryly comedic way. Steph was partly based on a student of mine called Cynthia, in the same year as Sue Birtwistle (who went on to produce *Pride and Prejudice*). Cynthia liked to have fun, but was desperately serious as well, on one occasion being heard to yell: "Yer all SHALLOW!" Great line, which of course went into the play. I did five radio plays altogether featuring Steph Smith, and Cynthia is still a good friend.

Tony told me I should try my hand at stage plays. I said I couldn't. My idea of theatre was all Ibsen and intensity, grand entrances and dramatic pauses – and, crucially, I couldn't think of how to get my characters offstage except when they had to go to the toilet. "No, no," Tony said. "Plays don't have to be like that any more." And, just like that, he showed me how to adapt my radio pieces, beginning with *Filthy Fryer and the Woman of Maturer Years*. It was more cabaret than conventional drama. Characters stepped into the spotlight and said, "Hello, I'm so-and-so and this is my life," and then boom, you were inside the scene. I loved it. It felt cheeky and immediate. No pretending the audience wasn't there. I'd always found that odd anyway – rude, almost – like ignoring a roomful of eavesdroppers who paid to be there. It seemed weird not to say hello, if you see what I mean.

*

Tony had a relationship with the Orange Tree pub theatre in Richmond, and he managed to get *Filthy Fryer* produced there. The audience lapped it up. And suddenly I was a stage dramatist, of a sort. I wrote several more pieces for the Orange Tree and other small venues. And a few years later, in 1979, and with a handful of plays and a TV series about the legend of King Arthur under my belt, I had enough swagger to say to Ed Thomason, who at the time ran the Belgrade Studio in Coventry, "I could write a better play than what's on here now, and it would fill the house."

I had an idea about a primary-school teacher, a story very much drawn from Diana's life and her complicated relationship with her mother. I knew the material and what I was doing. Write a play about a teacher, and you'll fill the place with teachers. The first version of that play was called *Diary of a Desperate Woman*, and I staged it like a cabaret. The audience arrived to find Rose and her mother already sitting at a table, drinks in hand, murmuring crossly. No curtain, no lights down. Their argument gradually swelled until the audience realized that the play had begun. At a climactic moment, the mother stormed off, and Rose looked out at the audience and said, "You think this is a play about my mother. It's not. It's about me."

And we were off. The play plundered material from both of our lives, mostly Diana's. It did well at the Belgrade – the teachers flooded in. A London-based producer took an option on it. He wasn't exactly high-profile, but he had energy and a gambler's instinct. He sent the script to Glenda Jackson. In those days, if Glenda said yes, theatres moved mountains to accommodate her. I'd written several plays I was deeply proud of, yet they'd never got anywhere near London's West End. The usual response was, "It's a very difficult time at the moment. Very tricky."

But *Rose* was different. Glenda read it. She liked it. She wanted to meet. I wore a pink suit to our lunch, which probably spoke louder than anything I managed to say. I was awestruck. I could barely eat, let alone speak. She was everything you'd hope Glenda Jackson would be: direct, funny, intelligent, unafraid. She said most of the new plays she'd read were awful. She liked that *Rose* had bite. Her only note? "Beef up the other characters. As it is, I'll blow them off the stage." And she was right. It was good advice, and I listened to it. Glenda knew herself very well, and she knew what she wanted.

Alan Dossor, the brilliant and eccentric director who'd made his name at the Liverpool Everyman, came on board to direct. He liked to finish rehearsals by lunchtime and spend his afternoons in the pub – where, presumably, the rest of his ideas fermented. We opened at the Duke of York's on St Martin's Lane, and the theatre was full every night. I'd walk past posters for musicals, tourists trailing scarves behind them, and then, there it was: my name in lights – a real West End opening. It was a life-changing moment for me. It was 1979: the kids were young teenagers, Diana and I in our forties and still teachers – and suddenly I was getting a weekly cheque for £2,000 through the post, a lot of money in those days. My then accountant, Michael Henshaw, advised me to go and live in Ireland for tax reasons, which felt a bit extreme. And, besides, it was wholly impractical, as I still had a full-time teaching job, at Warwick University. "Well, you'd better turn yourself into a Limited Company, then," he said. Which I did. Was he anticipating that it was all going to be plain sailing from now on?

*

The play ran in the West End for six months, with rave reviews and packed houses. Glenda held the stage with effortless power, and when Broadway came knocking, she said yes to that too.

New York.

This time, we were doing it properly (there had been a rehearsal of sorts a few years earlier). Diana and the kids, by then fifteen and thirteen, came along. There were limo pick-ups and fresh flowers in the suite. We stayed on 42nd Street – back when it was still gritty and not gentrified. From the coffee-shop window we could see men sunning themselves on the steps across the road, their shirts pulled up to reveal stomachs and sores.

I sat in rehearsals while Diana and the kids saw the city. The cast was enthusiastic, the energy high. But something was off. There was a faint dissonance, a cultural static noise. American ears missed the nuance of provincial English rhythms. But we smiled, shrugged. It was fine. It was going to be fine. This was Broadway, after all. The preview audiences were polite, even appreciative – but not ecstatic. We said the show was settling in, finding its stride. Diana and the kids flew home, and I stayed on alone for the opening night. I was filled with existential dread and spent most of the first act in the hotel bathroom, paralysed by nerves, while on TV a Southern preacher shouted about hellfire and damnation. "It is all going to be OK," I thought. "Glenda is bringing her London triumph to New York." Why did it all feel as if cracks were opening in the pavement? I got back to the theatre in time for the curtain call. The applause was fine.

We went to Sardi's – because that was the done thing. Except, there was something in the air. The smiles were a little too wide. The food was unchewable. One actor came in with his whole family, and the restaurant stood and applauded him. I thought, "How lovely!" Then I wondered if they were applauding his courage for showing up on a doomed night. And then came the reviews. Piles of them. The wet ink still clinging to the pages… that smell… of failure. The room fell silent. Only one review mattered in those days: Frank Rich in the *New York Times*. His opening line: "It is always a pleasure to welcome Miss Glenda Jackson back to these shores." But basically he was saying: what is she doing in this pile of crap by some nobody called Andrew Davies?

Glenda rang me the next day. "These idiots know nothing. Come and have a drink at the Oak Bar in the Plaza." I did. Her agent paid – it was the first time I'd seen someone settle a bar bill with a credit card: March 1981. I drank too much – of course. Glenda was lovely and positive.

Recently, I looked up that review again. It wasn't nearly as brutal as I remembered. Frank Rich loved Jessica Tandy's performance as Rose's mother, who was, let's be honest, very much based on Diana's mother. His point about Glenda's Rose being too formidable? Fair, perhaps – balanced, even. At the time, it crushed me. The dream collapsed – the lights dimmed. And I got out of town while the cast kept going, dragging a wounded show through three months of quiet audiences.

Still, my name had been in lights. On Broadway. Twice.

*

The previous occasion was *Fearless Frank*, a small-scale musical. *My Life and Loves* by Frank Harris had long been one of my guilty favourites, equal parts autobiography and pornography. It was outrageous, gloriously excessive and absolutely irresistible. Harris wasn't just a writer: he was a phenomenon. A fabulist with a libido the size of Texas. He left England at seventeen, landed in America and did all sorts of things, from bootblacking and hotel-clerking to riding the range as a bona-fide cowhand. Then he came back to England and reinvented himself as a literary lion and friend of the famous. He moved in rarefied circles: Carlyle, Wilde, Whistler, even Maupassant – and, if you believe Harris, they all unburdened their most intimate secrets to him over brandy and cigars. He edited the London *Evening News* with flair, went to prison for offending public decency and dictated his magnum opus to a string of secretaries in Paris cafés when he was old, impotent and more outrageous than ever.

What fascinated me wasn't just the extravagant claims or the endless sexual escapades he recounted, but the sheer *zest* for life. Yes, he was a boaster. Yes, he was a liar. But his *joie de vivre* was infectious. From a young age, Harris had been obsessed with sex, not in a brutish or exploitative way, but in a manner he saw as reverent, generous and deeply focused on women's pleasure.

Louis Marks was my favourite producer at the BBC. He had script-edited my second BBC show, *Is That Your Body, Boy?*, and he was keen for me to write more for him. When he became a full-time producer, our careers hung by the same slender thread for a while, but things turned out fine for us both. I suggested to Louis that we tell Harris's story theatrically, in the studio, no elaborate set, just the intimate setting of a café in Paris, with Frank holding court and the secretary playing all the women from his scandalous past. It would be playful, subversive, non-naturalistic. This was the 1970s, and TV was obsessed with realism. What we proposed was something different, bold, fearless. Fearless Frank. Leonard Rossiter was cast as Frank, and Colin Bucksey directed. The play was like a cabaret of confession, and the critics didn't know what to make of it.

Dan Crawford, the delightfully eccentric American impresario of the King's Head Theatre in Islington, adored it. He saw its potential as a stage musical, of all things. Dan introduced me to Dave "New York" Brown, a composer with flair and bite. Together, we turned *Fearless Frank* into a rollicking, raucous show that packed out the tiny King's Head for six glorious weeks and earned rave reviews. We were ecstatic. The kind of excitement that makes you believe "maybe this really is going somewhere".

And then along came David Black. An American producer with Broadway credits and a fondness for Langan's Brasserie, he had bushy black eyebrows and a wicked grin. Groucho Marx could have played him in the movie. He'd started out in menswear, and moved to Wall Street – "Yeah, from socks to stocks" – and now dined exclusively on spinach soufflé with extra hollandaise and anchovy sauce. He insisted we do the same. (It was delicious, by the way. I think you can still order it there.) Anyway, he loved the show and insisted it could transfer to New York. So, Broadway, here we come!

It was summer in Manhattan – a brutal, sticky, furnace blast of a season. That city, in the *Taxi Driver* decade – grimy, dangerous, electric – was both thrilling and slightly terrifying. Cool auditoriums were the only refuge, but ours, the Princess Theatre, had air con so deafening it drowned out half my witty lines. Worse still, the American cast and director missed the tone entirely. They played it earnest when it should've been wicked – sedate when it should've been saucy. The spark, the cheek, the subversive delight all vanished. *Fearless Frank* closed after just three weeks.

The feeling of having a Broadway flop is like getting punched in the gut while bystanders loaf around sneering. One day it's all limos and flowers, martinis on the house. The next, it's like you've contracted leprosy. And everybody knows. No one will sit too close. No one returns your calls. Even the guy at the deli truck gives you a strange look. But here's the truth: even that was fun. Those three weeks on Broadway? I was drunk for all of them, drunk on Bloody Marys at 10 a.m., martinis at noon and the thrill of simply *being there* – staggering between bars to escape the swelter, eating the world's worst club sandwiches in hotel lobbies, watching steam rise off the asphalt and cab drivers hurl abuse at each other. If the show had been a success, I'm sure it would have been even more fun, but even failure had its glamour. And there was a hundred dollars a day in per diems – "walking-around money", they called it. Would I do it again? In a heartbeat.

*

Having a flop on Broadway, or indeed anywhere, is instructive. Failure teaches you things that success never does – like who your real friends are, for example. When everything goes wrong, the actors miss the joke, the critics damn you with faint praise or lambast you, you're forced to take a good, long look at the wreckage.

Actually, it hurts to do so, and I avoid it for as long as possible. It doesn't get easier – but it does get familiar. Nobody actually died. "Count your blessings," I told myself. I had a wife who loved me, even though she loved someone else as well. I had two lovely, interesting kids. And failure is a rich source of material. Think of *The Crack-Up* by F. Scott Fitzgerald and J.P. Miller's *Days of Wine and Roses*. I got a couple of good short stories out of my New York humiliation. Nothing really bad can ever happen to a writer: it's all material – and the worse the experience, the better the material. You learn to notice how everything looked, sounded, felt, smelt, even while you're hurting. You'll use it all later. Writing is turning pain into money.

Some Notes on Writing

I think I was always writing my own story.

There was a bridge near our house when I was a boy, an ordinary concrete bridge across the stream, in the middle of the village. I remember walking across it and, without any conscious decision, narrating myself.

"The tall, slender boy paused on the bridge."

I wasn't tall – nor slender, really. But in my mind I was. We are all the protagonists of our own stories. And this "boy on the bridge" stuff was the beginning of something, seeing myself from the outside as a character in a tale. Third person, past tense, like a proper narrative. It would be years before I wrote a screenplay.

Writing has preoccupied me for most of my days. If I add up the hours, it must be the single activity I've done more than any other, including sleeping and eating – I'm eighty-nine as I write this, so that's saying something. I write first of all to please myself. I have to like what I write, or I can't go on. But don't you write for an audience? Yes, but initially a very small one: myself, then there are two or three people who know me well and know my stuff. And I want them to like it – I need them to like it. If they do, I feel pretty well armoured. Anyone else, if they don't like it, they can go to hell. Arrogant? Writers have to be.

There's a huge difference between writing a memoir like this and writing a play or a film. With this, it's all me. With a drama, I can always say: that's not what I think, that's what the character thinks. But I know that's not true, not really. I know that everything I write gives me away. Writing sex scenes is particularly exposing. People read them or watch them, and think, "Does he really think that's how people do it?" I once said, in public, about a well-known novelist: "He writes about sex like someone who's never had a shag in his life." Well, you have to speak as you find, don't you? But that's the sort of fear that all writers have, I guess: that people will point and sneer, or even fall about laughing when you've been deadly serious. That's why I like to run things by my two or three trusties before letting them go free.

Increasingly, as I get older and older, I like to write characters who are not like me, especially young female characters. I love to inhabit them for a while, carefree young girls like Louisa Musgrove in *Persuasion* before she cracks her head on the Cobb at Lyme Regis: "Jump me down, Captain Wentworth!" There is a physical thrill when I slip fully into a character's head and think their thoughts as if they were mine. Stepping into other people's consciousness, especially those who are nothing like me, remains one of the great pleasures of the job. Women in particular. Writing them frees me from the gravitational pull of the Welsh male voice (not to mention that of the paunchy eighty-nine-year-old Welsh male body) that might otherwise dominate everything. It's a way of escaping from myself while using myself at the same time. A pleasant paradox.

*

When I was twenty-one, my parents gave me a portable Olivetti Lettera 22. I loved it. It was a design icon of its day – Caryl Churchill had one, I read in *Vogue*. I taught myself to touch-type on it, and I used it for years. You didn't need to plug it into anything: it was always ready to go. Carbon copies. Ignore typos, just bash on. It meant I was a lot faster then than I am now. Computers let you fiddle about endlessly with small changes, which slows you down. There are still some writers – I believe Alan Bennett is one – who write their first draft in longhand. I did that for a while – a reporter's notebook gave you a page a minute in my handwritten scrawl. Now Final Draft lets you do the same thing.

No one ever taught me how to write: I learnt by reading and watching. In the Fifties I managed to find a book of TV scripts by eminent writers, which I devoured, thinking, "Ah, that's how it's done! Got it! Many years later, in the late Eighties, I found myself in Robert McKee's Story Seminar ("found myself" is disingenuous: I paid two hundred quid of my own money to find out what the fuss was all about). For the uninitiated, this is not a seminar in the proper sense: it is a word marathon delivered at high decibel levels by McKee. For him, every problem is an opportunity in disguise. (That sounds so slick and simple, but it is a profound truth, I believe.)

McKee lectured us for three whole days, but I got three or four gems of wisdom that made the weekend worthwhile for me. The above is one of them. The next one was "Identify the inciting incident (the thing that sets the story going) and foreground it". I was writing *Pride and Prejudice* at the time – or at least thinking about it. What gets the story going? Bingley deciding on a whim to rent Netherfield Hall. Wow! So we don't start with the Bennets: we start with the men who are about to disrupt their lives. Brilliant! Next: "Where there is sex, put it right on the spine of the story." Huge insight! I was writing *House of Cards*. Of course, Francis Urquhart has to shag Mattie, the girl reporter! And she can call him "Daddy" when they're doing it! Next: "Never let the resolution slip out of the hands of the protagonist." No deus ex machina. Good advice. I used it when adapting *Falling*. She can't rely on friends: she has to save herself.

*

Things were very different when it all began for me. There was no industry machinery humming around me, no sense of joining an established conveyor belt. It was more a matter of pushing a manuscript into the world and hoping someone would catch it. I was a solo adventurer – with support, certainly (Harvey Unna, my first agent, in the background, and those early producers who decided to take a punt on me), but essentially I was on my own. At first, I regarded producers and script editors with suspicion. They were, after all, the people who might tell you what was wrong. It took me a while to realize that they were not the enemy. They wanted the piece to work as much as I did.

*

When I write, the hardest moment is always the beginning. The first couple of pages are often a painful, hesitant business – then it gradually becomes easier. I write all the time, both what I'm paid for and other things that may never earn a penny. Writing rarely leaves my mind. Even now, as I'm about to hit ninety, most days I'm at the desk. If I go a day without it, I grow slightly restless – not tortured, just unsettled. It keeps me sharp, like walking in the woods, like the gym, which I still go to, to the amusement of some. It may sound obsessive. It isn't. I'm not inclined to despair at three in the morning over a clumsy sentence. I'm generally a decent judge of my own work, and I trust my instincts. The panic tends to arrive earlier, at the scale of the whole undertaking.

Occasionally, before I've even begun writing, I'll see a face: a presence I've never met will wander into my imagination. It's instinctive. That's the character. Not the actor. That's the essential person. Then the real work begins, and I hope whoever is cast is better than my private fantasy. Sometimes they are startlingly different from what I imagined. Jessie Buckley as Masha in *War and Peace* is perhaps the most striking example. On the page Masha is subdued, melancholy, wary of happiness. Jessie is none of those things in the flesh. She arrives with vitality, humour, force. The joy was watching her contain that energy, restrain it and then allow it to emerge slowly as the character's circumstances shift. That kind of transformation is one of the rewards of adaptation. You write one thing – an actor delivers something more complicated. And you think: "Yes, good, better than I'd planned." That's the pleasure of it all. Not control, but surprise. Not perfection, but the moment when something larger than your own effort begins to live.

Stephen, my agent, thinks I'm getting better and better. His enthusiasm is touching. Agents are meant to believe in one's continuing brilliance: it's in the job description. But Stephen has been around long enough not to waste hyperbole. So perhaps he does have a point. Age, after all, is not a straight line downhill. One does not automatically decline into irrelevance. It is possible that one will improve. You shed certain anxieties. You worry less about what people will say and more about whether the thing works.

There was a period when producers would lean in with that speculative glint and ask, "What would interest Andrew?" It's an agreeable position to find oneself in. I was regarded as a sound investment. Now people worry I might be dead before I finish the pilot episode. A lot of executives in the business, especially in the States, don't like writers who are older than they are themselves. And there's that prevailing industry wisdom that most TV writers are finished by the time they're fifty. But I don't feel like yesterday's man – rather, like today's man with a lot of yesterdays under his belt. The best may be yet to come. And there still seems to be an appetite for my work.

*

I enjoy getting mail through the post, and still get excited by that moment between opening it and knowing what it contains. I do like a letter, especially when the writer is saying something lovely about some of my older work like *A Very Peculiar Practice* or *Game On*. That means a great deal to me and flicks the switch back on.

It's rare now, though, to hear the soft thud of paper on the carpet. In the days before everything migrated online, letters arrived in envelopes. One turned out to be unexpectedly significant. It was from a young graduate who'd watched *Pride and Prejudice* with enormous enthusiasm and had written to say how much she loved it. She then added, with commendable directness, that perhaps she might come and work as my assistant. At that point I'd never had an assistant and hadn't felt any pressing need to acquire one. Writing is not obviously a team effort. Still, curiosity got the better of me, and I looked at her CV. It was clear enough that what she really wanted wasn't to make tea for a writer, but to work in television drama properly. Script-editing, in other words. So I wrote back and said, in effect, "You don't want to be my assistant. You want to be a script editor." I was working on *The Line of Beauty*, adapting Alan Hollinghurst's novel. I suggested that she read the book and write a few pages for me: how she thought it might be adapted, how many episodes it might sustain, what the structure could be. It was a small test, really – the sort of exercise script editors do every day. She did a very good job. The young woman was Laura Lankester. She went on to become an extremely accomplished script editor, and later a producer in her own right. She developed a formidable reputation within British television drama for intelligence, rigour and an ability to see the structural bones of a story. Years later, when she was working at the BBC and we were discussing possible projects, it was Laura who first suggested that I might consider adapting *War and Peace*. At the time the idea seemed faintly mad. Looking back, it's one of those moments that alters the tapestry of life. A letter arrives. You answer it. A conversation begins. Years later you find yourself writing a six-part adaptation of one of the great novels in world literature. It makes one slightly wary of ignoring the post. Who knows what might not have happened if I had simply put that letter aside…

*

Losing work is a writer's nightmare. It's happened to me. Once, I was holidaying in Cape Verde and I was also writing a television script – an hour or so of writing in the morning was just enough to keep the machinery turning over and good for the holiday. My laptop was stolen at the airport on the way home. Panic. Then I remembered I had emailed the latest draft to one of the producers. The panic subsided. Just a matter of buying another laptop. Lessons are often learnt the hard way. Mine was simple enough: always ensure that someone else, somewhere, has access to the latest version of what you're doing.

Writing Partners

I'm always excited by the prospect of having a writing partner – and, sometimes, it genuinely feels necessary. The problem is that I'm quite fond of getting my own way. Most writers are. A writer's room is particularly dangerous territory for me, because I soon revert to my schoolboy self, trying to make everyone laugh while trying, at the same time, to write all the scripts myself. People get all sensitive and touchy about that, as they often think that they are better than they are. I'm the same – I think I'm brilliant and always want to be right as well. In short, I am not the best team worker.

It was different for me at the beginning, as I was writing original plays on my own and was suspicious of anyone trying to change anything, but in the end it's always about making a better show, and when the notes are good, I'll take them. If somebody has a genuinely better idea than mine, I'd be a fool not to use it. The trouble is... that's not always the case.

At the moment, I'm working on *Mansfield Park*, and part of it is set on a plantation in Antigua at the turn of the nineteenth century. Everyone thinks – including me – that I ought to have a writing partner, for all the obvious reasons. As I said, the prospect of meeting potential collaborators is always enjoyable. Working with them is where the difficulties begin. However, I've had a few writing partners over the years that I've enjoyed working with.

*

My first writing partner was George Moore, my colleague at Coventry College. As I mentioned before, we were very close for a while, and during the five years between my first and second drama commissions we co-wrote comedy material for *Little Big Time*, other kids' shows, schools programmes and an educational soap.

Then it all went a bit sour, but we managed to repair the friendship. Sadly, he passed away a couple of years ago.

*

Steve Attridge had been a student of mine, and became a close friend. When he broke up with his partner, he came to live in our house, in the top-floor flat that had been my son Bill's. Steve was in a state my doctor friend described as "agitated mourning". There was a lot of pacing up and down, a lot of pointless driving in the dead of night. Steve had a talent for writing, and a small son, and I suggested we write a kids' show together, so we wrote one about a junior school where the teachers all go mad and the kids take over. It was called the *Boot Street Band*. We would talk each episode over, then one of us would write the first draft. We had a good time doing it – we could make each other laugh, and Steve cheered up considerably. Even better, the BBC bought it, and Steve became a successful writer for children's TV for quite a few years. He is still a good friend. We used to play tennis every week until he got too good. And his small son is now six foot five, with a wife and daughter of his own.

*

Bernadette Davis was Stephen's assistant back in the late Eighties. She told me how much she had liked *Getting Hurt*, a novel about a destructive love relationship I published in 1989, and how she wanted to be a writer too. She was in a problematic domestic situation: she'd been living with her best friend, but somehow this had turned into sharing the flat with her best friend's brother and his friend, whom she didn't like at all. She made it all sound so dire and so funny at the same time. I realized that this could be great material, and told her so. She didn't see how it could be made into anything, so I found myself offering to help her. And I got more and more into it. And eventually we had the sitcom that became *Game On*. It took time, and we had some setbacks. We originally saw it as a stage play, and sent it to various producers, who all turned it down, saying it was very funny, but the characters didn't develop. This made me furious. Anyway, we were not too downhearted, because we'd had fun writing scenes, and we could both make each other laugh – a lot. Then Geoffrey Perkins asked me if I had anything that might make a situation comedy – and of course I had! Characters in sitcoms don't "develop", but stay the same or get even more like themselves. Hat Trick, who produced the sitcom, could not have been nicer or more accommodating. And we got a super cast. Ben Chaplin was very funny and also kind of scary at the same time. He was our perfect Matthew. Samantha Janus was a bombshell as Mandy – not a bit like Bernadette herself, but a new person who was a delight to be around. And Matthew Cottle was sweet and funny as Martin. We wanted it to be shot on film without a studio audience, but Geoffrey was adamant that it needed one, and as he was so much more experienced than either of us in this genre, we followed his advice.

When a show is brand new, the studio audience is made up of people who just want to see a show for free: they don't know anything about it. Later on, when the show has established itself, people come because they are already fans and understand the tone of the thing. Anyway, a large section of the audience laughed at absolutely every line, including the ones that weren't supposed to be funny. It was excruciating. But Michael Jackson, who was controller of BBC2 at the time, said, "I like the graphics, and I like the demographics." No, I don't understand that either, but he liked two things about it, and we were deemed to be a success. We did the first season together. Bernadette took more of a lead on the second, and she wrote the third on her own, by which time she was an established writer. We did another show together, *Wilderness*, a drama about a woman who turns into a wolf, starring the extraordinary Amanda Ooms. And Bernadette went on to write two more excellent sitcoms, *The Wilsons* and *Some Girls*. I love her writing, and I hope she goes on to do lots more.

*

I first worked with Stella Merz when she joined as a junior script editor on *A Suitable Boy*. I wasn't sure about her at first – she struck me as very cheeky – but we bonded over a shared love of *Top Boy* ("Wagwan, fam?"), and she got me into *Love Island* in that great Maura Higgins season. "Fanny flutters" and "the ick". Script-editing was not enough for Stella: she wanted to do all the jobs, so she became a freelance producer (*Gentleman Jack*, *Miss Austen*, *Film Club*), and now she is my writing partner on *The Watsons*, based on a Jane Austen fragment. We have a lot of fun working together, and each of us thinks the other is wonderfully talented and funny. Sickening, really.

Kingsley Amis

I once heard Kingsley Amis on the radio talking about his writing process, with specific reference to *One Fat Englishman*. He said that, when creating a character, he'd often take some aspect of himself he didn't particularly like and push it until it became something recognizable but entirely other. I found that fascinating. Also, a salutary exercise and a useful tip. I'd read *Lucky Jim* soon after it was published in 1954. I'd laughed so much that it hurt. It was the iconoclasm of it, the release, the sense that he'd said something transgressive which also felt true, and therefore liberating. He seemed to know exactly how I felt about institutions, about pretension, about being young and angry and not quite knowing where to put it all. After that, I read all of his books as they came out. I didn't think them all wonderful, but they all had at least something in them that made me think, "Yes, this is what it's really like." A tone, a way of looking sideways at the world. That was enough.

The BBC used to have parties for writers. That seems almost unbelievable now, but they really did. The first one I went to was in the BBC Club on the second floor of Television Centre. It must have been sometime in the 1970s, and it was a hell of a hooley. All the writers were there – all drunk, most of us ungratefully abusing the BBC. Writers are a bit like that – always biting the hand that feeds them. Anyway, there was Kingsley Amis, larger than life, booming away, holding court without any obvious effort. I thought I ought to tell him how much his books had meant to me and how important they'd been. So I did. And, what do you know, it seemed to go down pretty well with the great man. And then I heard myself saying: "But I didn't think *Girl, 20* was quite up to your usual standard." He sized me up and said, "And what makes you think I would be interested in what a young shag like you thinks? What makes you think you're such an expert?"

"Well," I said, "it's just that I've read all your books and—"

"Have you? Have you really read all my books?"

"Yes," I said.

"Right," he said. "Let's give you a test."

So, he asked me a series of questions about his books – details, characters, plot turns. And, by some miracle or luck, I got all of them right. By this point we had acquired quite an audience. He flung his arm round my shoulders and addressed the crowd:

"This young shag here has read all my books – and, what is more, he remembers what's in them!"

So I was Kingsley's best friend for one night. Later at the same party I fell in love with Fay Weldon, and she with me. We shared a taxi going God knows where. I remember her saying: "This is dreadful. What are we going to do about it?"

And I said: "Well, nothing, probably."

And so it transpired.

It was some years before I met Amis again. *The Old Devils* had won the Booker Prize. When asked what he would spend the money on, he said: "Booze. And then, curtains." It wasn't entirely clear whether that meant his demise or drapes for the posh house he shared with Elizabeth Jane Howard. Ruth Caleb, who was then in charge of Drama at BBC Wales, asked me if I'd like to dramatize it, and I said yes. Tristram Powell was named as director because he sounded Welsh (he wasn't), but he was a good director and, as it turned out, a lovely man who became a good friend, which always helps. Adrian Mourby managed to get himself a role as producer. He was middle-class Welsh, a rare breed, and wore a smart dark suit and carried a shiny briefcase, like a spy.

Adapting *The Old Devils* was a real pleasure. Kingsley Amis had written a novel that was both wickedly funny and melancholy, always an attractive combination. The book follows a group of ageing Welsh friends – retired academics, teachers and hangers-on – who meet regularly to drink heroic quantities of whisky and reminisce about the past. Into this comfortable pattern comes the return of Alun Weaver, a celebrated writer who has spent years abroad building a reputation that may or may not be deserved. His arrival unsettles the group's fragile equilibrium, stirring up old rivalries, disappointments and half-buried grievances. What begins as a portrait of convivial old age gradually reveals itself to be something sharper: a study of regret, self-delusion, loyalty and the humiliations that accumulate across a lifetime. People who have spent years telling themselves agreeable stories suddenly find those stories challenged.

My father did not approve of *The Old Devils* at all. His principal objection was that the women in the novel drank far too much. He felt this reflected badly on Welsh womanhood. Kingsley, I suspect, would have regarded that criticism as evidence that he had observed things accurately. One of his great strengths as a novelist was his ability to listen, really listen, to how people talk to one another. The women in the novel are observed with a mixture of affection and ruthless clarity. They are not idealized: they are entirely recognizable. Curiously, very few people seem to have noticed the small, heartbreakingly understated poem that appears at the end of Kingsley's own memoirs, which is revealing. It hints at something much more vulnerable beneath the sardonic exterior – a recognition that he had found real love early in life and not valued it as he should have. The lines have lingered with me:

> Well, that was much as women were meant to be,
> I thought, and set about looking further.
> How can we tell, with nothing to compare?

It is a bleak admission, the casual arrogance of youth recognizing, too late, what it dismissed. By then, after the collapse of his marriage to Elizabeth Jane Howard, Amis was living as a lodger with his first wife Hilly and her second husband in Primrose Hill. He had come to the conclusion that Hilly was always the one for him – he had simply realized it too late. There's a rather beautiful poem he wrote about catching a Camberwell Beauty butterfly as a boy, not knowing how rare it was. Later, when he falls in love, he thinks she'll be the first of many. Only in hindsight does he realize she was the one. That rang a bell with me too.

The BBC paid for Kingsley and me to discuss the adaptation of *The Old Devils* over a posh lunch at the Orangery in Holland Park. Those were the days. We met, and Sir Kingsley, as he was by then, said he needed two double single malts before going into the restaurant. I had the same, not to seem rude. He appeared to have forgotten our previous meeting, and I didn't remind him. Over drinks he was very entertaining, talking about how morose his old friend Philip Larkin had become – the implication being that Amis himself was bonhomie personified. Inside the restaurant there was some unobtrusive background music and only a few tables occupied.

"Are you enjoying this music?" he said to the room at large. Total silence.

"I beg your pardon?"

"I SAID, ARE YOU ENJOYING THIS MUSIC? DO YOU FIND IT NECESSARY?"

"Er, not really."

"GOOD! NEITHER AM I! WAITER! WE DON'T WANT THIS MUSIC. KINDLY TURN IT OFF!"

It was turned off.

As we talked, it became clear that the novel drew heavily from real life. I suggested, for the sake of symmetry, that Charlie, the third of the old friends, might also have had a moment with Rhiannon in the past. Amis thought for a while.

"No," he said. "I don't think that happened. I'd have to ask him, but I don't think so."

I realized that Alun was a dreadful, inflated version of Amis himself. Charlie also carried some of his traits: blackouts, fear of the dark, inability to drive. I thought it kind of him to share so much of himself, even if he did it more honestly in fiction than in life.

The adaptation went well. The performances were wonderful. Tristram handled the material with tenderness and restraint. Amis came to the screening.

"Not bad," he said. "Plenty of rumpy-pumpy!"

"Oh, for Christ's sake," I thought, but said nothing. "That's not you, not really. Underneath, you're as soft as the rest of us."

There were more lunches about more collaborations. One was at a pub that he liked, another back at the Orangery for an adaptation of *The Russian Girl* that in the end was never made. That lunch was a disaster. Mourby was there with us. Amis was in pain, furious with the food, the clientele, the sun and the clouds. We were very drunk.

Mourby paid the bill, and we all started to process out sluggishly. We were nearly at the door when I realized that Sir Kingsley wasn't walking quite upright. He was very slowly going over backwards, and as I was right behind him, I thought I could push him into an upright stance, but he was too heavy. I thought, "At least I can break his fall" – and we went down with me pinned under the great man, both of us unable to move. We must have looked like some huge, obscene eight-legged beetle as we ineffectually waved our arms and legs about. The waiters, who hadn't really taken to us much , came over stroking their beards and looked at us, wondering what to do. Finally they got us onto our feet, no damage done, and I'm sure they were glad to see the back of us. Amis said nothing. I did the same.

Outside, his taxi waited.

"I am going to the Garrick for a drink. Could I offer you shags a lift?"

"Very kind," I thought.

"I'm afraid I shall have to charge you ten pounds each."

He meant it. Needless to say. And I never saw Amis again. Or Mourby, come to that.

But I used Kingsley Amis's idea of taking something about yourself you don't like and pushing it further, to see where it takes you.

In my "Play for Today" piece, *Bavarian Night*, I mined the idea of using your nearest and dearest, and ended up with a story about a writer called Joe. He was married to someone rather like Diana, had two children remarkably like Bill and Anna, and lived in a house suspiciously similar to ours. Joe's wife accuses him of retreating into his work and of only paying attention to the family when something they say or do might be useful to his writing. The family gets fed through his imagination like some dreadful mincing machine. Her accusation was brutal, but honest. Because, of course, she had a point. I recently watched *Bavarian Night* again, and it startled me. I'd remembered it as a very funny comedy about middle age and parenthood, with a mad head teacher thrown into the mix. Watching it again forty years later, it was still funny, but also very bleak. Surely our marriage wasn't ever quite as rocky as this one? Maybe I'd pushed Kingsley Amis's little dodge too far. Maybe it was the performances – or maybe it's just that the truth hurts.

Another example where I used our family life was *Ball-Trap on the Côte Sauvage*. It was based on a very real and very glorious family holiday in Brittany during the blistering summer of 1976. We went camping. Well, "camping"… the tents were pre-pitched, and ours had three bedrooms and a stove. I wasn't wrestling with guy ropes. We lived al fresco for a couple of weeks, surrounded by other English families. The kids ran wild. So did we. A few tents down from us was a woman we nicknamed "Early Bird". She was always up first, eyelashes on before the kettle had even boiled – flimsy things stuck to her eyelids like upside-down caterpillars. Totally unnecessary: she was beautiful without them. A bit nutty too. She'd come blinking towards us, saying things like, "He's been awful. He won't give me any money. I can't buy a bloody thing. Anyway, how are your kids? Let's go to the beach, yeah?"

Her partner, whom we called "Smiley Face", never showed his teeth. Not once. Just sat at the back of their tent drinking wine. "I'm seeing if it's worth importing," he'd say, swirling his glass with an eternal frown. Then there was "Topless", a sun-kissed Adonis with a lovely fragile blonde wife and two toddlers. He was on a mission to find the ultimate topless beach. He dragged his poor family from coast to coast in search of this mythical nudist utopia. And then, of course, he was arrested – not for being topless, but for being bottomless on the topless beach.

"Ball-trap", in case you're wondering, is French for clay-pigeon shooting. They seemed to be very keen on this in Brittany, and there were notices advertising it all over the place: "BALL-TRAP 50 m". They seemed threatening until you found out their innocent meaning. In the film, of course, "ball-trap" had a double entendre. Early Bird was very attractive, and the version of me in the film had a moment with her that didn't quite turn into anything and was all the sexier for that. I haven't always plundered from our family holidays. At least, not knowingly. Writing about them now might be doing so.

*

Family holidays mattered to us. They were punctuation marks in the year, promises of togetherness, and occasionally proof that the writing had paid for something tangible. When a bit of money came in, we splashed out on a long weekend in Ibiza. Anna was about five. She'd been living in Bill's cast-offs, and we decided she deserved something of her own. We made a trip into Birmingham to buy a dress. It became known as "the Birmingham Dress". She wore it in Ibiza in the evenings, terribly proud of herself, and danced when the hotel band struck up something Mediterranean and faintly off-key. The weather was hot, the pool was enough, the food was good. No grand statements about lifestyle: just sun, children and the sense that we were doing all right. Afterwards, I folded some of that trip into a Marmalade Atkins story, *Marmalade Atkins in Space*.

Family holidays never stopped me writing. In fact, sometimes the ease of everyone being settled, sunburnt, fed, temporarily content, made it easier. Menorca was particularly memorable. We didn't have much money, and the place we'd booked was part of a complex that had seen better times. That didn't matter to us. We had a hire car, the island was beautiful, and every day became an expedition. The heat was ferocious. We would drive until we found a tiny bay, and then throw ourselves into the sea without ceremony. Bill once peeled himself out of the car and leapt straight into the shared pool fully clothed, unable to bear perspiration for another second. There was a small shop on the complex that sold what appeared to be oranges. They were hollowed out and filled with ice cream. Bill adored them. He spent days trying to work out how he could transport some home to show his friends. He never solved the logistical problem, which is probably for the best.

I was writing *To Serve Them All My Days* at the time. I'd get up very early and sit outside with my portable Olivetti before anyone else was awake. *Rumours*, the new Fleetwood Mac album, had just come out, and the reps, whose grotty apartment was next to hours, played it on a loop from 6 a.m. onwards. That record is now inseparable in my mind from pale dawn light, the sound of typing and the determination to finish a script so that perhaps next year we could afford somewhere marginally less disreputable. The man in the apartment next door on the other side spent his holiday photographing the cracks in his flat, cataloguing stains so he could argue for his money back. We preferred to go out. There was a rhythm to those days: early writing, Diana waking, breakfast, exploration, coming back sandy and exhausted, plunging into the pool, then down to the beach café run by a vast man who resembled a retired buccaneer. Then chicken and chips.

Mostly it was the four of us – Diana, Bill, Anna and me – and that felt sufficient. Then adolescence arrived, and Bill decided that staying home was preferable. Sensible of him, in retrospect. Anna brought a friend instead, to preserve the balance. By then, we had a bit more to spend and could manage a villa on a beach in Corfu. It was at the far end of a long stretch of sand, and you left the car and walked along the shore to reach it. Fig trees shaded the steps to the house, and we ate the fruits greedily and without sophistication. One evening, Anna and her friend, both fourteen at the time, announced that they had met a couple of Welsh boys and would like to go clubbing. We said yes, with the complacency of people who think that Welsh boys must be trustworthy by definition. Midnight came. Then one o'clock. Then three thirty. Mild anxiety turned into panic. What would we tell Lorna's parents? Why had we been so relaxed? And then they walked in, cheerful and indignant. The club, they explained, didn't get going until midnight. They hadn't wanted to leave just as it started. Nothing had happened beyond dancing and noise. We allowed ourselves a long, silent exhalation and attempted not to appear ridiculously anxious parents.

The second villa that year was on an even quieter beach. No clubs, no lurking Welsh boys. Everything slowed. I would sit in shade or sun and let my mind idle. Out of that stillness came the story of the previous summer in France, which had been frenetic and full of incident. Details resurfaced – people I had half forgotten returned fully formed. The mother in that piece carried a current of sadness. That, I realized later, I had taken from Diana. Her father had recently died, and she was grieving in that contained, practical way she had. So, am I borrowing? Plundering? Retelling? Perhaps all three. What I know is that the life was lived first, properly, imperfectly, and the writing followed. If I take something from those holidays, it is not out of a thieving impulse, but because the moments insist on being shaped. And because, in the quiet of early morning, with a typewriter and a half-finished script, they are simply there. These stories lived in my head, waiting for the moment I was ready to write. And I usually was, until the one time I wasn't at all – or, more precisely, the one time I found that I couldn't.

Full-Time at Fifty and Writer's Block

I didn't formally leave teaching until 1986, when I was fifty. I'd spent months dithering over whether to take early retirement or apply for a sabbatical. In the end, I said "Fuck it" and handed in my resignation. I'd fallen out of love with the university – not the students or the teaching, but the bureaucracy, the grey-faced administrators who regarded students and lecturers as inconvenient necessities in their mission to corporatize higher education. The other reason was far more enticing. Off the back of my first big TV success, *To Serve Them All My Days*, broadcast in 1980, the BBC asked if I'd be interested in creating an original series.

I came up with a story about three mature students at university getting a second chance at life, their complications with resentful husbands, and so on. Good concept, but I couldn't make it work. Was it a comedy or something more serious? I had written three limp episodes when Ken Riddington broke it to me. The BBC were going to bin it. But they had paid me £17,000 in advance. Would I like to pay it back or write myself out of trouble? Having spent the £17,000 already, it was an obvious choice. Desperation is the mother of invention.

I'd always wanted to write a medical series, but not the usual po-faced story about the wise old doctor and the modern thrusting new one: I wanted to write about real, mad, useless doctors. I thought back to my third radio play, written over two decades before: *The Hospitalization of Samuel Pellet*. That had weird doctors: a Marxist, a Freudian and a fearsome surgeon called Doctor Grendel. And the leading character could be based on my nervous gloomy hero from *Heartattack Hotel*, and his uninhibited girlfriend could be in it too. And it would be set in a university! With nuns! Now we were in business. Diana's cousin Elaine was married to a handsome and very congenial doctor called Tom Kelly, who worked in the student-health-care centre at University College London, so he could be my deep throat. Jonathan Powell, Head of Drama, said it was heaven on wheels.

Ken said: "Do there have to be nuns?"

I said, "There are always nuns."

"But do there have to be two of them?"

"There are aways two of them, Ken."

"But do they have to *speak*?"

I had a think, and said, "No, not necessarily."

Ken sighed with relief: non-speaking nuns would be much cheaper.

So we went ahead and got down to bringing *A Very Peculiar Practice* to the screen. There were lots of jolly meetings at Tom Kelly's flat, and the writing went well. Hugh Laurie wanted to play Stephen, our hero, but we went for Peter Davison, who projected a sort of goofy integrity that everyone liked. We had a problem with Rose Marie, the feline feminist: the first actress we cast looked great but didn't understand the character. I said I couldn't understand her either: she was based on one or two women who had frightened the wits out of me in the past. Then Barbara Flynn came in and said, "I know exactly how to do this" – and she did. Critics didn't get it at first, and then it clicked, and we were nominated for a BAFTA after the first season.

I loved writing the characters in this show and watching them being brilliantly brought to life. Jock McCannon, the mad old fart, was based on a doctor I had known when I was at UCL, who was a pioneer of personal care and studied the many forms in which mental illness can manifest itself. Tom knew the same man when he was old and half crazy. He was fun to write, because there was always a sliver of truth in his wild diagnoses. Bob Buzzard was another joy to write – a doctor who saw people as badly functioning machines, a Thatcherite who was all bombast on the outside and a quivering heap of neuroses on the inside.

The myths associated with doctors are often also applied to universities, with some campuses imagined as rarefied enclaves of pure intellect. Yet anyone who has spent time within their walls knows that madness, subdued and at times operatic, haunts their corridors. Authority does not neutralize instability: sometimes it amplifies it. I've been threatened more than once, in tones that made it quite clear my performance was not good enough. It can be a genuinely frightening experience. For the avoidance of doubt, none of the characters in *A Very Peculiar Practice* were portraits of my colleagues at Warwick (well, maybe the vice-chancellor in the first series, just a bit). I always used to tell my colleagues that none of them were interesting enough to be used as inspiration.

Peculiar things do happen, though, once an institution acquires a sense of its own importance. Warwick University, for example, became briefly entangled in Sir Clive Sinclair's C5 electric-car experiment. Several of the vehicles were presented to the campus, and senior staff took to using them to travel between meetings. The sight was irresistible: elegantly suited professors gliding solemnly across the grounds in low-slung plastic contraptions, reviewing their territory like minor dignitaries. They could keep their dignity intact until the campus pavement rose. On the gentlest incline the machines would falter and lose speed and be overtaken by undergraduates ambling uphill without effort. What fascinated me was the total denial embraced by the drivers and the pedestrians' polite refusal to notice their mechanical distress. The professors in their turn, out of pride, declined to acknowledge the pedestrians passing them. An entire moral ecosystem – hierarchy, embarrassment, self-importance – played out in miniature. One does not need to invent farce: one simply needs to observe it.

Peter Davison's character, Stephen Daker, became the audience's way into this world. On the surface he embodied everything the public expects of a doctor: articulate, attentive, composed, apparently humane. But beneath that composure lay lack of confidence, sexual insecurity, existential dread. What was great was that people at other universities recognized a common truth. They'd say, "How did you know about how bad it is at Lancaster University?" when I had never been anywhere near it. It was successful – not a big hit, but a cult one, which is even better in some ways. A second series was commissioned.

And just when life seemed full of potential and I had decided to give up my day job, it suddenly hit. The block.

When I talk about it, I tend to say it started in October 1986 – but there had been signs before that. On the surface I felt fine about leaving Warwick. Underneath, I was trying to ignore a growing sensation of disquiet. There had been a group of postgraduate teaching students with whom I hadn't quite hit it off. They were an earnest lot, and I'd assumed a rapport that hadn't been there. I'd always been good at reading the room. With this bunch I'd missed cues. It was rattling. If you don't quite get it, how can you be a writer? Might this be the burnout so many writers get at forty-five or fifty?

Professor David Jenkins, our splendidly eccentric Head of Department, proposed sending me up in a balloon for my leaving party. A delightfully mad idea that seems to me now something I'd say yes to in a heartbeat, but then it just made me cross. I think I was already in a depression without being aware of it.

So, October. The leaves fall, the students return, the campus buzzes with possibility. But I wasn't there. I was at home, alone, facing the blank page. And nothing came. At first I thought, "Well, this is new." And then, "Well, this is annoying." And soon after, "This might be the end."

It continued. Days spent watching daytime television. I'd sit there, staring at quiz shows and property programmes, thinking, "Christ, what am I doing?" But whenever I tried to haul myself out of it, everything I wrote felt thin, false and hollow. The voice in my head, the one that usually said "That's it!" had gone very, very quiet. I felt uninteresting. And uninterested. The show, as far as I was concerned, was over. Why didn't I go to the doctor and get something for it? I guess I didn't know, or couldn't admit to myself, what was happening to me.

Diana was thinking, "Oh God, do I have to support him now?" A primary-school teacher, two kids and a washed-up writer husband living in his dressing gown. Not what she'd signed up for all those years ago. It got urgent. The BBC needed scripts. My agent

Stephen decided attack was the best means of defence. "You need to do something," he told them. "You've got to re-energize him."

Eventually, salvation arrived in the form of David Tucker, the director of *A Very Peculiar Practice*. "Come and live with me for a bit," he said. "We'll go to the pub every day, talk it through, and I won't let you leave until we've got a workable outline." It worked. The ideas returned, the energy came back, and the block lifted as quietly as it had arrived – as if it had never happened. David saved me. It wasn't just a case of jollying me up. He convinced me that the show had to develop or die. We very sadly decided to lose our vice-chancellor, who had been so wonderful in John Bird's vainglorious performance. We needed something more sinister. There was a lot of apprehension in the Eighties that there would be a war with Russia and that the UK would be in the front line. Universities would be weaponized. Our new vice-chancellor was to be American, a Jack Kennedy lookalike with a dark agenda. Our other decision was to give Stephen a new love interest, the prickly and quarrelsome Polish art historian Grete Grotowska, played by Joanna Kanska. She was wonderful. So all was well again. We did another feature-length one-off, *A Very Polish Practice*, set in Warsaw. Bliss. *A Very Peculiar Practice* remains one of my favourite shows.

*

The block disappeared, but I've never forgotten the feel of it. It's always there, lurking somewhere in the wings. These days, I know that when something stalls, I can go for a walk, take a nap, step away, have a shower, sleep on it. And the words, more often than not, return. Since then, the writing has more or less flowed, although sometimes not exactly when you most need it to.

In the mid-1990s, I was wrestling with Defoe's expansive novel *Moll Flanders*, and found it hard to make any progress. Moll had simply lived too much life. There were too many husbands and crimes, too much narrative girth. I couldn't see where to begin, which is always the problem with a story of epic proportions. So I decided to forget about it and go on holiday.

Our vintage BMW was very temperamental, as it showed on that trip. It failed in stages: little sulks at first, then outright mutiny – until we rolled into a dealership in Carcassonne like a train out of steam. We were on our way to a painting holiday in the Luberon in southern France and looking forward to lavender fields, sunshine and wine. Our friend Steve Attridge had come along for the ride, because he needed to meet his son somewhere en route.

Everyone had a purpose on the trip to the south of France. The car did not. Our arrival coincided, with exquisite timing, with the Feast of the Assumption. France, understandably, had holier preoccupations than the mechanical problems of an ageing German engine. The garage man had wrapped up for the evening. There was to be no salvation for the BMW that day. Fortunately, Diana had done what she always did: taken some precautions. She'd insisted that I take out an expensive insurance policy with the AA covering hire cars and emergency accommodation. I had grumbled – I often did. She had quietly filed the paperwork in one of her fireproof boxes. Without her foresight, we might have spent a few days in Carcassonne. Despite the insurance, however, there was no room at any inn. We rang and rang. Hotels, auberges, private lodgings. All full. Eventually, through the garage man's persuasion skills, a room was secured. It was small, hot and carried a preternatural stench we couldn't identify. None of us slept. The air, just like our car, didn't move. We lay there, contemplating mortality and our poor life decisions. Even grappling with *Moll Flanders* felt a comfort at that stage.

Morning arrived. We were all already overheated. The bad smell persisted. Bells rang inside and outside our heads. Steve, pale from lack of sleep, surveyed the scene and announced that he supposed he should head to Marseilles as planned. And then, rather ceremoniously, on that stifling mid-August morning in Carcassonne, he put on his thick woollen socks. There was something deeply British about it, totally incongruous and yet oddly reassuring. The sight of Steve regally pulling on those socks while our world felt slightly unhinged has never left me.

Steve set off to meet his son Jake, and Diana and I retreated to an open-air auberge nearby to save the day. It was perfect: shaded tables, good bread. We ordered cold dry white wine in quantities. The heat softened – the pressure lifted. And somewhere between the second and third bottle, I got it.

"I know how to do *Moll Flanders*," I said.

It didn't descend from heaven: it had clearly been lurking in my unconscious. At home I had been paralysed by the scale of it: a whole life, from cradle to transportation. I'd been trying "to begin at the beginning", as Dylan Thomas said. The sun slipped below the horizon, and I saw it plainly: begin in prison, Moll addressing us directly.

"*What do you think of me, then? What would you do?*"

Let her argue her case. Let the audience decide whether she is victim, opportunist, survivor, rogue or all of the above. We raised our glasses – to the car being mended, to insurance policies and fireproof boxes the world over, to painting in the Luberon, to Steve's socks and to the curious truth that, occasionally, creative solutions require mechanical failure.

The BMW, in the end, was fixed. *Moll* too. But when something isn't working, the sensation is bleak – a suspicion that perhaps this time there will be no solution. Then usually the knot loosens: a line comes, a scene clicks into place. You remember how to do it. You carry on. And here's a solid tip for writing, or any problem really: think hard about it before you go to bed, then forget about it. Then, in the middle of the night, or maybe next morning under the shower, a new idea will pop into your mind unbidden.

Well, it works for me. Sometimes.

Vital Support

My agent, Stephen Durbridge, has stuck by me through thick and thin. Ours is another kind of marriage. I've come to value his enthusiasm for the creative stirrings of my elderly mind, while being faintly bemused by it. At my age, most people are praised for merely staying awake through *Newsnight*. Still, I accept the compliment, albeit with the seasoned scepticism of a man who's been around long enough to know the difference between genuine encouragement and well-intentioned flattery. With Stephen, it's the real thing, a "glass half full" man in a world edging on empty.

But he wasn't my first agent, That was Harvey. Harvey Unna. It all began, rather surprisingly, with my third radio play, *The Hospitalization of Samuel Pellet*, a little absurdist number about a new psychiatric hospital preparing for its grand opening by the queen. The premise was that there weren't enough mentally ill people to fill the beds, so volunteers were rounded up with the promise of three meals a day and a nice lie-down. *Catch-22* with a British twist: once you're admitted, something *must* be wrong with you. The doctors weren't much better, Freudians, Jungians, Marxists, all rigidly clinging to their belief systems as the chaos unfolded around them. It was silly, sharp and, I thought, rather good.

Martin Esslin thought so too – at least enough to accept it for the Third Programme, which was what they called Radio 3 back in the day. At the time it was known for poetry and avant-garde drama as much as music. Dylan Thomas, Samuel Beckett and, now, Andrew Davies had work aired on it. It felt like I was among my heroes. The play more or less slipped into the ether unnoticed, until, a few weeks later, the BBC forwarded me a letter from someone called Harvey Unna, who introduced himself as a literary agent and offered to represent me for ten per cent of my literary earnings.

A few weeks later, the *Sunday Times Magazine* ran a spread on London's top literary agents, and there was Harvey, labelled as one of the leading lights in film, TV and radio representation. I scrambled to find his letter and wrote back saying that I was interested in being represented by him. And so I found myself sitting in his first-floor office in Beaumont Mews, just off Marylebone High Street, a genteel corner of London that I hadn't known existed. And there was Harvey beaming at me rather as if he was looking forward to eating me.

"Mr Davies," he boomed, in his lush Mittel-European accent. "I enjoyed your little play. Very clever – very amusing. I should like to exploit you in all media."

Exploit? Did I want to be exploited? Harvey explained, in the way a patient tutor might to a slightly dim pupil, that literary exploitation was simply about extracting the full potential of a piece of work. Translate it, adapt it, merchandise it. I surrendered, and he became my agent, remaining so until he drifted gently into retirement and, eventually, decline.

To say Harvey was enigmatic is like saying Oscar Wilde enjoyed a witticism. He once told me he had worked in scrap metal before becoming an agent. "Very similar, dear boy." I thought it was a joke – but it turned out to be true. He had, in fact, been a respected lawyer in Germany, destined for the High Court, but, being a Jew, was forced to flee to England in 1933. He did a stint in scrap metal with his brother before returning to the law as a translator at the Nuremberg Trials. A hell of a backstory for a man who helped bring Paddington Bear to the masses. Harvey had strong opinions and an almost preternatural ability to snuff out nonsense. He once told me I shouldn't write series for television. "You have a proper career already," he said. "As a teacher. You should write only what moves you." He meant, of course, that I shouldn't be a gun for hire. I had a job that would pay the bills. I could afford to write what I wanted to write.

Though unfailingly courteous, he maintained his aura of mystery, which I rather liked, No hugging it out for Harvey. In the early days I think he regarded me as an indulgence, a rank outsider, a long-odds bet. It wasn't until I had a sold-out play in the West End that he invited me to his house, a breathtaking gem of modern architecture on the fringe of Hampstead Heath built to his own design. (I guess he didn't want to upset me by letting me see how rich he was before I had any money myself.) Afterwards I asked another client of his if he knew about Harvey's house, and he said, "Ah, yes, the one that Paddington Bear Built."

There were classic Harvey moments. For example, the time I was invited to lunch at the Connaught by an American producer who'd allegedly fallen in love with one of my plays. Harvey raised an eyebrow and whispered to me at an opportune moment: "Enjoy the lunch, dear boy. He has no money."

"But he's staying at the Connaught!"

"He may be staying at the Connaught, but he has no money. Enjoy the lunch."

The producer ordered a Coke. I ordered a first-growth claret. I never heard from him again.

And then there were the pantomimes – yes, pantomimes. Actually, there was only one. I wrote *Robin Hood and the Babes in the Wood*, which had a run at the Haymarket in Leicester. Harvey came to the first matinée, stood in the stalls counting heads and said approvingly, "Good house. A lot of children." And then, after a pause: "I hope they're not getting in half price."

In truth, Harvey didn't get me a huge number of jobs, but he made me feel like a real professional writer. He protected me from crooks, charlatans and... a famous academic publisher. ("Notorious throughout Europe, Andrew. I shall strike out these clauses with extreme prejudice.") And whenever I had a show on, he would ring me. Sometimes with praise. Occasionally with something more muted. Once, I swear, he said, "Not up to your usual standard. Not one of the better nights on the box, dear boy." He later claimed never to have said any such thing.

When his agency grew and moved from Beaumont Mews to Pottery Lane in Notting Hill, where they used to make the bricks that built London, Harvey remained as senior partner like a rock while the stream of life swirled round him. I was now mostly being looked after by Stephen Durbridge, but while he was still there I continued to think of Harvey as my "real" agent.

As Harvey began to lose his edge and drift slowly towards dementia, Stephen stepped in. At first, I wasn't sure. He wasn't Harvey. Too eager, too smiley, too… optimistic. But he grew on me. Slowly. I remember one night in New York, just after the ill-fated opening of *Rose* on Broadway. The reviews were dire, and we were reeling. Stephen turned to me, full of manic glee, and said, "Let's get a limo and go to a party!" And we did, crashing Tony Harrison's soirée, where no one had heard the news yet and everyone was far too drunk to care.

Stephen's origin story is perfect. His father, Francis Durbridge, was a household name, a wildly successful writer of thrillers and detective fiction. As a young boy, Stephen apparently listened to the shouts and anguished wails of his father wrestling with contracts and vowed that one day he'd grow up to help writers. And he did. And he still does. He has certainly helped this writer a lot. He laughs first, then solves the problem. He never used to read novels, then writers like William Boyd and Ian McEwan saw he was doing their movie deals so well, they asked him to be their book agent too. When I get myself into trouble, professionally or otherwise, Stephen listens, chuckles and says: "Let's see how we can turn this to our advantage" – which has faint echoes of Robert McKee.

Having supporters behind the scenes has helped me enormously, and very early on, when I was starting out and still juggling teaching and writing, the producer Louis Marks encouraged me to write as much as I could and for as many people. He didn't try to keep me for himself. In many ways he was better than an agent for me at that time, and he'd recommend me to like-minded producers saying, "He's very talented, he's very quick and he's very cheap." I am still quite talented and quite quick.

Rosemary Hill was one of those producers. They don't make producers like her any more. Small, sharp-eyed, formidable. You didn't pitch to Rosie: you turned up, and if she liked the way your brain ticked, she sent you home with a commission. Rosie had a penetrating gaze. I was in awe of her at first, but later became very fond of her.

We first worked together in 1976 on *The Signalman*, my first Dickens adaptation. It was a ghost story – short, austere, unsettling – and it scared the hell out of me, not least because I had no idea what it meant. A traveller encounters a lonely railway signalman who's been experiencing eerie premonitions, each one followed by a real-life tragedy. The tale ends with the signalman's death, struck down by a train, as the engine driver echoes the exact same gestures and words the traveller used when they first met. Was it fate? Madness? Or some terrible alignment of the two? I didn't know. Rosie didn't care. She believed in atmosphere, ambiguity, unease. She believed in writers figuring it out on their own. She didn't reassure. What she did was based on trust – which, in the early days, was worth its weight in gold.

I dramatized the story more or less as Dickens wrote it. The only flourish I added was a bride, the "beautiful young lady" who dies in the story, who I had tumbling out of a carriage window in her wedding dress. It was grisly. It was visual. It worked. Denholm Elliott gave a performance so perfect it made me look far cleverer than I was. I got paid £500. The scaffolding, I noticed on the production budget, cost £560.

Now I had Rosie, Louis, Stephen and Harvey watching with dry amusement and support behind me. In 1984, nearly a decade after *The Signalman*, Rosie rang me in a state of high agitation. She'd been let down by a writer and needed something quickly.

"Can you write something? Preferably Welsh. Or at least set in Wales. And soon."

We hadn't worked together for quite some time, but loyalty lingers – and, besides, I liked Rosie. So of course I said yes. I wrote about a man who had made a name for himself in Hollywood

– modestly successful, you understand, but successful enough. Wish fulfilment? Possibly. Of course, it was all about me, and Rhiwbina, and Beulah Chapel, and a girl called Jane Hughes. He returns to his Welsh village for his father's funeral, and the visit unearths all sorts of things best left undisturbed: adolescent humiliations, chapel politics, eccentric neighbours and a teenage love affair that had ended badly and therefore remained unforgettable. The village, as villages do, remembers everything. The hero pretends he doesn't. Richard Pasco played the writer with a lovely mixture of hauteur and vulnerability. The film's title was *Pythons on the Mountain*, which I thought suitably grand for a story set in a place where the most dangerous wildlife was usually a disgruntled ram. By this time Rosie was drinking more than was wise. She'd always enjoyed a glass or two – now she seemed to regard that merely as a preamble. There was a pub in the village where we were filming, and she and her chosen companion would repair there every evening with grim determination. She took a particular shine to my father.

"Wynford!" she would call across the room. "We want Wynford! Come here, Wynford!"

My father would comply politely, though I could see he was saddened by the spectacle. He was of a generation that believed in composure. It always amazed me that she remained upright at all. She was tiny, bird-like, as if one strong gust might carry her off, yet she could absorb alarming quantities of wine without visible damage – at least temporarily. For all that, she and her husband Ayton were generous and loyal friends. In my early days, when I had a play on at the Belgrade Theatre in Coventry, they took me out to dinner afterwards. There wasn't much choice in the neighbourhood at that hour, so we ended up at a slightly dubious curry house populated mainly by late-night drinkers and the already defeated. Ayton, with immense courtesy, leant towards the waiter and said, "I don't suppose you might have any bottles of claret that we could try?" The transformation in service was immediate. We were no longer strays looking for sustenance: we were connoisseurs. Bottles appeared. The staff regarded us as a refined clientele – which, by the end of the evening, I'm not entirely sure we were. But it was rather marvellous to be treated as if we were. Rosie was chaotic, occasionally worryingly so, often hilarious, and professionally brave and always brilliant.

Life and Art

Life. It can never be neatly parcelled. It's messy, sprawling and inconveniently emotional. Take *Getting Hurt*. It began as a novel and later found its way to television. Charlie Cross, the protagonist, is absolutely nothing like me – except, of course, that he *is* me, or a very particular version of me. And, like many things I write, it was born from a very real situation I found myself in. A simple story, really – man falls in love with a woman, and she breaks his heart. That's it. That's the whole story, boiled down to its aching core. But behind that clean line lies a wilderness of feeling.

I was dreaming a lot at the time – feverish, violent, almost melodramatic dreams – and I gave them all to Charlie. He became my vessel. The woman in the story, Viola, is an amalgam: part Gabriele (a sharp, enigmatic German woman I got myself tangled up with) and part a beautiful Polish girl I'd had a foolish, helpless crush on. That strange, heady cocktail of desire and loss found its way onto the page, and then onto the screen. Gabriele was ferociously clever, and I was slightly in awe of her: ten years younger than me, and so bright and uncompromising. She was very straightforward, and would express her thoughts with no filter.

We'd be having an argument, and I'd be trying to soften it, and she'd glare at me.

"Why are you smiling?"

I felt out of my depth, and when Gabriele decided that enough was enough and dumped me, I was really upset.

Diana, who was still serenely carrying on her own affair, was understanding. It was utter madness at the time, though, as I drove at breakneck speed to Leicester and we engaged in literary debates which she always won, saying about a play by Shakespeare:

"Rubbish – how does he expect us to believe that you can go to bed with somebody and not know who it is straight away? I would know if it was you or not – straight away!"

I would have liked to have sat in on the Shakespeare lecture she was due to give in the morning. The experience was intense, all-consuming. At the time, it felt like I was carrying a stone at the centre of my body, a sick weight lodged behind the ribs. Sometimes, love is like that: heavy, exhausting, not meant to last.

When the novel came out, I received letters, mostly from men, saying, "Yes, this is it. This is exactly what it feels like." One of the strange comforts of heartbreak is its universality. Some things get remembered as stories. Others become poems. I gave this one both. Here's the poem, written for Viola, who wasn't really Viola, and wasn't really mine.

For Viola

Bright-brown hens stamping about,
Glossy crows amongst the silver birches,
Sky grey as the dead wood underfoot;
You pale in your light camel coat,
Fragile to me as the birches
Shivering in the wind.

A child had left a blue book on a green bench,
A scruffy dog marked past it,
He alone had the park for his purposes –
You called to him.
He stopped, half-turned,
Barked without conviction and went on.

Aniela talked trouble about flat and car.
Krystyna: "Is John Fowles a major writer?"
Barry walked on ahead in his neat duffel;
You told me about selling vegetables.

I saw you standing in a green overall,
Fumbling through confusions of apples
And potatoes, your hands red with cold,
Naming all the wrong prices in your sweet voice.

I could do nothing with my love for you
But let it happen –
Language a mantrap, dead work underfoot.
We talked of dogs and families,
Separate words, hanging heavy in the mist.
Later, I blundered into mud and brushwood,
Shambled like a drunken bum down hot, dark corridors.

Your tears: "I don't want to talk to you – go away!"
Not understanding one thing,
I sat to comfort you and squashed your Polish flowers
Under the English arse I'd left my brains in.

You gave me three kisses at the station,
But the park was the best.
Here's how I'd hold you –
In a child's swing,
Smiling,
Your eyes wide,
Caught, still, at the top of a rising curve.

Looking back, I suppose what I feel most about my marriage to Diana is gratitude. I knew her and loved her for such a long time, from when she was a shy girl from York trying her best to be sophisticated to when she was an eighty-seven-year-old grandmother. All the books we read together, all the conversations, all the private jokes. She was the constant one. We knew such a lot about each other. And we were never bored with one another. It's tempting, with the benefit of years and hindsight, to frame the whole thing as a series of trespasses and near-misses – lapses in fidelity, yes, but never in affection. I loved her. Even when I wasn't being particularly lovable. Even when I was behaving appallingly. I always came back. Not because I had to, but because part of me never left.

*

Diana and I always enjoyed being together, with the kids or without them. There were so many things we shared: five dogs in the course of our marriage, and many cats, a host of jokes and memories, the books and films we would reread and rewatch together over and over again. And when she retired from teaching, she took a degree in Fine Art and became a painter and brought a whole new world into our marriage. And somehow those sex-mad students turned into this elderly couple – a writer and a painter sharing a house and so much more. Two companionable old dogs, one at each end of the sofa.

In essence, Diana was my best collaborator, in both life and art. When both our kids were safely stowed at school, Diana took a teacher-training course and got a job in Coventry teaching four- to seven-year-olds. The school was on what was known as a "sink estate", where the council put problem families, for convenience. The headteacher had instituted "family grouping". The idea was that the older children would nurture the younger ones. In practice, that meant big kids beating up little ones in the classroom as well as in the playground. It was not an easy placement for anybody's first job. I used to have lunch with Diana on Friday and then go in and help her, mostly just doing storytelling and singing songs. The stories they liked best were those about themselves, about how Mrs Davies's class went on an adventure and met an ogre, and stuff like that, with heroic roles for them. I would be acting the monster generally, and some of the little boys would get so worked up I feared being overpowered. I could play the guitar in those days, and I made up songs they could all join in on. One was about our first dog, Chowder.

Had a little dog, and his name was Chowder –
You can bark loud, but he could bark louder.
Bow! Wow! Bow wow wow wow wow!

And so on. Not exactly John Lennon and Paul McCartney, but they liked it. My best song was 'Cyril the Squirrel'.

Oh, my name is Cyril, I'm a big fat squirrel,
And what I like best is nuts.
Every year, when the leaves go brown,
I'm shinnin' up the hazel trees and flingin' nuts down –
More and more
In me store.
I'm happy as a king –
Oh, nuts nuts nuts, I shall stuff 'em in me guts,
From now till half-past spring!

After a couple of years, Diana was able to move on to somewhere a bit more genteel, and she became a very skilful and much-loved teacher. And she enjoyed the power too – to hold a class of kids spellbound, and sometimes the whole school. I still wasn't fond of carrying a conventional briefcase, and for a long while I carried my stuff in a very fancy French schoolkids' satchel, deep blue and yellow, with shiny fastenings. Diana made up a whole school assembly based on it. In her version, the satchel belonged to a teacher. A small boy became covetous: since he liked it and wanted it, he decided it must be his. So he took it. What followed was a tale of crime, panic, conscience and eventual restitution. It was received with awe, the whole school hanging with bated breath on every word. Diana told it brilliantly. She had timing. She understood where to pause, when to lower her voice, how to let a roomful of five-year-olds lean in. Storytelling was not an "activity" in her classroom: it was how she taught. The children adored her for it. Inevitably, we began shaping ideas together more deliberately. We would sit at the kitchen table after supper and see if something might grow. We wrote things down – we sent them off. Occasionally, they were published.

Stoke Infant School had a large number of Sikh children, many newly arrived in England. Quite a few began school speaking no English at all. There was one little girl, Poonam, who went through an entire term without uttering a word. She was lively, attentive, entirely engaged – she simply did not speak. Then, one day, she did. And when she did, she spoke in full, perfectly formed sentences. It was as if she had been listening, waiting, assembling the language carefully in her head until she was certain she would get it right. When Diana told me that story, we both knew there was something in it. The book became *Poonam's Pets*. In it, Mrs Wig, Diana's lightly disguised fictional self, announces a special pet assembly. The children may bring in a pet, she says, provided it behaves itself. The classroom erupts: dogs, cats, goldfish, rabbits. Mrs Wig turns to Poonam and asks what she will bring. Silence. Then a whisper in the teacher's ear. Mrs Wig straightens herself and says, "And Poonam will bring her lions." There's some laughter. No one takes it seriously. On the day of the assembly, every child is in place. Every pupil and their pet have arrived except Poonam. The door creaks open. In she walks, followed by six enormous lions. Real lions. Golden, magnificent, perfectly calm. Some children dive under desks, others freeze. Poonam, who has barely spoken all year, says with authority, "It's all right. You don't need to be frightened. These are nice lions." One by one, the children climb onto their backs, and Poonam leads the parade with solemn ceremony.

We sent the manuscript to Methuen, not expecting very much. They found a wonderful illustrator, Paul Dowling, who understood the tone – not too cute, not too dissonant – and it became a beautiful picture book for early readers. We only did one more book together after that. We should have done more. That's one of those regrets that sits there among the list of things "not done" and "not finished".

The second story, *Raj in Charge*, arrived as an idea when we were on holiday in Portugal. I had recently been in hospital with a peculiar stomach complaint. Once discharged, we decamped to the Algarve, so that I could convalesce in the sun like a Victorian invalid. I was

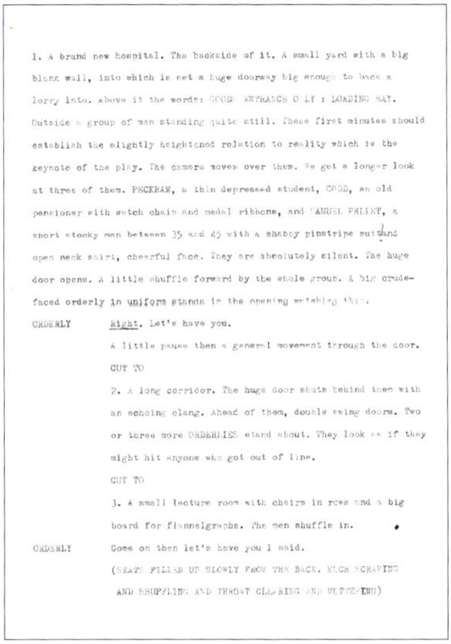

1. A brand new hospital. The backside of it. A small yard with a big blank wall, into which is set a huge doorway big enough to back a lorry into. above it the words: GOODS ENTRANCE ONLY : LOADING BAY. Outside a group of men standing quite still. These first minutes should establish the slightly heightened relation to reality which is the keynote of the play. The camera moves over them. We get a longer look at three of them. PECKHAM, a thin depressed student, GOOD, an old pensioner with watch chain and medal ribbons, and SAMUEL PELLET, a short stocky man between 35 and 45 with a shabby pinstripe suit and open neck shirt, cheerful face. They are absolutely silent. The huge door opens. A little shuffle forward by the whole group. A big crude-faced orderly in uniform stands in the opening watching them.

ORDERLY — Right. Let's have you.

A little pause then a general movement through the door.

CUT TO

2. A long corridor. The huge door shuts behind them with an echoing clang. Ahead of them, double swing doors. Two or three more ORDERLIES stand about. They look as if they might hit anyone who got out of line.

CUT TO

3. A small lecture room with chairs in rows and a big board for flannelgraphs. The men shuffle in.

ORDERLY — Come on then let's have you I said.

(SEATS FILLED UP SLOWLY FROM THE BACK. MUCH SCRAPING AND SHUFFLING AND THROAT CLEARING AND MUTTERING)

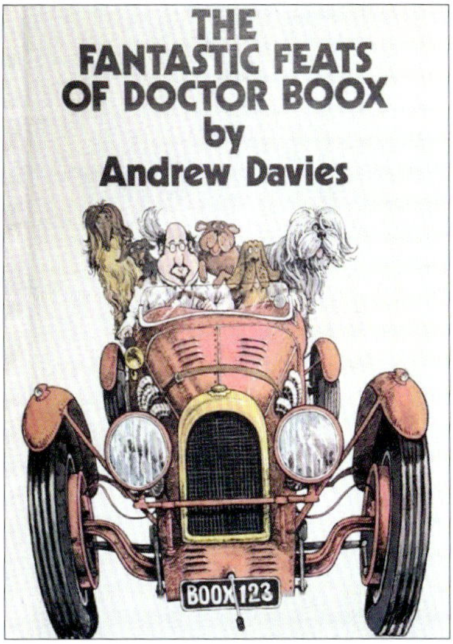

The first page from the typescript of my third radio play, *The Hospitalization of Samuel Pellet* (1964); my first published book, the children's story *The Fantastic Feats of Doctor Boox* (1972); my first film adaptation of a classic: Charles Dickens's *The Signalman* (1976).

(Left) The front cover of the playbill for *Going Bust* (1977), the first big-stage production of any of my plays, written when I was still working full-time as a teacher. (Right) A poster advertising another of my early plays, *Stabs at the Simple Life* (1978).

Posing with the young, talented team of *Stabs at the Simple Life*.

Fearless Frank (1978): a staggering success as a musical in the UK (left) – a pitiful flop on Broadway (right).

The brilliant Leonard Rossiter and Susan Penhaligon in the BBC2 Play of the Week production of *Fearless Frank*.

Rose (1980), starring Glenda Jackson – a runaway success in the UK, another Broadway flop.

(Left) The front jacket of *Educating Marmalade* (1983), the third book in the Marmalade tetralogy. (Right) The naughty Marmalade Atkins, played by a teenage Charlotte Coleman.

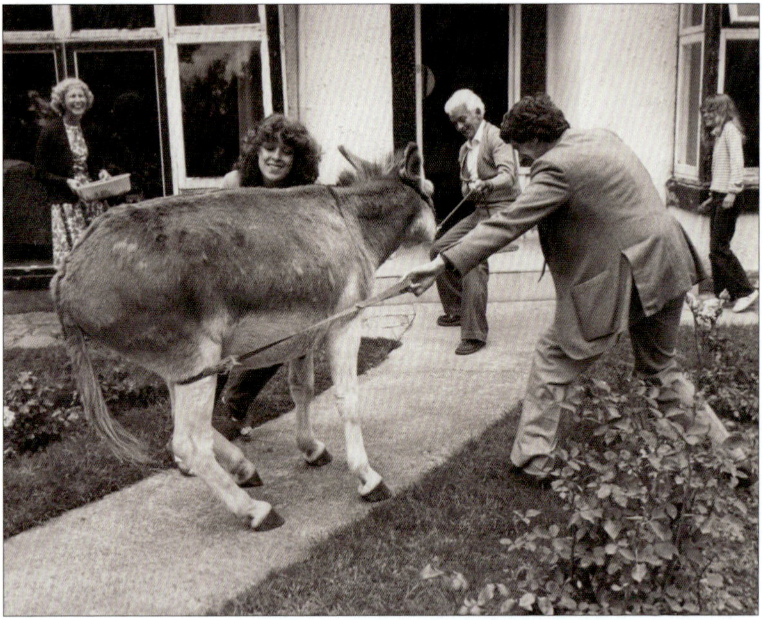

Rufus the donkey at his recalcitrant best.

(Left) The front cover of one of the books based on my TV series *A Very Peculiar Practice* (1986–88). (Top right) *Inappropriate Behaviour*, a Screen Two TV play that, together with *A Very Peculiar Practice*, won me the Royal Television Society's Writers' Award in 1987. (Bottom right) *Lucky Sunil* (1988), another Screen Two TV play.

On the set of the feature film *Consuming Passions* (1988) with Tyler Butterworth, who played Ian Littleton in the lead role.

(Above) A candid shot of the filming of *Ball-Trap on the Côte Sauvage* (1989), a Screen One TV play based on a family holiday in Brittany during the summer of 1976. (Below) The front jacket of *Poonam's Pets* (1990), a children's book I wrote with Diana, illustrated by Paul Dowling.

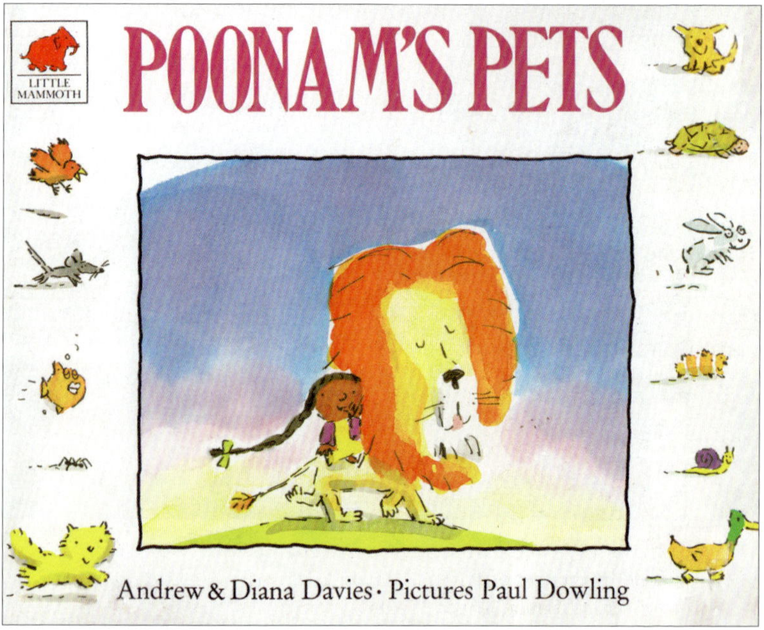

At the 1991 BAFTA Awards ceremony with the team from *House of Cards* (1990). The show was nominated for seven awards, and Ian Richardson (sitting next to my wife Diana in the photo) went on to win Best Actor.

Surrounded by the cast of *Filipina Dreamgirls* (1991), a Screen One TV play set in Manila, featuring many non-professional actors.

Discussing the adaptation of Kingsley Amis's *The Old Devils* (1992) with "Welsh-sounding" director Tristram Powell.

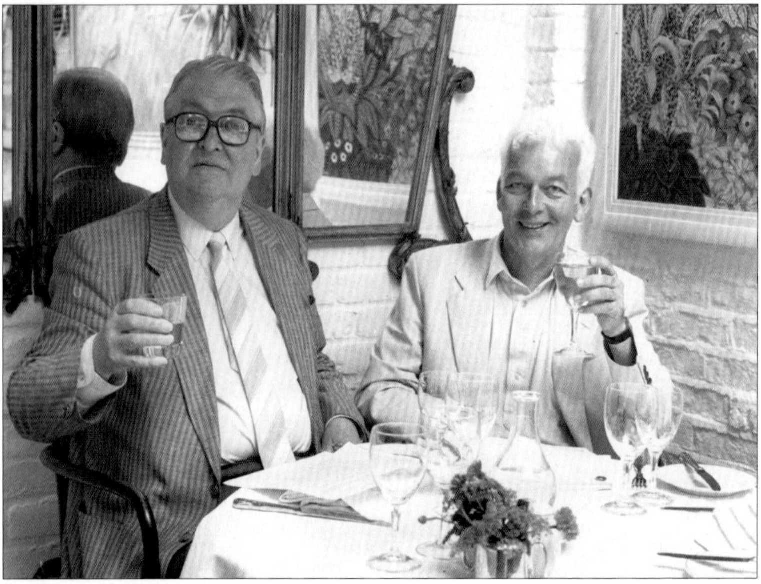

One of those hard luncheon meetings with Kingsley Amis.

under strict instructions about what I could eat and, worse, what I couldn't drink. There was a rigid no-alcohol rule. On holiday! In Portugal! So, instead of wine, I had mineral water. And we made up stories. As ever, the seed came from Diana's classroom. There was a boy called Raj who specialized in petty mischief: snapped pencils, pilfered rubbers. Diana decided that the solution was not to punish him, but to promote him. Raj would be in charge of the pencils: he would distribute them, collect them, guard them. Responsibility as a path to reform. In our story, this noble experiment grows into something rather grander. Raj becomes excessively conscientious. The pencils are counted, audited, held in safekeeping. He dreams that enormous rats are invading the school at night and gnawing through the pencil hoard. He imagines himself alone in the corridors, defending HBs and 2Bs from rodent marauders. The burden of office begins to weigh. Even an eight-year-old can only take so much anxiety. Eventually, in both fiction and life, Raj realizes that power carries consequences. He approaches Mrs Wig – our fictionalized version of Diana – and politely asks to be relieved of his duties. He understands now, he explains, that looking after things properly is harder than breaking them. It was a simple tale: morality, imagination, mild peril, redemption. Debi Gliori illustrated it beautifully, bringing out all the warmth and humour we could only hint at in words. Like *Poonam's Pets*, it had grown directly from Diana's classroom soil.

Looking back, I can see a pattern. *Conrad's War* and *Marmalade Atkins* sprang from Bill and Anna – those vivid creatures who happened to live in our house. *Poonam's Pets* and *Raj in Charge* came from Stoke Infant School. They were all, in different ways, about children negotiating the business of growing up, learning power, fear, responsibility and the small dramas that feel enormous at the time. As Bill and Anna grew older, that rich, noisy laboratory began to change: fewer invented games; fewer imaginary friends with telephones; more doors shut; more privacy. Perfectly natural. But the raw material shifted – the family dynamic altered, as it must – and I drifted back towards adult worlds and adult compromises. We should have done more of those books, Diana and I. They were our purest collaborations: her instinct for children, my instinct for narrative. No career ambition attached, no grand strategy. Just the two of us on a hot balcony in Portugal inventing a boy who took pencils too seriously – while I took mineral water more seriously than I cared to admit.

Children were at the centre of our lives for so long that it was hard to imagine a version of ourselves without them rattling about in the background. Family holidays, Sunday breakfasts, dogs under the table, arguments about nothing in particular – the ordinary fabric of it all. Then, gradually, the fabric thinned. They kept coming on holiday with us for as long as we could persuade them to do so. There was a gentle campaign each year: offers of sun, sea, decent food, minimal parental interference. It worked for a while – not long, though. That's the way it goes. Bill settled in Manchester (he works at Salford University, lives in Didsbury). Anna went off to university and then, happily for us, came back for a year afterwards. That was a gift. It felt like borrowed time. I'd have had either of them move back in permanently, if they'd asked. They were good company. But children are meant to peel away. It's their job. When they did, Diana and I had to recalibrate. The rhythm shifted. A quieter house.

Diana threw herself into work. She became a deputy head, which meant arbitrating playground dramas, navigating staff politics, soothing fractured marriages, disciplining errant pupils, as well as the actual job of teaching. She continued to teach art, which was her real passion. She did an access course in Leamington and then went on to take a fine-art degree at Coventry University. She always did things properly. I had my writing, which by then occupied most of my mental landscape. Even when I wasn't at the desk, I was there in my head. It was around this period that we settled into a way of being that carried us right up to that fateful October Saturday in 2023. I occasionally found myself asking unhelpful questions: "Why are we still together? What is the glue? Habit? Loyalty? Fear of loneliness? Mutual toleration?" All of the above, perhaps. But also something simpler: we were good at letting each other be. I learnt early that even during our more combustible periods, she had no interest in wounding me. And I had no interest in wounding her. We rubbed along remarkably well. Work, pets, occasional drama. Bill and Anna stepping further into their own lives. It was solid. It was ours.

During her post-university year at home, Anna did an office-skill course at the local technical college, and we talked about her future. Script-editing seemed right for her: she was intelligent, curious, emotionally literate – she'd been around writers all her life, particularly this one. Sally Head gave her a start as a "baby script reader", reading piles of hopeful manuscripts and writing notes. She was very good at it, and Sally recommended her to Keith Richardson at Yorkshire TV. Keith was old-school, and taught Anna the trade. One of her earliest jobs was on *Heartbeat* – that sturdy Sunday night institution which cast a warm, nostalgic glow over crime in the Yorkshire Dales of the 1960s. It was policing as pastoral theatre: gentle misdemeanours, wayward farmers, the occasional morally instructive scrap and, at the centre of it all, a handsome constable riding over hill and dale on his motorbike attempting to restore order. The only difficulty was that the actor in question was, by all accounts, not entirely at ease with the motorbike. He was a nervous rider and had a habit of parting company with it. But the audience loved him. When she'd been there a while, I asked her what it was like working on a popular series.

"Dad," she said, "you wouldn't like it. We come up with the storylines, then we send them out to the writers. The scripts come in, and they're rubbish. We ask them to rewrite them. They're still rubbish. Then we rewrite them and give them to the actors. They rewrite all their own bits, and then we shoot it." I was impressed. But she was right. I wouldn't have liked it.

It was during that year Anna spent at home with us that I started writing my adaptation of *Pride and Prejudice*, then intended for ITV. I was sitting at my desk downstairs (or "dining-room table", as Diana preferred to call it). Anna was upstairs in her room.

The opening of *Pride and Prejudice* is probably the most famous in English fiction. "It is a truth universally acknowledged..." If I started with that, I'd be grovelling humbly though all six episodes. I needed to make my mark on this thing.

Robert McKee's words echoed in my mind. "What's the inciting incident?"

Of course! If Bingley and Darcy don't ride into Hertfordshire and see Netherfield Hall, there's no story. So let's start with that. Men on big horses, kicking up the dirt. Tight breeches, testosterone and sweat! I started pounding the keys.

FADE UP: *Ext. Netherfield Park. Late September. Day 1.*

(*Pounding hooves really close, the horses snorting and the screen full of glossy flanks as* DARCY *and* BINGLEY *gallop across a meadow, the horses snorting and kicking up dirt, all that immense power under control. They rein in their horses, looking across at the very pleasant prospect of Netherfield Hall. Very calm, very peaceful; the educated English countryside. A few gentle chords of music to tell us that everything is in its proper place in the ordered society.*

BINGLEY *is quite out of breath.* DARCY, *characteristically, more together. Doesn't like even his best friend to see him out of puff. They are dressed for exercise rather than for business or society. We'll see their formal manners later. Now we're seeing two very virile young blokes.*)

BINGLEY: It's a fair prospect.

DARCY: Pretty enough, I grant you.

BINGLEY: Oh, it's nothing to Pemberley, I know. But I must settle somewhere! Have I your approval?

DARCY: You will find the society something savage.

BINGLEY: Country manners? I think they are charming!

DARCY (*smiling*): Then you had better take it.

BINGLEY: Thank you! I shall! I shall close with the attorney directly!

(*And he kicks his horse up and rides off down the hill towards the house.* DARCY *follows.*)

It sounded good to me. Especially the bit about the attorney. I ran upstairs and showed it to Anna.

"What do you think?"

Anna read it carefully.

"Very good, Dad."

It feels apt now that Anna should have been the first person to read the first page of a production that would remodel our lives. We didn't know that then, of course. She had grown up sitting on the sofa beside me watching what might loosely be described as "adult drama". She developed a taste for it at about eight or nine. She didn't always follow the politics or the sexual subtleties, but she had an instinctive grasp of motive. Within minutes she would identify who was to be trusted and who was not, who was posturing, who was dangerous, who was merely vain. She was rarely wrong. Our living room – where that sofa sat and still sits – was the true centre of the house. It was open, democratic, slightly chaotic. People drifted in and out. We had always been permissive parents: sofas were to be jumped on by nine-year-olds or snogged on by teenagers. Dogs underfoot. Television in the background. The dining room was my monastery. The living room was communal, and Bill's friends often colonized the space. They were bright, loud, occasionally outrageous. On one such evening, they were all watching something on television that Anna deemed unworthy.

"I don't think this is very good. Shall we have it off?" she said.

One of Bill's friends instantly replied, "Oh Anna, I didn't know that you cared."

She went scarlet and fled the room.

There were only two years between Bill and Anna, which is nothing in adult terms. Watching Bill and Anna negotiate their closeness and difference was a kind of education for us both. And, through it all, Anna sat beside me, absorbing the story. Looking for truth. Spotting false notes. Which is perhaps why it felt entirely right that she should be the first reader when Bingley and Darcy came clattering into our lives on horseback.

Asset-Stripping

To me, there's not a huge difference between writing original material and adapting someone else's. I never feel particularly handcuffed by the source material. *House of Cards* is an extreme example. My adaptation was basically asset-stripping: the plot was the asset. I changed the characters and the dialogue, the central relationship and the ending. Michael Dobbs's novel ends with Francis Urquhart throwing himself off the roof of the Palace of Westminster. But my Francis? My Francis wasn't going to do anything so wet. No, my Francis threw the girl off instead. Even though he loved her. In the book, she's having a love affair with another journalist. Boring! Robert McKee says that, where there is sex, put it right on the spine of the story – which is Urquhart's rise to power. The implication is he has to have a sexual relationship with Mattie, who is young enough to be his daughter. All the better! And she can call him "Daddy" when they're doing it! The first actress we cast for Mattie wouldn't say the lines. So she was replaced by Susannah Harker. I remember watching the rushes for the first time, in a BBC van with Michael Wearing, the BBC Head of Drama. Her despairing cry of "Daddyyyyyy", then a second or two of silence. Then... bang – that awful, sickening sound as she hits the car below and slides down the roof. I thought, "Oh God. What have I done?"

Michael loved it. And Ken Riddington, the producer, pointed out that the new ending opened the door for a second series. I hadn't thought of that. It was simply that this was where the story took me. Urquhart wasn't a quitter. If he was going to be stopped, it would have to be for ever – which, eventually, he was. When the American version came along, Dobbsy and I were both thrilled: huge budget, huge reach – and, best of all, a lovely cheque. The only condition was that we weren't to say anything negative about it. And that was fine – until I forgot. I was in LA, promoting *Sense and Sensibility*, chatting to a journalist who seemed more like a new friend than someone on the job. We talked Austen. We talked adaptations. And then he said: "Have you seen the US version of *House of Cards*?" Without thinking, I said, "Well, it looks fabulous. We'd have loved that budget. Great writing too. But, I must say, Kevin Spacey doesn't have the charm or subtlety of Ian Richardson."

Six weeks later I had my agent Stephen on the phone.

"Andrew, did you say something about the American *House of Cards*?"

"Don't think so."

"Well, a journalist claims you did."

"Oh, bloody hell, I didn't know that was an interview!"

Stephen laughed. "I'll smooth it over. But try not to do it again, eh?"

At that moment the relevant clause in the contract flashed in my mind with alarming clarity. One of the occupational hazards of writers, I've discovered, is that we are rather fond of giving opinions – sometimes before checking whether we are legally permitted to do so. Fortunately, the matter was resolved without too much drama. No lawsuits ensued, no lawyers descended from the skies, and the American version went on to become an enormous success. In fact, it was oddly satisfying to watch our original story mutate and expand in a completely different political ecosystem. But it did reinforce a small professional lesson: when a contract says "Do not say anything negative", it is wise, however conversational the circumstances may feel, to remember that someone is probably writing it down.

My run-ins with the press have been few and far between, thank goodness. However, when I said I wanted to write "a really sexy version of *Pride and Prejudice*", the press got very excited. Roy Hattersley wrote a full-page outrage piece. Austen societies had their bonnets on fire. I hadn't written a single word, and already people were scandalized. It was glorious. By the time the series aired, the nation was ready for a corset-ripping romp. They were looking for sex behind every sidelong glance. The whole thing turned into exquisite foreplay. And, of course, there was nothing remotely pornographic in it. But we had the country hot under the cravat.

People were already titillated by a version of *Pride and Prejudice* that existed only in their imagination. It was rather wonderful. By the time we began filming, the public conversation had gathered such momentum that the audience seemed to be waiting for something outrageously indecent to happen. Which meant that when the series finally aired the entire country watched it with a heightened sense of anticipation. Every moment of tension between Elizabeth and Darcy carried a faint electric charge, because everyone had been primed to expect something shocking. There was, admittedly, a wet shirt. Colin Firth emerging from that lake turned out to be one of those television moments that entered the cultural imagination. It was replayed, parodied, written about endlessly and discussed with the seriousness normally reserved for matters of state. Meanwhile, the series itself drew audiences of around eleven million viewers in Britain and travelled happily around the world, turning Austen – briefly, at least – into the hottest property on television.

But mostly what we had done was simply restore the physicality and emotional intensity that is already there in Austen's writing. People forget that her novels are not genteel museum pieces: they are about attraction, frustration, pride, humiliation, jealousy and desire, all the things that make human beings behave rather badly. In the end, the supposed scandal turned out to be the best publicity imaginable. The nation tuned in to see just how outrageous this new *Pride and Prejudice* might be. A little scandal, I've found, goes a long way.

A Man Walks into a Town: Tackling George Eliot

But before Austen there was Eliot to be tackled.

I've always loved *Middlemarch*. I'd wanted to adapt the novel for ages, and when Brian Eastman at Carnival Films proposed it, I was keen. But my agent, Stephen Durbridge, thought Brian and I might end up at each other's throats, so he suggested we run it past the BBC instead – which we did. Michael Wearing, to whom we were trying to sell *Pride and Prejudice* at the time, was very much into things that were a bit more rugged and gritty and less about frocks.

"It's not about frocks," I said. "It's about sex and money."

"Well, look," he replied, "if we do *Middlemarch* first, then perhaps, if it's a success, we can do *Pride and Prejudice* as well."

Deal.

Michael had not actually read *Middlemarch*, but he had formed a view of it by asking a lot of people.

"The way I see it, Andrew…" he said. "A man rides into a town…"

I waited for more, but that was it. Michael was famous for his brief and enigmatic pronouncements. What did he mean?

"Ah yes! Got it! It's a Western!"

Middlemarch starts with Dorothea and her sister Celia discussing whether they should wear the jewellery of their mother, who has recently died. All very good, but typical nineteenth-century woman centred stuff. Michael wanted to foreground Lydgate riding into Coventry to revolutionize community medicine and make some breakthrough in medical research. Magic! With the forces of provincial conservatism lining up to gun him down. *Middlemarch* as a Western! Genius!

Then came the fun part: working with the producer. I was paired with a bright-eyed fellow who said, in our very first meeting, "The thing about *Middlemarch* is it's written in long chunks. I think we need shorter scenes, something more like *EastEnders*."

"Not exactly like *EastEnders*, I hope?" I asked.

"No. Not exactly."

Middlemarch as soap opera. My heart sank, but I nodded politely and set about doing a first draft, something with heft but also energy. I knew it wouldn't be exactly what he wanted, but I figured we'd find our way to a middle ground. We'd negotiate, finesse, collaborate. I'm ever the optimist! At the script meeting, he stood up and announced, "I don't think Andrew and I see eye to eye on this. I'd like to pursue the project with another writer."

I was gobsmacked. I felt betrayed, really. I had thought we were working towards something together, not lining up for a duel. I rang Stephen immediately.

"The man's trying to sack you," he said. "Let's get *him* sacked."

So we did.

Michael Wearing groaned when he heard. "Oh Lord," he said. "I really thought you two would get along."

"Get along? That man tried to sack me!"

"All right," he said. "Of course, we'll continue with you. But who's going to produce it? I suppose it'll have to be Louis."

Which, honestly, was a stroke of luck. Louis Marks and I had worked together many times before, and it was a joy to be reunited. He was a George Eliot devotee, and understood the kind of structural work *Middlemarch* needed. And the BBC brought in a young script editor named Susie Conklin, an American, who had asked to be on the show. *Middlemarch* was her first drama – and she and I hit it off straight away. She agreed with my ideas: make it physical, kinetic, filmy, and allow the characters to breathe. George Eliot has this habit of writing a brilliant, subtle scene with lots of subtext, then you turn the page and she's telling you what she's just done, and what to think of the characters. Back off, George. We want to make up our own minds!

Michael wanted Anthony Page to direct, which was a coup, since he'd done all sorts of acclaimed stage work. But there was one small problem: Anthony was of the "Isn't *Middlemarch* marvellous?" school of thought. He wanted to lift chunks of the novel directly into the script. "So much wonderful material," he kept saying.

"Yes," I said, "but that's not what screenwriting is about. You can't just plop a novel on the screen. I admire Eliot deeply, but she can be, let's say, *emphatic* – always worried the reader might be missing the point, always explaining, re-explaining, and then throwing in a footnote for good measure..."

Anthony favoured a slower, more reverent style. I favoured pace and momentum. Things came to a head one afternoon in Louis's absurdly tiny office on the fourth floor of the BBC building. It was winter, and I'd dressed in layers for the train journey: overcoat, jumper, shirt, undershirt. As the argument heated up, so did I. By the time I was shouting "But we're making a film, and you're supposed to be the fucking director!" I was down to my T-shirt and sweating like a pig. Anthony stood up and said icily, "I AM the director! I AM the director! And I think you're being VERY RUDE!"

I stormed out.

Halfway down the stairs, I realized I'd left half my clothes behind and had to slink back, red-faced. I found Louis with his head in his hands, like a man in the throes of an existential crisis. We didn't sack Anthony. He was much too distinguished for that. Louis decided that we should be kept apart, with Susie as the go-between – a role she performed brilliantly. I would bark, "What the hell is he playing at?" – and she would translate it into "Andrew was wondering whether you might possibly think again about..." And so on. And it worked. At one point, mid-production, Anthony turned to Susie and said, "You know, I've been thinking... and d'you know what: *Middlemarch* is rather like a Western."

Eventually, Anthony and I managed a civilized conversation again, and I kept all my clothes on – which was an improvement. And, I must admit, he did a great job.

*

George Eliot has a way of lingering in one's mind. So in 2001, years after *Middlemarch*, I turned to her last, most sprawling, most maddening novel: *Daniel Deronda*. I came to that book very late. And, at first, I found I agreed with the critical consensus: half of it is a great, penetrating portrait of an abusive marriage, the other half is ridiculously dull and earnest. Here's the story in brief: a beautiful young woman (Gwendolen Harleth) is playing roulette in a German spa and losing. A young man (Daniel) watches her and later follows her as she pawns her last piece of jewellery. He returns it to her – she is embarrassed and angry. But something's happened between them.

A bold flashback to a year ago: Gwendolen's provincial beginnings. Soon after the death of her stepfather, Gwendolen moves with her mother and sisters to a new neighbourhood. Her family's precarious finances depend upon her making a profitable marriage. Enter Henleigh Grandcourt: titled, elegant, coolly self-contained. But he is also cruel and cold-hearted. Gwendolen toys with him, as she does with most things. She thinks she holds the reins. That illusion collapses when she encounters Grandcourt's mistress. Gwendolen flees to Germany, which is where the story begins. She is strongly attracted to Daniel, but marries Grandcourt, who asserts his dominance on the wedding night. She realizes that she's walked into marital hell. Meanwhile, Daniel has rescued and befriended a penniless young musician, which leads him to London's Jewish community and the Zionist cause, and all sorts of earth-shaking revelations.

Music is an important motif, and so is water. The problem is that George Eliot was so sympathetic to the Jewish cause that all the characters from that community, including Daniel, are too good to be true. Casting helps. Hugh Dancy made a spirited and engaging Daniel, and Jodhi May was very moving as the Jewish girl Mirah. ("All tears and snot," said Jane Tranter, "but you have to love her.") Romola Garai was terrific as Gwendolen – brittle, beautiful, infuriating, heartbreaking. And Hugh Bonneville was chilling as the sadistic Grandcourt.

The path to production was not smooth. I proposed the concept to the BBC, started to develop an outline with Louis, and then it turned out that Stephen Evans was trying to put together an independent film based on the book, so we combined forces for a year or so, and had a series of long and unproductive meetings while the ducks refused to get in a row. I remember one proposed scene (maybe I came up with it) had Daniel knocking Grandcourt down in a fist fight. Louis, a George Eliot purist, was very shocked. Anyway, eventually we found some common ground and went back to Michael Wearing, and he commissioned three episodes just before he got the boot, apparently for saying some rude things about the BBC management.

We had a new exec producer, Kate Harwood, and a young director called Tom Hooper, who then went on to win an Academy Award for *The King's Speech*. He had just done an adaptation of Nancy Mitford's *Love in a Cold Climate*, which had been a success. I must say I didn't take to Tom very much. One of his ideas was that Grandcourt needed to be more sympathetic. I couldn't believe my ears: Grandcourt is a monster, surely. If you soften him, you destroy the whole moral structure of the piece. Kate Lewis, our script editor, agreed with me – and so did Hugh Bonneville, who decided to ignore Tom's notes. This is the sort of solidarity a writer prays for. *Daniel Deronda* remains one of my favourites: I can watch it all without wincing once.

*

In 2007, five years after *Daniel Deronda*, I found myself working with Hugh again on *The Diary of a Nobody* (Hugh thinks it's one of the best things he's ever done). It's quite a different creature from Deronda, of course. No grand moral architecture, no philosophical foundations: just a lowly City clerk, Mr Pooter, diligently recording the minor triumphs and humiliations of suburban life, and, in doing so, revealing something devastating about English self-regard, aspiration and unease. I've always loved it. The tone, the absolute seriousness applied to the essentially trivial, is extraordinarily hard to sustain. Most writers, given half a chance, will reach for the joke. The Grossmiths don't. They simply let Pooter proceed, convinced at every turn of his own propriety, and the comedy takes care of itself. What struck me, as ever, was how little one needs to add. The voice does all the work. Get that right, and everything else falls into place. Get it wrong, and you're left with a man who is merely silly – which is fatal. I remember scribbling in the margin at one point: don't improve this. It's a useful note for any adapter. Improvement is very often the problem.

Back in the Seventies, Rosie Hill did it as a fully dramatized show. We, on the other hand, did it as a one-man show. Hugh has that rare ability to convey decency without making it dull, and to reveal vanity without any hint of sarcasm. There's a particular kind of Englishness he carries very lightly: self-aware but not arch; precise but never showy. You believe him entirely as a man who might spend a whole morning composing a letter of complaint and then be wounded when it is not properly appreciated.

What we discovered was that the less we did, the better it became. The smallest inflection – a pause, a misplaced confidence, a faint tightening of the jaw – could carry an entire scene. It's delicate work, and oddly unforgiving. Push it, and it dies. In a way, it's not so far removed from what I was doing with Eliot – just played at a different pitch. Both works are concerned with how people see themselves and how the world contradicts that view. Deronda searches for moral coherence in a vast and often indifferent society; Pooter is simply trying to get through the day without social embarrassment. But the impulse is the same, and the secret is to make their contradictions become visible. And perhaps that is why *Diary of a Nobody* has endured.

Pride and Prejudice

"Andrew, do you want to talk about doing *Pride and Prejudice*?"

Sue Birtwistle and I had already begun treading a measure with this particular Austen novel some years earlier. Sue had pitched it to Nick Elliott, who was then at London Weekend Television. Nick had several teenage daughters, and Sue pitched it as a book about a man with five daughters, all brimful of hormones, for whom he has to get blokes. Nick said: "Great, are the rights available? Can we meet the author?"

But even after Sue revealed it was Jane Austen, Nick gamely commissioned the first three episodes. I wrote the scripts, and Nick loved them. But his bosses didn't think that was what LWT was about, so Sue started all over again with Michael Wearing, and eventually he said yes on the strength of the *Middlemarch* success. Looking back, it's funny to think how many people didn't want us to do the series. After it became a hit, all the BBC execs lined up to say "I fought for this show" – whereas we knew they had been against it.

Coming back to it was harder than I'd expected. The first half, which I'd already written, had rolled along easily. There are plenty of wonderful dramatic scenes in the book. All it needs is a little pruning – one of my Jane Austen mantras is: "When in doubt, copy it out." The second half of the book is another matter. I've occasionally wondered if the book began life as a more straightforward epistolary novel, and whether Austen never quite got round to dismantling its original scaffolding. But, as Robert McKee would say, "Every problem is an opportunity in disguise."

The pivotal letter is Darcy's, delivered to Elizabeth after she has contemptuously refused his first proposal. He wants to explain himself – particularly his conduct towards Wickham. On the page, it's narration – on-screen, it would risk becoming a boring recital. So I decided to dramatize it as a sequence of flashbacks. Two boys, Darcy and Wickham, close companions. Affection, ease, then fracture, betrayal. And Georgiana. In the novel, Georgiana Darcy is hardly present at all. In drama, that isn't good enough. If Wickham nearly ruins a fifteen-year-old girl, we should see her, feel for her. Emilia Fox was perfectly cast. When Darcy discovers Wickham's scheme and rescues her, we glimpse something else in him: tenderness, real feeling. It gives Elizabeth, and the audience, a new angle from which to see him.

I wasn't particularly involved in casting decisions. That was more Sue's domain. Colin Firth was initially only given the first three episodes to read. At that stage, he hadn't read *Pride and Prejudice*. Nor any Austen. He said, "Well, I suppose that's the end of the show for Darcy." Sue replied, "No. That's the beginning."

She was clear-headed about the whole enterprise. She also had at her disposal the invaluable resource of her husband, Richard Eyre, who knew every serious actor worth knowing. Richard was an early and firm Colin Firth enthusiast. Once he'd realized that Darcy stays in the story, Colin read the second half of *Pride and Prejudice* and then the rest of Austen's novels. He took it all very seriously. I can remember seeing him in costume for the first time – hair darkened, long limbs, boots. He was sprawled over a sofa during a test, and I thought: "Women are going to go mad for you." Jennifer Ehle turned up having dyed her naturally blonde hair to a deep brown. She understood Elizabeth instinctively: the intelligence, the irony, the refusal to perform femininity for anyone's benefit. Pretty soon it was obvious that Darcy and Elizabeth were enacting something quite charged – both on- and, to a smaller degree, off-screen. That helps, sometimes, so long as there's no fallout during filming. The plot engine is simple. Darcy fancies Elizabeth. He doesn't approve of her family. He doesn't think she is socially suitable. He can't help himself, though. She mocks him, outpaces him intellectually. He doesn't understand what's happening. Underneath it all, it's Darwinian. The Darcy line requires vitality, intelligence, unpredictability. Elizabeth supplies all three. Sex matters. It always does.

At the full read-through, I looked around the room and felt elated. Alison Steadman's first lines as Mrs Bennet changed the temperature in the room. I had imagined Mrs Bennet as fluttery and nervous... Alison made her loud, vulgar, magnificent – explosive and utterly alive. It worked far better. Years later, in 2025, at the thirtieth-anniversary reunion, Alison admitted that a critic – just one – had savaged her performance, and that she'd been deeply upset by it. I was surprised. She'd seemed indestructible. But then I guess most actors aren't. Most writers aren't, either. David Bamber's Mr Collins was another revelation. He lifted him off the page: absurd and authentic at the same time. The read-through ended with the distinct feeling that we had somcthing of a substantial nature. Then they all decamped to Wiltshire for the beginning of a six-month shoot, and I returned to my dining room in Kenilworth and resumed work on *Moll Flanders*.

Once the shoot was in the can, I'd visit the edit intermittently. One scene in particular, Darcy in the lake, intrigued me, and I was curious to see how it had come out, since the idea had been mine. In my head, Darcy has just returned from London, where he's endured the Bingley sisters and a thousand assorted social obligations. He has a day alone at Pemberley before hosting yet another house party. It's hot. He's riding, not travelling in a carriage. He sees the lake. He thinks: "Sod it." He goes in.

My instinct was that he should be naked – not for titillation, but for animal freedom: a shedding of etiquette. No waistcoats. No expectations. Just a man in water. In the event, for reasons I can no longer precisely remember, most of the clothes stayed on. He emerges, sees Elizabeth, freezes. Social paralysis returns at once. Words fail him. In a modern romantic comedy, they'd kiss. They don't. Instead, they fumble in awkward conversation while one of them drips. The refusal to acknowledge the dripping is part of the awkward comedy. I never thought of it as a sexy moment, but I'm very happy if that's how it's seen.

The scene shifts to the music room. Pay-off. We know Georgiana because of the flashbacks, and we understand Darcy's sensitivity.

Miss Bingley makes a cutting remark. Elizabeth defends Georgiana. Darcy registers it. That look across the room (my favourite moment in the whole series). The next day, he dons his best green coat and heads to the inn to propose again. But Austen, being far better at plot than most of us, pulls the rug. Lydia has run off with Wickham. Darcy retreats. Elizabeth believes him lost.

As for production difficulties, I tend to remember only the good parts – "euphoric recall", they call it, a useful condition for getting through life, though perhaps not the most reliable when writing a memoir. The sharper edges blur, the arguments fade and what remains is the sense that everyone was having a rather marvellous time. If there were battles, they were most likely between Sue Birtwistle and me. We are both fairly strong-willed. As I mentioned before, Sue had been a student of mine at Coventry many years earlier, already quite determined to do things her own way. That tendency had not softened with time. As producer on *Pride and Prejudice*, she cared about it fiercely. Sue had a very clear sense of what the series should be and how it ought to look and feel. When two people with strong views care deeply about the same project, sparks are inevitable. We argued from time to time about tone, emphasis and, occasionally, how much liberty one could take with Jane Austen. Sue fought hard for the production when it mattered – casting, locations, the look of the whole enterprise. She had formidable determination and a great deal of energy, which is exactly what a project like that requires. More often than not, she succeeded in getting what she wanted – which, in retrospect, was usually a good thing.

As everyone knows, *Pride and Prejudice* was a huge success. It redefined costume drama. I am still very proud of it. There was one marginal note in the script that caused some amusement. Elizabeth has walked three miles through mud to Netherfield: her petticoats are dirty, her face is flushed, alive. She bumps into Darcy. In the scene direction, I wrote: "Darcy is surprised to find that he has an erection." It was intended as a private joke about male response, not something for the camera. It was a note about intensity and aliveness. Jane Austen, I suspect, would not have approved.

It does feel faintly alarming that *Pride and Prejudice* is now more than thirty years old. I don't feel thirty years older. The show seems to have, by any reasonable standard, stood the test of time, which I allow myself to be pleased about. I'm perfectly content to be known as "the man who wrote *Pride and Prejudice*", or even "the man who sexed up Jane Austen". It's a slightly vulgar badge, but I've worn worse. I suspect it's less convenient for Colin Firth to be for ever Darcy in certain eyes. That's the hazard of emerging from a lake in a wet shirt. Am I sensitive about newer versions appearing? In truth, I'd be a little cross if people preferred them to mine – which is unreasonable. My version is thirty-plus years old. Most things are considered dated after ten. The fact that people still tell me they watch it again and again is immensely gratifying. I have the same experience with *Last of the Mohicans*: I think I'll watch five minutes and suddenly I'm at the end, wondering where the evening went.

Looking back, I can see that our structural approach, the flash-backs, the muscular plotting, letting Darcy be a sexual being rather than a drawing-room ornament, helped reshape period drama. It also opened doors for me to more literary adaptations, a renewed appetite for the classics and, eventually, the modern heir to Austen: Helen Fielding.

I read *Bridget Jones's Diary* as soon as it appeared, prompted by the reviews. I thought it was very funny indeed. It came out in 1996, just on the back of *Pride and Prejudice* being screened on television, though it was some years later that I was approached about the film. I was pleased. It covered familiar ground. I also wanted to meet Helen Fielding. So I added a small rider: I'd do it on condition that I could drink Chardonnay with Helen in what-ever establishment she deemed suitable for Bridget. And we did, meeting at one of those West London places that aren't exactly posh but are determinedly not ordinary. We got along beautifully, except for one fundamental disagreement. To my mind, *Bridget Jones* ought to be a romantic comedy in the classical sense: Bridget and Mark Darcy end up together. This Darcy should be closer to Austen's: proud, awkward, emotionally stunted, but redeemable, and less of a comic character. Helen's argument was altogether different. "Romantic relationships," she said, "are fundamentally unreliable. What endures is the 'urban family' – the tight circle of friends who are there for you whatever happens." That notion made it into the film, and it's meant to be touching and witty. My reasoning was simple. What would make Bridget happy? Being in love. Being loved back – preferably by a handsome man resembling Colin Firth. Helen said, "No, it's about the friends." It did not escape me that Helen, at that particular juncture, was unattached and very much embedded in her own urban family. Shortly afterwards, she fell in love and relocated to the Caribbean. The urban family was forgotten, at least for the time being.

When I joined, there was already a script bearing Helen's name, with input from Richard Curtis. It was extremely funny, but rather loose at the joints. I met Eric Fellner at Working Title and said, politely but firmly, that it needed reshaping into a romantic comedy and that Darcy needed to be more Mr Darcy. Several writers are credited on the finished film, but it was Richard who did the final polish, as was always understood. He's a bloody good writer. There is barely a line of mine that survived intact. But it *is* a romantic comedy, and Mark Darcy is much closer to Austen's character of the same name than he initially was, so I feel that I left fingerprints somewhere. Working Title were charming throughout, and there were a great many lunches and the odd crate of wine. A few years later, I was asked to be the first writer on *Bridget Jones: The Edge of Reason*. Being first out of the gate means inventing more of the architecture yourself, and as such I was consequently more attached. I also knew, in my bones, that much of it would be rewritten. That's the ecosystem. At one point there was hope of securing George Clooney, so I wrote him into the script as a heightened, faintly absurd version of himself, a man for whom taxis materialize and doors open. Naturally, he couldn't be signed. All the Clooney material went. Frustrating, yes, but again, the wine was excellent. In the end, I find I don't mind too much. Films are collaborative efforts.

Marc Munden and *Vanity Fair*

Hot on the heels of *Pride and Prejudice* came *Moll Flanders* and another weighty adaptation. Gillian McNeill was the producer on *Vanity Fair*, and she was absolutely determined that Marc Munden should direct. At that point he hadn't done very much in television drama, but she showed me a couple of documentaries he'd made – one about a loan-shark enforcer, another about two working-class girl friends. Both had an extraordinary degree of intimacy and tenderness. They were quite unlike anything I'd seen before, and I could see why she was so keen.

What intrigued me was how that sensibility might translate to William Makepeace Thackeray, whose world, on the surface, is all glittering rooms, social manoeuvring, reputations made and unmade in drawing rooms. But Thackeray, of course, is far less superficial than that. *Vanity Fair* is a savage book. It smiles as it dismantles people. Becky Sharp is not a heroine in any conventional sense: she is charming, ruthless, opportunistic and, crucially, unrepentant. One of the pleasures of adapting the novel is that Thackeray refuses to moralize. He simply shows you the machinery of society and lets you decide whether to laugh or wince.

Marc didn't want much input on the script – which is always nice. But everything he did surprised me, and nearly always in a good way. He approached the material as if it were happening now, not then. The music, for instance: no Regency daintiness, no genteel tones. Instead, he asked Murray Gold to write a signature theme for a mariachi band – raucous, strident, completely counter-intuitive. My first reaction was alarm. Then delight. It captured something essential: the noise beneath the manners, the appetite beneath the etiquette.

I had imagined Becky as forthright, cheeky, slightly confrontational – someone who pushes her way into a room and dares you to object. Marc cast Natasha Little, who did something much more interesting: she drew you in – which meant that when the ruthlessness emerged, it landed much harder. You weren't resisting Becky: you were complicit with her.

Visually, too, Marc refused to behave. He put a huge grunting pig in the foreground of the opening episode, which felt, once you'd recovered from the surprise, entirely appropriate. This is a story about greed, after all. He gave us enormous close-ups where one anticipated establishing shots, and long, distancing frames when we were expecting intimacy. He constantly shifted the goalposts of how the story should be told, which kept the whole thing alive, slightly unstable.

He assembled a terrific cast and directed them with a mixture of tenderness and, occasionally, something close to brutality. He wasn't interested in smoothing edges. There's a scene where everything has gone wrong for Becky, and he had Natasha sobbing uncontrollably, the camera held close on her face, refusing to look away. It goes on longer than is comfortable. That was very much his instinct – to stay, to insist, to let the moment become awkward rather than aesthetic.

Many critics disliked *Vanity Fair*. They found it too strange, too stylized, not what they were expecting. But I think they were looking for reassurance, for a comfortable "period drama". Marc wasn't interested in that. Nor, really, was Thackeray. It remains one of my absolute favourites.

Of course I wanted to work with Marc again. I tried to get him for *War and Peace*, but it never happened. Perhaps it's just as well. There is something satisfying about a single collaboration that feels complete – one piece of work where everything aligns, unexpectedly, and holds.

Eastern Promise

Looking back at the list of my credits, you could be forgiven for thinking there was a neat, linear progression. One thing leading sensibly to another, career marching forward in tidy steps. Of course, it never felt like that. The broadcast dates suggest order; the actual work unfolded in a jumble of overlaps, false starts, abandoned projects, others revived years later. It's only in retrospect that you can persuade yourself there was some underlying logic to it all. In one version of the story, *Circle of Friends* begat *Pride and Prejudice*, which begat *Bridget Jones*. Somewhere upstream of that sat, quite implausibly, *Filipina Dreamgirls*.

It was the late Eighties, and Ruth Caleb, a BBC producer, hit on this idea of sending writers into challenging locales to see if they could turn them into drama. "Gonzo research", they called it. (One poor chap was sent to the Amazonian jungle, and he got lost and went mad.) Her first offer was: would I like to explore the high suicide rate among Welsh hill farmers? No, I didn't think so, thanks. Her next offer was sex tourism and mail-order brides in the Far East. I thought I might give that a go. Ruth's idea was that I would accompany a small group of British men to the Philippines, where they would (or wouldn't) find Filipina brides. How far I would involve myself in the high jinks would be up to me. Oh, and there was one condition: my sex punters would have to be Welsh, because it was to be a BBC Wales production. No problem. Ruth had found a likeable rogue who ran an organization called "the Filipina Friendship Club". He had a Filipina wife who lived in the UK, while he himself spent most of his time in Manila.

So it came about that I found myself on a flight with half a dozen British men, some of whom had already singled out possible brides, others flying blind, as it were. They had seven days and nights to get engaged. And they were an unprepossessing lot, to put it mildly. They had a bleak view of UK women, who had not been good to them. And they had a bafflingly high opinion of themselves. There was one chap from the Forest of Dean who said to me: "I see you got a shirt on. I was going to wear one, I does have a shirt, but I couldn't get him on, must have got fat or something." When we got to the airport, his girl took one look at him and ran away. "Never mind," said Arthur, our genial host. "Plenty more where she came from."

And there were. In fact, when we all piled out of the jitney at the clubhouse, the girls were lining up: pretty, intelligent young women who spoke reasonably good English, who were keen to engage themselves to middle-aged British… how should I put it? "Arseholes" was how Arthur put it. Economics, of course, was the explanation. A young Filipina who married an Englishman could send home enough money to support her family, and in two years she would be a British citizen and able to divorce her husband for a more suitable partner – and most of them did. The Filipinas were on the whole bright, brave and resourceful, and went into it with their eyes open; the "arseholes" were blind to their own true nature, and got what they deserved. (There were exceptions, of course.) I was happy to see that the whole thing could be regarded as a comedy, rather than another bit of colonial exploitation. It was that, of course, but the exploitation went both ways.

On our first night, Arthur led us on a tour of the girly bars. This was, he said, so that the men could make up their minds what they were there for: sexual tourism or a partner for life. (Another reason was that Arthur liked going to the girly bars, which gave him a kickback for bringing in clients.) And the answer to Arthur's question was a resounding "Both".

On first impression, the bars seemed quite tame – seven or eight girls in bikinis dancing on the bar. But Arthur explained that they were all available. One had to pay the bar a small amount to take the girl away from her dancing duties and then make a separate deal for sex. This process was known as the "bar fine", and "bar-fining" became a euphemism for shagging, as in "See that guy? He bar-fined six girls in one night." I worried about my companions, who were recklessly bar-fining away without worrying about STDs, getting robbed or mugged, etc., while their prospective brides waited patiently back at the clubhouse. Arthur counselled caution, explaining how cheap life was in Manila, how easily you could end up with your throat cut, but really he didn't care that much. His contempt for his "arsehole" clients was barely hidden.

There was one irritating little chap called Jordan who had three prospective fiancées lined up at the clubhouse, all between eighteen and twenty years old. But he formed an attachment to one of the bar girls, and bar-fined her almost every night for a week. I asked her what she saw in him, and she said seriously: "Jordan very good lover – very big dick." At the end of the week, though, the chap chose one of his three fiancées, leaving the other two and the bar girl in tears.

I had a research date myself with a beautiful young woman in her early thirties, who spoke excellent English and worked as a secretary. We had a posh lunch in the best hotel in Manila, and it cost about ten pounds for two. She took me to see where her family lived, in a shanty town down by the water, with no proper sanitation. If I had been a real punter, I could have lifted a whole family out of squalor.

I made a mass of notes that week, went home and wrote the script. And a year later I went back to watch them filming it. It was an uncanny experience to be back in that same girly bar with actors. In fact, they inhabited their roles with such enthusiasm that they became indistinguishable from the real thing, and they all started falling in love with the Filipina girls playing Arthur's clients. The dreamlike quality went up a few notches when they couldn't find the right actress to play Jordan's bar girl, but the real girl was still right there dancing on the counter, and played herself with conviction and panache.

The writerly lesson was rather similar to the one about adapting Jane Austen or Tolstoy: if it ain't broke, don't fix it. With Austen, you simply copy out the best bits. For *Filipina Dreamgirls*, I wrote down what happened, pretty much. Slightly embellished, but not much really. Gonzo scriptwriting.

The show was a big hit, and got great reviews, especially in *The Sun* and the *News of the World*, and Arthur's business got a lot more clients. Ruth Caleb was very pleased, and sent me to Hong Kong to research a project about the impending Chinese takeover seen from the point of view of a young English sex worker. Brilliant idea, but somehow it never got made, or even written.

*

I was drawn back to the Far East years later by a novel about an Englishwoman who marries a Japanese man. A small independent American producer managed to scrape enough money together to send me on a three-week research trip to Japan, where I had never been before. She had fixed up an hotel for me, a modest businessman's place, with small but very well-designed rooms. I could just about fit in and reach everything without moving. Surprisingly, it was not too claustrophobic. I had a card with the hotel address in Japanese characters, so that if I got lost I could always show it to a taxi driver. So far so good. But she hadn't got me enough contacts: just a few phone numbers of European and American women who had married or otherwise shacked up with Japanese men. Every day I would cold-call women and say, "You don't know me, but I'm a writer interested in what it's like for a European woman with a Japanese man." Of course they were suspicious and slammed the phone down.

But then a Swedish woman agreed to meet me, at her child's nursery school. Once she realized I was not a sex pest, she was eager to talk. She'd met her husband in Germany, and they had communicated in English. Before she went to Japan, she learnt Japanese – but the wrong variety. She told me that men's Japanese is quite different from that used by women. Men tend to sound as if they're in a bad temper or barking out orders. Women's Japanese has a sort of sickly, wheedling melody to it that did not suit my new Swedish friend at all. She said there were quite a few things for which there were no words in women's Japanese. It was ruining their relationship, so they had to go back to communicating in English. She also told me that men's relationships with their mothers were a big problem in Japan.

So I'd got something, but not made enough progress. I panicked and phoned Stephen, who came up with the number of an English journalist who lived in Tokyo. And this guy was wonderful. First of all, he told me how to order a beer and how to navigate the subway (which was remarkably easy – the only problem is when you surface: which way do you go?). He said that people under twenty-five often spoke English and would help me find my way. He also took me out for the evening, drinking *shōchū* with Japanese businessmen. I baulked at eating live prawns, and they laughed at me. "Which is worse, having your head bitten off or being fried in hot oil?"

I asked if he happened to know the novelist whose book I was adapting. Miraculously, he did. She lived in Osaka. So I travelled there by train. The meeting went well. She was charming, intelligent, amused by my quest. At one point she said, almost casually, "You should go for a drink with my husband." He looked, to my untrained eye, like someone who might run a port or a small, discreet criminal syndicate. He spoke little. We drank whisky. We nodded gravely. I felt as if I were being assessed for something undefined. When we got back, she remarked, perfectly lightly, "Osaka is full of gangsters. They pretty much run the town." That information would have been more useful earlier in the evening.

*

Sometime during my adventure in Tokyo, I met up with a Kenilworth neighbour called Robert who happened to be there on business (Mister Obrod was what they called him in the hotel). When you're travelling in a place as culturally distant as Japan, the sight of someone from home can be very reassuring. We agreed to meet in a yakitori restaurant tucked down a narrow street. The meal was agreeable enough. Sake, charred skewers, polite conversation drifting gradually into more personal territory. He confided in me about his first marriage, how he had pressured his wife to try swingers' parties, and she had taken to them all too well, and swung away from him. And it was all his fault – she had been the love of his life. He told it well. I was quite moved.

Then he said, "Look, I've got this address."

He showed me photographs.

"We could go and have a couple of girls."

I had had enough strange experiences in Tokyo without seeking them out. I told him I didn't fancy it.

"Oh well," he said, putting his hand on my thigh. "Maybe you and I could manage something?"

I removed his hand, feeling ridiculously prim.

"No," I said, "I don't think that would work either. Sorry."

It was a very English moment.

"No worries," he said.

We paid the bill, shook hands cordially and parted. Later, back in Kenilworth, I heard that he retold the story to mutual friends with our roles reversed. Fortunately, nobody believed him.

*

It was an odd trip all round – disorientating, occasionally comic and even faintly alarming. I was tense and stressed pretty much the whole time, except when I was asleep – and even then I was often troubled by one of my recurring bad dreams. In it, I've written several novels in school exercise books. They've poured out of me without effort. I'm calmly pleased with myself. The problem is not whether they are good – they are obviously masterpieces – but how best to publish them. Should I send them to my agent Stephen immediately? Release them one at a time? Offer them as a box set? I can't remember much about them except that one is a passionate love story. I wake in a state of mild professional anxiety, wondering whether I have in fact written these books and mislaid them. I haven't written them, of course. It's very disappointing. I think the dream is about unfulfilled potential.

I did, in fact, write a script from this trip: we called it *Foreign Languages*. It dealt with cultural misreadings, with desire misunderstood, isolation inside marriage. Never made. Looking back, I sometimes think the real drama was less in the fictional couple and more in my own pilgrimage: an Englishman abroad, understanding nothing.

*

Before I leave the Far East, let me return for a moment to the Philippines. I was sitting on the toilet in my hotel room in Manila when a phone went off right next to my ear – a great big wall phone I hadn't noticed before. Quite upsetting. I ignored it for a bit, then I thought it might be the front desk telling me the hotel was on fire, so I picked up gingerly and said hello. "Andrew, it's Ken Trodd." I recognized the familiar velvety tone I first heard back in 1966. How did he know I was in that hotel in Manila? "How would you like to do a Maeve Binchy book as a movie?" whispered Ken.

And that was how I came to meet Arlene and Alex, and was introduced to a different sort of world entirely.

The Dorchester Chronicles

Arlene and Alex were staying in Suite 201 in the Dorchester. I went up in the lift and rang the bell. The door of suite 202 opened, confusingly, and a small, elegantly dressed man in his sixties smiled and said, "Come in."

"Er... I'm here to see Arlene Sellers, Suite 201?"

"Sure, come right in, she's waiting for you. I'm Alex Winitsky."

So I went right in – and there she was, a formidable blonde in her seventies.

"Mr Davies, we're great admirers of your work – now, do you think there's a movie in *Circle of Friends*?"

The novel was a real baggy monster of over five hundred pages. I had speed-read it on the plane coming back from the Philippines. The story: three little girls have their first Communion together and become best friends. Years later, they all meet again at University College Dublin. Plump, sweet-natured Bernadette (Benny) falls for rugby star Jack, and he for her. Nan, a raving beauty, hooks up with Simon, the son of local gentry. And orphan Eve, brought up by nuns, is pursued by nice Aidan. There are betrayals and untimely deaths, but finally Benny gets her happy ending.

"It's a bit unwieldy," I said, "but I think there could be a sweet little sex comedy there, if we cut out the sub-plots."

"Alex," she said. "I knew we had the right guy."

"Champagne?" said Alex. "I hope you say yes: she won't let me open the bottle if it's just me drinking."

I said I would have a glass of champagne, and so began a beautiful friendship. Arlene and Alex were property developers who owned a lot of prime real estate in Hollywood and Beverly Hills. She had a passion for producing quality movies, and he went along with it. Arlene was old Hollywood money, and had stayed at the Dorch off and on since she was a little girl.

Arlene and Alex were both kind, wise and good at detecting bullshit. Over time they got to know Diana, and grew fond of her too, and she of them. I still have a tie that Alex lent me so I could be admitted to the Dorchester Grill. Lunch there felt less like eating and more like participating in a well-rehearsed ritual. Plates arrived and disappeared with discreet efficiency; wine materialized without being explicitly requested; and Alex presided over the proceedings with the relaxed assurance of a man entirely at home in such surroundings. I kept the tie. He never asked for it back.

Arlene insisted I visit Maeve Binchy to pick her brains about University College Dublin in the Fifties. Maeve and her husband Gordon lived by the sea in Bray, about half an hour south of Dublin, if the traffic behaved itself. Bray, with its long promenade, the Irish Sea blowing in with determination, chip shops, faded hotels that had seen better decades and a scattering of comfortable houses nestled in the hill, wasn't the popular commuter town that is today. However, Maeve and Gordon's house was welcoming in every sense.

Maeve was physically and temperamentally larger than life. She was generous in spirit and immediately disarming. She had the sort of presence that filled a room. By then she was already one of Ireland's most successful novelists, producing books that sold in astonishing quantities, though she retained the manner of someone who had wandered accidentally into literary fame. She'd begun as a journalist at the *Irish Times*, writing sharp, observant columns before discovering that she had an almost preternatural ability to tell stories about ordinary people – teachers, shop assistants, bank clerks, families negotiating love and disappointment. Her novels were not fashionable in the metropolitan literary sense, but readers adored them because they recognized themselves in them. At the table Maeve talked and listened with equal enthusiasm, laughed loudly and ensured that nobody's glass remained empty for long. It was a household run on conversation, food and the cheerful assumption that life was best approached sociably – which suited me perfectly. I'd arrived at eleven in the morning.

"Oh God," she said, "Gordon and I usually open a bottle of champagne about this time." An excellent habit, I thought.

Over the next three hours, and more champagne than would be strictly advisable, she spoke about college life: desire constrained by Catholic guilt, intellectual awakening, the shock of lecturers who dared question the Church. She confided that "Jack" was based on a friend, not a lover. She herself had been a "good girl" in those days, yearning occasionally not to be. After graduation she travelled to the Holy Land and experienced a moment of revelation – religious and otherwise. It suddenly came to her that everything she'd been taught about God, virtue and sin was made up by the priests – and that night she hooked up with a soldier and lost her virginity. She told me she could never say such things publicly, as her readers would desert her in droves. She was hilarious, sharp and utterly without vanity. Out of that conversation in Bray came Professor Flynn, who doesn't exist in the novel, but who lectures about Malinowski and the sexual lives of remote islanders, thereby detonating a little controlled explosion in Benny's conscience. Maeve didn't object. Great stuff, and I was so glad I went to see her. Writing the script came easy, and I found my memories of Babbie and her venial and mortal sins very useful. Perhaps my favourite line was one that I wrote for Eve, the one brought up by nuns: "All right, I'll hold it – but I won't jiggle it about." There was nothing like that in the book, of course.

I suggested renaming the film *Good Girls*. Maeve objected to that on entirely commercial grounds. It would harm book sales. She was right. We appeared together once on *Woman's Hour* at a live event. Just before going onstage, she leant into me and murmured, "I'm always terrified before this sort of thing. It would be nice to have some of that cocaine people have now." Then we walked out, giggling like conspirators.

The film had a budget of eight million dollars. One million of that went to Chris O'Donnell, who was hot property and worth it. Minnie Driver received thirty thousand. It was her first film. She was glorious. Funny, tender, entirely unforced. It was my first movie too, and the only one in which my script survived almost intact. A rare experience. We shot in Ireland. Diana joined me, and we stayed in a cottage in County Wicklow. The kitchen was stocked with unfamiliar tubes of something called "Pringles". We were early adopters. Another film, Mike Newell's *An Awfully Big Adventure*, based on Beryl Bainbridge's novel, was shooting nearby, and we all became fairly sociable with each other. At a party the casts mingled. Alan Rickman was present; Hugh Grant hovered somewhere between youth and legend – *Four Weddings and a Funeral*, also directed by Newell, had just been released. I asked Rickman if he might consider playing a darker Mr Bennet one day, an early version I had in my head, which bordered on the nihilistic.

"Certainly not," he said crisply. "Darcy or nothing."

Colin Firth was playing an upper-class cad in *Circle of Friends* at the time. With his fair hair, confidence and moustache, I couldn't yet imagine him as Darcy. Hair dye is a wonderful thing. Saffron Burrows, extraordinarily beautiful but also politically engaged and entirely grounded, talked Labour politics and education with Diana as if they'd known each other for years. Pat O'Connor directed beautifully. He didn't like writers hovering on set. Nor did he care to discuss the script once filming began. Many directors prefer their autonomy. I don't blame them. I'd done my work. Arlene and Alex, without whom the film wouldn't have existed, were occasionally made to feel like Hollywood intruders on an Irish set. I thought that unfair. Ken Trodd, anxious to protect his director, perhaps felt it necessary. Film politics are often a delicate arrangement of loyalties.

After that I wrote more scripts for Arlene and Alex that were never made. Arlene found and bought a wonderful novel by Elizabeth Jenkins called *The Tortoise and the Hare*, and I wrote the screenplay. Arlene and Alex never quite managed to get it off the ground, then Arlene died. Robert Altman said he would direct it, then *he* died. I must really find out who has the rights now and see if I can set it up before *I* die.

So many of the projects have begun over a long lunch or a meeting in a hotel, and the Dorch was a favoured place. Fast forward to 2009 – that terrible year (more of which later).

Fernando Ghia was a wonderful Italian film producer, known for *The Mission* and *Nostromo*. He was also a kind and lovely man. I can't remember how he found me, but he took me for lunch in Holland Park and told me about a book he had been trying to set up as a movie for decades, *The Purple Land* by William Henry Hudson. Written in the late nineteenth century, it relates the adventures of a young Englishman in Uruguay: cowboying with gauchos, falling in love with senoritas and getting caught up in a revolution.

"It's a very fun-n-ny book, but in a sly way," he told me. "You must read between the lines. You will get it. You can write this kind of thing: serious, but also very funny. And if you like it, we can go exploring Uruguay before you write the script."

I was sold already, before I'd read a word of the book. I loved his lush vowels, the way he dwelt lovingly on the double consonants, and I'd never met a producer before who took writers on recces before anything was written.

It turned out that Fernando, like Arlene and Alex, always stayed at the Dorch when he was in London. We were dining there, and he told me he had wanted Albert Finney to play the young hero when he first tried to set the film up in the Sixties, but now there was a great part for him as the old revolutionary general. Fernando and Albert had been pals for over forty years. So I flew to Montevideo and met Fernando, who was there before me, and we started by eating an enormous amount of meat, which is what you do in Uruguay. The cowboys in the book fed on nothing but beef, and it turns out that it can be quite a healthy diet. Fernando introduced me to George Hilton, who, despite his English-sounding name, spoke hardly a word of English. He was Uruguay's only international film star, and a very useful contact. He was a good friend of the president and charmed him into lending us an army helicopter that could fly us all over Uruguay. Extremely convenient, but scary and noisy.

It was an amazing week. We flew to a gaucho *estancia*, watched them wrangle huge herds of cattle, ate a lot more beef, went to an ostrich farm and packed away large quantities of ostrich meat. I remember a field with five hundred wild horses in it. I felt very hampered by my limited Italian and Spanish, but found that you can get by surprisingly well with *perché?* and *por qué? Por qué no?* Three men together for a week: without a common language, little made sense, but the bond was powerful.

Then it was over, and I was back in Kenilworth writing the script. It went well – Fernando was happy, but somehow those damn ducks would not get in a row. Fernando had secured Kevin Reynolds to direct, and we all met in Rome and got on very well… And then Fernando died. And so did the movie. A few years later, I adapted my script as a radio play for the BBC, and David Tennant played the young hero. It felt a bit odd going back to radio, where I'd started back in 1960. But very rewarding. Radio is so light and flexible: it costs nothing to shoot in Uruguay, because the place is in the listener's head. Five thousand horses? Not a problem. A bloody massacre? Easy, and no one gets hurt. The only thing is that the pay is lousy.

*

Around this time, I met Eileen Quinn, who had been something of a protegee of Fernando's, and she talked me into doing a new adaptation of *A Room with a View* for ITV. We were on a hiding to nothing, of course, since the Merchant Ivory film is so beloved, but I thought I could put a new spin on it, punch up the class issues and the humour and the sexiness. I also pushed the ending, going from a consummation scene in the room with the view to a sequence in which George is killed in the trenches and Lucy is revisiting Florence in the 1920s as a young widow. Elaine Cassidy played Lucy quite delightfully, and I had the great casting notion of Tim and Rafe Spall as *père et fils*, which worked brilliantly. Track it down: it's worth a viewing if you didn't see it at the time.

And, of course, it meant that Diana and I got to go to Florence for a few days. I know, nothing to stop us going any time, but there is something special about being in a place where a film is being made and you are a part of that film – especially when the place is as lovely as Florence. You're walking along the street and suddenly there's a familiar face – Tim West, beaming, in a straw hat. What could be nicer? He's dead now, of course, but he still crops up in dreams.

*

Eileen invited Diana and me to stay at her place in Umbria, very near Fernando's country house. The deal was that Eileen and I would work each day for an hour or two on the script and the rest of the time we would be relaxing in Umbria, drinking Orvieto and so on. Eileen advised to fly to Rome and hire a car at the airport, so we did that. Have you ever tried to hire a car at Rome airport? Not for the faint-hearted. We found ourselves in a snarling rush of traffic that swept us inexorably towards the city centre, when we needed to head north. It was nightmarish, and the Roman drivers showed no mercy on us. Eventually we stopped by a garage, and a kind man told us how to get out of that jam. And so in the end, wrung out and traumatized, we managed to struggle up to Eileen's hill village, which was admittedly very pretty indeed. It turned out that there was a very good rail service connecting the airport and Eileen's village, and she had got us to hire a car so that we could drive her about. When Diana realized this, she was furious, although of course she didn't say anything to Eileen – but I am sorry to say she harboured dark thoughts about her for the rest of that trip.

Serendipity, Polanski and Bob Altman

I was sitting at home one evening with a whisky in my hand, comfortably bleary-eyed, when the phone rang.

"Hey, this is Andras Hamori – we were just talking about you at lunch. You don't know me – I got your number from X—— Y——. She sends her best."

"Send her mine," I said, instinctively polite, but having no idea who he was talking about.

"Yeah, she's a nice girl, everybody likes her, everybody's fucked her, but she never gets anything made. So, we were talking about *House of Cards*... great show, Andrew... and I said, 'Hey, you know what he should do next? *The Count of Monte Cristo*. And you know who should direct it? Polanski! Roman would love that!' And you would be the guy to write it – what do you think?"

I blinked.

"I think it would be great," I said, because what else do you say when a Hollywood Hungarian in a hurry drops Polanski's name?

"OK, Andrew, great talking to you – I'll let you go now."

Click. Gone.

I put the phone down and, frankly, forgot all about it until, a few weeks later, my agent rang me.

"Andrew, what's all this about you writing *The Count of Monte Cristo* for Robert Lantos?"

"I've never heard of Robert Lantos. I've heard of *The Count of Monte Cristo*..."

"Well, Andras Hamori says you've had a conversation in which you agreed to write them a script."

"Ah, yes. I didn't realize that was a serious offer."

"You know Roman Polanski is attached?"

"You're joking."

"No. They want you to meet in Paris next week."

"Fuck. I'd better read the book, then."

I was vaguely aware of *Monte Cristo*. I'd read a children's version when I was about ten, in one of those illustrated, abridged editions. I remembered betrayal, imprisonment, escape, revenge – classic stuff. But when I sat down and tackled the full version, it turned out that, yes, I'd already read all the best bits. The revenge, so lovingly drawn out over endless chapters, was as exhausting as it was emotionally detached. But there was one thing that genuinely touched me: his lost love, Mercédès.

So did I say no to the project? I did not. I thought that, with my talent and Polanski's flair, we could make something rich and strange. Maybe even better than the original. Of course, there was good reason to say no – that being Polanski himself. He had, as the whole world knew, pleaded guilty to the rape of a thirteen-year-old girl in California, and was now permanently based in France to avoid extradition. A non-starter for many, understandably. But I'd grown up in admiration of his films, from the haunting surrealism of his short *Two Men and a Wardrobe* to the exquisite melancholy of *Tess*. I didn't hesitate, and even now I doubt I would. The chance to collaborate with a cinematic legend was too good to pass up, however problematic his past. I was immediately on a plane to Paris.

We met for lunch – me, Roman, Andras Hamori and the elusive Robert Lantos. The latter was a large man, still-faced and funereal, like a well-dressed executioner. Andras, in contrast, was fizzing with animal energy, half producer, half street magician. Roman was tiny, sharp-featured, with those long tentacular arms that seemed to reach beyond the rest of his body. The first topic of conversation was how much they all hated Hollywood. And then Roman told a joke – a long, grotesque, unapologetically vulgar joke involving shipwrecked men, cannibals and an unending ordeal called "buggaloo". It was, I gathered, a metaphor for the American film industry, and for life in general.

The tone of the conversation was then raised and turned to *Eugene Onegin*. Ralph Fiennes had just made a film adaptation, and the table agreed that, while noble, it wasn't quite Pushkin. To my surprise, they all began reciting Pushkin aloud, in Russian, handing the baton from one to the other like a Soviet poetry relay. Then they looked at me. I was a Welshman in exile, surrounded by Pushkin-loving Eastern Europeans. I was briefly tempted to say "I'll get me coat", like the man in the *Fast Show* sketch. I had not even read *Eugene Onegin*. I had to content myself with raising an eyebrow and pouring more wine. Still, despite the poetical faux pas, I got the job and wrote a first draft of the *Count of Monte Cristo* script. A few months later we reconvened at the legendary Hôtel du Cap, a short drive from Cannes, where Roman had a preferred nook and the views were obscenely beautiful. There was an unreasonably long debate about mineral water. Then came the verdict.

"This script…" said Lantos, with the solemnity of a man who's about to reveal a cancer diagnosis, "it's good."

There was a pause.

"But it's not great."

"Oh, fuck," I thought. "There you go. This is the bit where I get fired." But no.

"Andrew," said Hamori, ever the impresario. "Would you be prepared to go to Paris and work with Roman on a second draft?" I said yes, obviously. I would've said yes if they'd asked me to go there on my hands and knees – well, maybe not, but you know what I mean.

But before that there was fun to be had in Cannes, where everything gleams: the sea, the chrome, the teeth. The yachts sit in the harbour like floating office blocks for the super-well-paid, and along the Croisette there is a slow parade of sunglasses, lanyards and perfectly poised indifference. Posters the size of small houses hang from the Palais. Young hopefuls stride about with scripts under their arms. The rest try to look as if they belong. Robert Lantos had a substantial motorboat moored at Cap d'Antibes. He offered me a lift back to my own rather less glamorous accommodation. Cannes has a way of revealing your exact place in the world. We left the harbour in a theatrical sweep through the blue sea. The villas along the Cap rose behind walls and cypresses, all discretion and inherited wealth. On deck, someone pressed a drink into my hand, and for a moment I allowed myself to imagine that this might be my normal life. Then we pulled up near the marina closest to my hotel and I clambered off, trying to look as though I frequently travelled by private boat between meetings. On the day I was flying home, I stood in the hotel reception with my bag at my feet, feeling sunburnt and a bit of an impostor, waiting for the car to take me to the airport. The lobby was marble-floored and very calm. A man in an impeccable suit approached me with purpose.

"Mr Davies?"

He had the manner of someone used to striking deals, but I assumed he was my driver and handed him my bag with cheerful efficiency. There was a fractional pause.

"I'm sorry," he said, not sounding sorry at all. "I'm not your chauffeur."

I recognized him then. It was Tim Corrie, an agent of roughly the same status as Stephen, and not pleased to have been mistaken for my driver. We parted politely, and my actual car arrived.

*

But back to Polanski and work with him in Paris. This time I stayed in a plush hotel near the Arc de Triomphe, and every morning strolled grandly down the Champs-Élysées to Roman's apartment – a huge, elegant place full of expensive silence and well-polished furniture. Our meetings took place in a room dominated by a rather startling artwork: a jigsaw of a woman's nude body, legs splayed, with several of the more essential puzzle pieces missing – distracting, to say the least.

Was working with Roman fun? No – no, it was not. I'd propose a change, and then, after a long pause, he'd say,

"Yes, but it won't work… because…"

Repeat ad infinitum.

He was reverent, almost religious, about the book. I, on the other hand, viewed it as a bloated melodrama crying out for a rewrite.

I dared suggest that perhaps the count and Mercédès could reunite – I liked the symmetry, the romance. Roman practically growled:

"No, Andrew. You must never go back."

There were long lunches at the local bistro, where he had his own table. Occasionally someone would stop him in the street, curtsey and kiss his hand as if he was the King of Auteurs. He took it in his stride. "You're very kind," he'd say. And on we'd go.

Working with Roman was torture – but a very pleasant sort of torture, with good food, nice wine and a soft bed at night. Eventually, I gave up trying to please him, and wrote a draft entirely to my own liking. I delivered it, waited and was told: "It's very good, but still not great."

Enter Julia – a beautiful, steely, smart New York script editor, fluent in literary theory, postcolonialism and emotional rescue. She flew to London. We talked for hours about orientalism, power, betrayal. She was magnificent. When the Hungarians suggested Paris again, I baulked. But this time I suggested Julia come too. Roman bristled.

"I hate those people" – meaning anyone American.

"You'll like Julia," I said. "I promise."

And he did. She charmed the dragon. She acted as an interpreter between me and him. She smoothed everything out and persuaded us that we'd been making the same film all along. In two days, we had our definitive screenplay. Roman kissed us both, crammed us into his yellow Beetle and took us out for cocktails.

And then – Kevin Reynolds released a cheerful, swashbuckling adaptation of Dumas's novel that audiences loved. Our version was no longer needed. The only consolation was that Kevin's ending was like mine: the count returns to Mercédès, and they live happily ever after. Great minds think alike, and all that. Kevin and I would later work on another ill-fated project. We got on like a house on fire. Naturally. We were both on the wrong bus – but what a ride. Looking back, it never really mattered whether the film got made or not. What counted was the people, the sparks, the lunches, the strange beds and mad phone calls and surreal walks through alien cities. That's the job. You write, you listen, you try not to take it personally when it all goes up in smoke, and you try not to get too cocky when it catches fire. I never got my *Monte Cristo*. But I did get Paris, and Cannes, and Roman, and a naked jigsaw puzzle I'll never quite unsee.

*

I went back to Cannes several times after that first brush with Hungarians, motorboats and mistaken chauffeurs. I was generally in one of two states: either mildly hungover or slightly inebriated. Lunchtime rosé slides into late-afternoon champagne, which slips into something stronger on a boat, and, before you know it, you're discussing international co-production treaties with a man called Luc while staring blankly at the sunset. I enjoyed it far more when I was in the company of friends – Faith Penhale, Simon Vaughan, the Welsh contingent. There is comfort in familiar faces when everyone else looks as though they've stepped out of a fragrance ad. We'd go from meeting to meeting, debrief, laugh at ourselves, find something decent to eat and restore perspective.

Cannes can be glorious in the sunshine, the palm trees and the flickering sea doing their best impression of the Riviera cliché, but glamour falters in bad weather. I remember one beach party in particular: marquee flapping, sand damp and uncooperative, shoes sinking, everyone pretending it was marvellous while scanning the sky. For all that, Cannes matters. That's where the deals are done, so now and again you *have* to be there. Even writers. And whether you have a good time or not depends on who's paying. Some people talk about BBC extravagance. That, by and large, is nonsense. The BBC can make quality shows more cheaply than anyone, and they treat their staff like paupers. Whenever my daughter Anna was in Cannes for the BBC, she stayed in an airbnb and couldn't afford to eat in a restaurant. BBC Worldwide are another matter altogether: if they are taking you to Cannes, you'll be in a five-star seafront hotel, eating at fancy places and drinking as much rosé as you want.

BBC Worldwide are also comically inefficient, in my experience, because they tend to have five people doing a job better handled by one – five charming people who spend all their time asking each other if so-and-so has done this or that. BBC Worldwide splash lots of money peddling shows that basically sell by themselves but if you've been making these shows, it can be a lot of fun hanging out in Cannes with BBC Worldwide footing the bill.

*

It was 2016 when we launched *War and Peace* at Cannes. I was flown over on the same plane as Lily James and Tuppence Middleton, which felt faintly surreal. They were bright, funny, entirely grounded. We were taking Tolstoy to the Croisette. What could possibly go wrong? The show went down extremely well. At the party afterwards, at the Hôtel du Cap, no less, Lily and Tuppence came up to me and, half laughing, half serious, said, "Stay close, Andrew. Harvey's on the prowl. Don't let him get us!" I felt very proud to be chosen as their knight in shining armour – and they were such fun to be with. Everyone knew that Harvey had a bit of a reputation, but no one took it seriously – he couldn't *really* do anything, could he? It was a year later, in October 2017, that all the allegations tumbled out in the *New Yorker* and the *New York Times*.

Allow me to digress for a moment. Harvey Weinstein had drifted into my orbit when he became involved with the adaptation of my novel *B. Monkey*. He sacked the director I'd worked with, ordered a new screenplay, and, in my view, spoilt the film. Not one of his better efforts, I thought. So why did I get involved with him again? God knows.

It was about 2005. I'd written a screenplay of *Northanger Abbey* for Jo Wright at London Weekend Television. First draft done, notes addressed. We had more or less been given the green light. It was going to be a perfectly respectable Sunday-evening Austen: intelligent, ironic, gently romantic. Then word came that Harvey

Weinstein was interested. He wanted to make a version that would appeal to fourteen-year-old girls. That phrase alone should probably have set off alarm bells. But we were flattered, we were intrigued – we were, in retrospect, naive. Of course, he wanted to option our script and then bury it. A meeting was arranged at his suite at the Savoy, another of those grand London hotels where, from time to time, one suddenly finds oneself conducting business, as if this were the most natural setting in the world. Going to the Savoy for a serious meeting, you expect suits and polished shoes, mineral water in elegant bottles. What we got was something else.

Harvey appeared in a rather grubby sleeveless vest, enormous trousers, ample belly, braces, slippers. Not a pretty sight, to put it mildly. He was seated like a monarch at the centre of the room, surrounded by about a dozen immaculately dressed underlings, all very tense and fidgety. Around him were packs and packs of cigarettes arranged in formation, as if he were planning a military attack rather than a conversation. They weren't casually strewn: they were lined up, stockpiled, ready for deployment. Jo Wright looked at them and said:

"You sure you've got enough cigarettes there, Harvey?"

I remember thinking: "Brave."

He didn't blink.

"You should be grateful. Normally I'd be smoking cigars."

The room exploded, because everyone laughed if Harvey made quips. But the air was thick with fear. He had his people around him – assistants, lieutenants, anxious young men clutching folders, who visibly tightened their buttocks every time he shifted in his seat. He would bark an instruction and they would scuttle away. It was dominance as performance art. We weren't scared: we were curious.

"I'd like to option your script, Andrew. I wanna use it as the basis of a movie."

That was it. The lure of a *real* theatrical movie. But I remembered the adaptation of my fourth novel, in which he had become involved, and it was as if he'd read my mind. "You weren't very well treated on *B. Monkey*," he said. "This'll be different." It was cleverly pitched: acknowledgement without apology. The promise of special treatment this time.

In the end, Harvey's *Northanger Abbey* never happened. He got Martin Amis to rewrite the screenplay: his script was even more closely faithful to the book than mine. Years later I decided I'd quite like my script back. It turned out Harvey hadn't renewed the rights, and the script was free again. Eventually ITV made *Northanger Abbey* after all – which felt, in the circumstances, a relief and a homecoming.

At the time we had seen Weinstein as a powerful impresario with a commercial instinct. What we didn't yet see, what the industry did not yet fully acknowledge, was the darker pattern that would later emerge in public. Hindsight rearranges memory in uncomfortable ways. That Savoy suite has a different tint now. But the script survived to tell its own story.

*

Sometimes I wonder if there's a genuine link between genius, creativity and outright eccentricity. And, if there is, then Robert Altman (Bob to his friends) was it. The director of *M*A*S*H*, *McCabe & Mrs Miller*, *Nashville* and a slew of other beautifully chaotic films where plot often seemed irrelevant, Bob had this wild, ragged brilliance that drew you in like a magnet. I was fifty-two when we met, he was seventy-five. And yet, the moment we started working together, it felt like I'd been sent back to school – except this time the teacher was funny, irreverent and fond of a whisky and a dash of trouble.

The first time we met was in the mid-Eighties. I went to his hotel in Piccadilly. An odd thing happened on the way: I was walking through Shepherd Market when a young woman stopped me and said something I couldn't quite hear. I assumed she was asking me the way, and said, "Sorry, what?" And she said: "Would you like to sleep with me?" And I thought this is like a dream come true – miracles do happen! Then I thought: "Hang on, we're in

Shepherd Market, which is famous for its high-end hookers" – so I said: "I'm awfully sorry, I'm late for an appointment" – and she said: "Shame, maybe another time." And we said bye-bye.

The hotel was called the Athenaeum, not to be confused with the stuffy gentleman's club in Pall Mall. The receptionist was Thai, and had a very shaky grasp of English. "Andrew Davies to see Robert Altman" seemed to baffle her. "Angie Davis to see Oblet Album?" I tried again. "How you spelling that?" I was starting to wish I was with the hooker. Finally, I got up to the room, which was on the eighth floor. I was expecting it to be a suite, like the Dorch, but it was just a room, and a very rumpled room at that, with an unmade bed and two women in fur coats. And there was the great man, also rumpled, but warm and welcoming.

"What do you know about Rossini, Andrew?" he asked.

"Nothing," I said.

"Want to find out? The Italians will pay."

He must have liked something I'd written, because he was clearly offering me a job. He told me some of his early thoughts about the movie, which would involve a lot of coach journeys and highwaymen and priests and prostitutes.

"You interested, Andrew?"

"Very," I said.

"Now look – I have to go down to the bar to meet this young actor I think could play Van Gogh."

"In the Rossini film?"

"No, no, this is another film – great idea though, Andrew. So, you want to come down with me, have a drink, meet the actor?"

"Why not?" I said, and down we went.

In the bar, he told me a bit about his Van Gogh movie, and then the door banged open and in came Tim Roth in a camel-hair coat with a spectacularly ripped pocket, doing his bouncy walk from *Made in Britain*. The talk was about a film he'd just finished, called *The Hit*. Tim was talking about Stephen Frears, who had directed the film.

"Think he's losing his edge now he's a fucking millionaire."

"Let me stop you right there, son," said Altman. "You don't lose your edge because you're a millionaire. We're all millionaires. I'm a millionaire. Andrew's a millionaire."

"I'm not, actually," I said.

"Well, you soon will be – as will you, Tim, so get used to it."

"Cocky little guy, isn't he?" said Altman when Tim had gone. "I think I'm gonna cast him."

By now he was treating me like an old friend. It felt great – I felt great.

He'd had his rough patches with alcohol, and was meant to be keeping it in check. "Not supposed to drink," he'd mutter, usually on the way to the bar. Then he'd grin sideways and say, "Shall we take a hit, Andrew?" – as if it was a bit of mischief, a small transgression to get the creative juices flowing.

We were in New York now – a couple of days, filled with a heady mix of Rossini research, meals at Elaine's (which was to him what Poms in Kenilworth is to me: a local place where they treat you like a friend), Altman movie indoctrination ("Who needs a plot? Life doesn't have a plot! Fuck the three-act structure!") and a lot of trouser talk. Bob was planning an extended stay in Europe to shoot *Vincent & Theo*, and he needed new pants. "I was a thirty-two waist for fifty years! Look at me now! Forty inches! I'd never get in a B52 now, I'd get stuck in the door." (He'd flown B52 bombers during the Second World War as a young man.) "Did you read that Stendhal book? Whaddya think?" It was hard to keep up with his restless mind, but thrilling to be in his company. "Get a fax! Get a modem! Get a Mac with Word installed! The Italians will pay!" I went home and ordered all this technical equipment – and, sure enough, the Italians paid.

The script was slowly beginning to take shape. There were going to be two Rossinis: an old one, shorn of creative ideas and racked by gout, piles and all the other curses of old age, and the young one, who effortlessly poured out melody after melody without any idea where they came from. And how the old Rossini hated the young one! How could they both exist in the same timescale? It was a sort of hybrid Altman–Fellini thing. It was going to be wonderful.

We were going for a family and friends' holiday in a villa in the south of France, and I found that Bob was shooting his Van Gogh movie only thirty miles away. I decided to take a day out and go and see him. I was glad I did. I got a big welcome.

"Andrew! Welcome to the movie! Do you wanna be in the movie?"

"Why not?" I said.

"Excellent! Put him in a suit!"

So they found me a suit, a very hairy tweed one, and a hat. (There were three huge boxes of hats, which were labelled respectively as "HATS", "BAD HATS" and "VERY BAD HATS". I chose a bad hat.)

Then it was lunchtime. French location catering is wonderful: no queuing in the rain, no grimy buses – everything stops for a couple of hours, and you sit down in a big marquee for a proper three-course lunch with wine. Then it was time for my scene. "OK, Andrew, you are an English art critic – you're not interested in Van Gogh's pictures, you just want to get your new girlfriend into bed, so that's your motivation. Can you do that?"

"I think so, Bob."

"Excellent. You know Geraldine?"

And suddenly I was face to face with Geraldine Chaplin. She wasn't officially in the movie: she'd just come to visit, like me. She was very nice. We did our scene in a crowded little gallery set, over and over. I told Geraldine how beautiful she was – but wouldn't she like a little lie-down? And she kept saying, "I think we should be looking at the pictures: it's rude not to." I thought we were pretty awesome. Years later, I saw the movie, and there was no trace of me in it at all. But Tim Roth was very good.

Now, with that movie shot, it was time for Bob and me to work together properly on Rossini. We were hosted at a farm near Montpellier owned by a former supermodel, still stunning in that casual no-make-up way. When I complimented her on the place, she replied with Gallic bluntness: "Buying a farm seemed a much better way of spending my money than pushing it up my nose."

The farmhouse was low and long and lopsided in the way that made you instantly fall in love with it. Built of pale, sun-faded stone, with bright-blue shutters and walls thick enough to resist cannon shot, it sprawled lazily across a rise in the land like a cat napping in the heat. My guest quarters were vast, cool and fragrant – and, as further proof that being a writer offers the occasional perk, we had a Michelin-starred chef from Montpellier to cook our dinners. Bob, who had simple tastes, preferred burgers.

At the heart of the house was a grand salon – half rustic elegance, half writing den. We'd eat at one end (long wooden table, mismatched chairs, flickering candles stuck into wine bottles) and work at the other, surrounded by stacks of scripts, notebooks and, in my case, overflowing ashtrays – because at the time I was still smoking, forty a day at least. Bob was full of cold and wheezing like a broken accordion. I tried to be polite: "I'm sorry about the smoke. It must really bother you." He looked at me piercingly and said, "Bother me? No. What bothers me is what the hell are you trying to do to yourself, Andrew? You're a good writer. You've got years ahead of you. I'm not telling you to stop – I'm just asking: 'Why are you trying to kill yourself?'" I think the smoke did bother him.

But that question hit home. When I got back to the UK, I bought *The Easy Way to Stop Smoking* by Allen Carr, a trifling little book that bamboozled you with words. It told you not to stop until the final page. By the time I reached it, I could barely stomach lighting one. I stopped – for good. And I still have dreams where I'm puffing away guiltily, and Bob Altman appears, shaking his head and scowling at me. "What are you trying to do to yourself, Andrew?" The odd thing was that he had no problem with smoking grass. He had a guy whose only job was ensuring a plentiful supply of it.

The days were spent talking each scene out in these intense forty-five-minute bursts. Bob would say, "Great work, Andrew, we're gonna make a great movie about Rossini together." Then he'd slope off to nap or disappear with his much younger, startlingly beautiful Italian girlfriend, reappearing later with renewed energy and the occasional idea for a new scene.

Evenings were a film-school masterclass. He'd insist on-screening his own back catalogue – *California Split*, *3 Women*, *Popeye*, *The Long Goodbye*, *Nashville* – adding a running commentary with punchlines. "This one… no plot to speak of… but look at the rhythm, the looseness, the jazz of it." I was beginning to feel that a bit more plot might be welcome. It was hard to concentrate, especially with all the grass being smoked, and often by the end of the movie half of us were peacefully asleep. Bob didn't seem to mind. He had this way of making you feel like you were part of something marvellous.

At the end of each writing day, he'd gather everyone, have me read out what I'd written and declare: "Great work, Andrew! That's the scene! That's it!" Wine would flow, conversation unfold. It was just a week, but it felt like a month, so intense was it. Oddly, it reminded me of when I was in hospital being treated for cancer – another immersive experience where the people around you, no matter how briefly known, become the most important in your life. My surgeon was brilliant. He wanted me to live. He had this group of assistants, who were clever, curious and keen to save me. And I remember thinking: "This feels like a crew: we're here now, we may never be again, but right now we're all playing our part." Bob wasn't saving my life, but he was lighting it up. He believed in me, fiercely. "Would I be working with you if you weren't great?" he'd say, as if it was self-evident. And I believed him.

One afternoon, Bob wasn't feeling too good, and he took his nap alone. His lovely Italian girlfriend asked me if I'd like to go for a walk with her. I said why not, and off we went. It was beautiful – soft sun, gentle breeze, absolutely no one about. She talked to me about how thrilled she was to be here with Bob. "I study him, Andrew, for a year, at film school! He is like a God to me! And then one day, he walks in the office, and I am just a… what you call, a temp? And he sees me! And now I am here! And I am his girlfriend! It's like a dream for me!" And a lot more in that vein. I didn't mind. It was a beautiful day, and it was pleasant to listen to her talking about Bob and how much she loved him. We walked and walked, and she talked and talked, and then I realized I had no idea where we were. The sun had gone down, and by the time we got back to the farmhouse we had been away for nearly four hours. Altman was in a bit of a state, to put it mildly. I explained about getting lost, but it didn't seem to satisfy him. He fixed me with a terrible gaze.

"Andrew," he said, "you are a good writer, and I like you. But if you have been fucking my girlfriend… I WILL kill you."

His words carried a terrible conviction. I stammered some further excuses, and his girlfriend joined in with her own protestations, and after a long pause Bob said: "OK, let's eat."

I returned home newly invigorated, and began revising the script. Bob and I stayed in touch – but then… the film never got made. Some fallout with the Italian financiers, I think. The money slipped away. Bob was mortified.

"I'm sorry, Andrew. That could've been a great movie. Rossini deserved us. But hey, how about something on World War One airmen?"

Home

It's ironic that a memoir should depend upon recall – on taking note, on remembering – when, over the years, I've been repeatedly accused, not without cause, of noticing very little at all.

Diana used to say that I walked through life as if much of it were irrelevant, that I'm unaware of my physical surroundings unless they are of immediate use to me. A kind of selective vision. "You don't see anything," she'd say. "You only see what you're looking for." Which is, I suppose, accurate. If I need a book, I see it and grab it. If I require a chair, I see it and sit on it. The decorative vase next to it? Invisible. What does this say about me? And yet I do remember certain things with clarity.

For example, I remember everything about our home.

The French doors open in summer. Sitting on the step, feeling the warmth soak into ageing knees. The sun lounger creaking slightly under the weight of manuscript pages and the dogs, who believed that any horizontal human existed primarily for their ascent. The scratch of pencil marking scripts. In winter the garden became something else entirely – snow transforming it into a monochrome stage set. The cats from neighbouring houses venturing into the whiteness, placing each paw with deliberation, affronted by the cold. The silence particular to snow. And the acer. We bought it as a small, decorous thing. It was never meant to become dominant – certainly not monumental. If memoir is an act of noticing, then perhaps it turns out that I noticed more than I thought – just not always what other people considered important.

Our home is a place that seems simple until you've lived in it for forty years and buried someone from it. Then it becomes layered. It's quieter now – just Jessie and me. But quiet is not the same as empty. There is still something to get up for. My alarm is set to BBC Radio 3. I like to wake gently – strings, piano, something civilized.

I lie there through to the end of "Bach before 7", easing into the day before the news headlines remind me of the state of the world. Then downstairs. Breakfast is predictable: fruit and yoghurt most days, occasionally scrambled egg on toast. Shower, dress and back downstairs by eight, more or less, to begin. Emails first. Admin. The mildly irritating by-product of a writing life. And then to the dining room: the desk – the work.

Routine is routine. It doesn't oppress me. It steadies me. I don't wrestle with it. The hours between eight and one are usually solid. I break for lunch, something simple, then back again until I feel the work thinning out. Some days that's three o'clock, other days it's six. When the writing goes well, time behaves differently. When it doesn't, it still must be sat through. Jessie has her own sense of schedule. Around late afternoon she materializes, jumps up onto the keyboard and makes it very clear that I have been upright long enough. Eventually I give in. She ushers me to the sitting room with an authority that would have impressed Diana: I'm not easily distracted during work hours. Occasionally a game of solitaire, a skim of the *New Yorker* – I've never once read it cover to cover, as it's absurdly long, but there's usually something worth reading.

At 5 p.m., Jessie begins miaowing for her evening meal. Technically, it should be 6 p.m. Diana was firm on that. I am less so. If I feed Jessie early, I can sit on the sofa and pour myself a whisky before watching the news. Then I'll cook something – nothing too extravagant. The routine holds the day together. Diana and I were very different cooks. If she sat down with a new recipe, she'd follow it religiously, as if its creator were in the room watching her. She wanted to understand what the dish intended to be before she would deviate from it. I, on the other hand, have always taken a more slapdash approach. I glance at a recipe and think, "Yes, yes… I see what you're up to… but surely we can get there another way…" I'm not quite sure why I do that. Impatience, perhaps. I'm always looking for structural shortcuts and abridgements – how to simplify without damaging the essence.

I'm fundamentally a stew-and-roast man. Once you've grasped the underlying architecture (thank you, Elizabeth David), you can make anything. A stew is simply a system. Brown something, soften something, add liquid, wait. After that, it's flavour and instinct. I'm an experimenter. I put things together that might not, at first glance, blend. Swede is tragically underrated. It's cheap, sturdy, faintly sweet, capable of depth, if you give it time. Great, if pickled. I've always liked rescuing the unjustly overlooked ingredient. Even now, when there's no imperative to hunt for a bargain, I enjoy one. It's a leftover reflex from leaner days. When Bill and Anna were small and Diana's working hours were longer than mine, I was the family cook. Both children became vegetarians early, and I found myself in an intimate, almost committed relationship with the aubergine. You can do a lot of things with it. Risottos became a staple – endlessly adaptable, capable of absorbing whatever had to be used up. No need for twenty-three ingredients. Structure first, embellishment after.

I've always thought that drawing, cooking and writing share a common rhythm. You begin with a line, a flavour, a character. You build outwards. You keep stepping back to see whether it holds. And, at some point, you have to stop fiddling. There's a danger in overworking a painting, over-stirring a risotto, over-revising a script.

After losing Diana, I decided, bravely or foolishly, that I needed to try to holiday alone for the first time – and so I headed to Morocco: guaranteed warmth, minimal requirement to engage. I sat by the pool, read, wrote, ordered food. It was fine. Everything was good. The loneliness not so. I told myself to be sociable the next time. Be careful what you wish for.

Once, I enrolled on a cooking holiday in Bologna – a part of Italy Diana and I had loved together. I imagined markets brimful of fruit and fresh vegetables, hanging prosciuttos, moon-sized Parmigiano wheels, communal pasta-making, laughter, heavenly aromas, the civilized clatter of cutlery. The cooking school was in the countryside, not far from the city – olive trees, long tables, flour scattered everywhere. That part was glorious. The company less so. We were a reduced crew. Several had dropped out. What remained was a middle-aged misogynist from Bristol, who had firm views about everything and felt no particular need to revise them; a pleasant but excruciatingly dull man who could speak for twenty minutes on the strategic advantages of living in Slough; a fast-talking, nervy woman who kept interrupting herself mid-sentence; an Irishwoman who spoke without fully opening her mouth, making it impossible at times to understand what she said. It was pretty excruciating, to be honest. Sometimes it's best to stay at home on your own.

*

These days the week has its own rhythm. Mondays always start properly: the gym in the morning with Eamonn for resistance training – bone density, joints, general defiance of gravity. In the evening, I drive to Leamington Spa for life drawing with Neil. The rest of the week runs smoothly, like a well-oiled car: work, reading, the radio, Paul and Georgia coming to clean once a week, Loz to do the garden… There are no bumps in the road. With the odd exception, of course.

One night, I had gone to bed just after midnight, having treated myself to a glass or two of whisky, and I relaxed into that deep, contented slumber you only attain when there's nothing outstanding and no script problems waiting to be solved.

At four in the morning the phone rang.

Now, there is no benign explanation for a phone ringing at four o'clock in the morning. My mind instantly raced to Bill and Anna and their children – accidents, hospitals, deaths: all the worst-possible headlines are conjured up in a split second. It wasn't them. A brisk voice said, "Can you go round and see if Mr Bausch is all right?"

"Who? What?" I said, still fumbling for consciousness. "Why?"

"He's pressed his emergency buzzer. He seems confused and isn't sure where he is. You're down as a first responder."

They were talking about Rainer Bausch, who lives across the road from me. We've been neighbours for years. In his prime he'd been a magnificent figure – tall, broad, commanding. Age, as it does, has whittled him down and fitted him with a Zimmer frame. I pulled on some clothes. The street lights were off. It was pitch dark and raining hard.

I rang the bell.

"Who's there?" came Rainer's voice – fierce, despite the hour.

"It's Andrew. From over the road."

"Andrew?"

There was a long pause.

"Oh, well. I'd better let you in, then. Wait a minute."

I could hear the slow, determined progress of the Zimmer frame along the hallway. He opened the door gingerly, and I slipped inside, manoeuvring around him so that he could shut out the rain.

"Well, come into the living room," he said, dignified as ever.

To my relief, he didn't look confused. He sat in his favourite armchair and regarded me calmly.

"Well, then," he said. "What can I do for you?"

I stared at him and blinked a few times.

"Well," I said, choosing my words carefully, "you pressed your emergency buzzer. The woman at the centre was worried about you."

"Oh, yes, a woman phoned. No idea what she was talking about. The thing is, Eva's not around. I think she's in Leamington."

Eva was his wife.

"OK. Shall we try calling Zoe, then?" I ventured. It seemed like contacting his daughter in France was something one ought to do in such circumstances.

"Yes."

I had just lifted the receiver when the living-room door opened and in walked Eva Bausch in her nightie.

Rainer looked up.

"Who are you?"

"I'm your wife, you silly old fool," she said. "What's Andrew doing here?"

Relieved, I said, "Is it all right if I go home?"

"Yes, yes. Of course. I am sorry."

I walked back across the road through the rain and returned to bed, far too awake to sleep. By morning the whole episode felt slightly dreamlike, and for a few days afterwards I had an odd, unsettling feeling. Surely somebody should be looking out for me at four o'clock in the morning, not the other way round. I have a buzzer too. After Diana died, I had a railing installed on the steps up to the front door. My balance isn't what it was. When there are two of you, one can always phone for an ambulance or whatever. When it's just you and the cat, you can't do that. My friend Lorna, who used to be a bereavement counsellor, said that in general women cope much better on their own than men do. About half the men would marry again in a rush, desperately grabbing for the lifebelt. I didn't, and never felt inclined to do so. Of course I miss Diana, but that doesn't mean I want to live with another woman. I like my own company, and my own cooking, and I like my own way of doing things. And I have Jessie, who is beautiful, affectionate and pleasingly independent.

*

I'm attached to this house in a way that has surprised me over the years. It's only bricks and mortar, after all, but, as I said before, it has acquired layers. Memory settles into walls. The light in the hall has seen arguments, reconciliations, birthday cakes, exam results, manuscripts, grief. Anna and Bill remain deeply attached to it too. It affects them in ways that perhaps they don't fully articulate. It holds us together. In its livelier decades it held rather a lot of other people too. For many years we had a standing engagement on 29th December each year. The invitation was simple: come to ours at lunchtime and stay as long as you like. Some of our friends treated it as two separate events. They'd arrive at midday in sensible jumpers, eat, drink, laugh, then disappear home at five to shower and change, and reappear in evening clothes as if attending a gala performance. Diana and I would simply soldier through, fortified by adrenaline and whatever was being passed around in the kitchen. It was the 1970s. Spirits were high in every sense. We'd lay out a vast spread across the dining-room table – cold meats, salads, puddings – and the house would fill up, room by room.

After my mother died, my father began joining us on our 29th December shindigs. He'd scoop up any children who had come along with their parents and keep them occupied. He made himself useful without fuss. It became not just a party, but a reaffirmation. When I walk through the house now, quieter, tidier, I can still hear the old echo of it all, the clink of glasses, the thud of feet on the stairs, Diana's laugh rising above the din. Houses don't remember, of course. But we do.

Giacomo Campiotti and *Doctor Zhivago*

It was the year 2000, and we were trying to develop a TV version of *Doctor Zhivago* for Granada Television – Andy Harries, Anne Pivcevic and me. It was problematic for several reasons. First, it would have to be a European co-production – a Euro-pudding. The Italians owned the rights, and we needed finance from Germany. That meant talent from all three countries. The second problem was David Lean's magnificent film version with Julie Christie and Omar Sharif. Could we come up with something that could stand comparison with that masterpiece? Well, we could have a go. The third problem was the book itself. Pasternak was a poet, and *Doctor Zhivago* is not an ordinary novel. He doesn't write the big scenes you want to see – for example, the one where Komarovsky seduces the schoolgirl Lara. You look for it, and it isn't there! Around page 59, Lara's feeling excited and anticipating the evening ahead; then you turn the page and she's back in school, a virgin no more. So I was going to have to write the crucial scene – and, what's more, write it in a different way from the Lean film, or we could get sued for intellectual-property theft. And there were lots more difficulties of that kind – but also opportunities.

Zhivago's father is important in the story, but he is nowhere in the film. I was able to write a whole opening sequence on a train, with the little boy, his father and Komarovsky, where the boy sees his father kill himself. So Anne and I wrestled the book into a three-act structure we felt happy with. Now we needed an Italian director, and we didn't know any. Anne found a film that had come out the previous year, *Il tempo dell'amore*. No narrative structure to speak of, but full of lyrical lovemaking scenes and full of tenderness. The director was Giacomo Campiotti. He came over to meet us – tall, handsome, unkempt, passionate. "This is my favourite book – all my life I have wanted to make this film! And I think we throw away this script and start again from the beginning!" I was appalled. I'd spent months perfecting the screenplay. I thought, either this guy goes or I do. And said so. Not in the room, but later, in private. Anne wanted both of us: my structure, his lyricism. And she started working on us both, rather as Susie Conklin had done years before with me and Anthony Page. And eventually we had a screenplay that pleased us both, which was not so far from the first draft, but contained some brilliant visual ideas by Giacomo. And he and I were becoming friends.

*

Casting was fun. Giacomo didn't know any English actors, so his view of them was fresh and bracing. Of one very well-regarded lead actor he said: "'E is no good! 'E is like a block of wood!" He really liked Kris Marshall though, and saw he had the capacity to go stronger and deeper than any of his previous roles. And for Lara he was determined to cast Keira Knightley, who was still only seventeen years old. "She will be a great star," he said. The Romanian-German actress Alexandra Maria Lara was a real find, so lovely and moving as Zhivago's wife Tonya. Other roles were taken by Bill Paterson as Tonya's dad, Anne-Marie Duff as the gritty survivor Olya Demina and magnificent Sam Neill as Komarovsky. Hans Matheson was our Zhivago – and he was excellent. I have often wondered why he didn't have a more glittering career subsequently.

Moscow and the Russian steppes were recreated in the Czech Republic, where the filming took place. Giacomo created many beautiful visual moments, and I longed to work with him again, but never did. One thing he said stayed with me: "Of course you can be in love with two women at once! I myself am in love with two women at once! It is natural!"

Tipping the Velvet and *Falling*

I've always spent a lot of time in bookshops. They can be a dangerous place for me. One minute I'm idly leafing through a novel, and within ten minutes I'm done for. There's a particular sensation, a tightening in the chest, a forward-leaning urgency, when a book starts murmuring, "You're mine." But that was not how I came across *Tipping the Velvet*. No, Sally Head sent it to me, as she had sent *Moll Flanders* years earlier, saying she thought I might like it. It was Sarah Waters's first novel, and the bookshops didn't think of her as a popular, bestselling novelist. In those days she would be in a niche called "Queer Romance" or "Lesbian Historical Fiction", in some out-of-the-way corner of the shop I would be shy to be seen in.

I took it with me to the Banff World Television Festival, where *Vanity Fair* was up for an award. Banff is bang in the middle of the Canadian Rockies. We were all staying in this huge old railway hotel, and you could have breakfast on the terrace with a view of the snow-covered mountains, which looked just like a child's drawing. So there I was, eating my pancakes with maple syrup and reading *Tipping the Velvet* – what a treat. And I came to this bit where our heroine enters wearing nothing but a guardsman's jerkin, black riding boots and an enormous leather dildo – and that's when I knew that I HAD to do this book, and I had to put that scene on the screen.

In *Tipping the Velvet* you're in the company of Nan Astley, an oyster girl from Whitstable who falls headlong in love with Kitty Butler, a male impersonator on the music-hall stage, and then, through heartbreak and hunger and desire, drifts into a succession of lives: backstage dresser, rent-boy in trousers, kept woman in a silk gown, socialist comrade in a borrowed overcoat. It's exuberant, erotic, political, funny and bleak by turns. Sarah's Victorian

London is sweaty and hungry, bursting with possibility. You can smell the gaslight and greasepaint.

There's always a question when a man adapts a story so rooted in female experience, but part of the craft of writing, and perhaps the fun of it, is transposition. We are constantly crossing borders: class, age, nation, gender. If you can't imagine yourself into the life of someone unlike you, what are you doing trying to be a writer? Love and sex are universal, though the details differ. And, as I told my school friend Graham in 1946, "I know all about sex now."

When I got back to England, I asked to meet Sarah, and we bonded over a shared love of Victorian pornography, which (if you don't know it) can be very tender and sweet and all about *jouissance*, as the French feminists say. I had some questions – for example, what would a girl like Nan think about dressing up as a boy and offering sexual favours to gentlemen down back alleys? Wouldn't she find it a bit off-putting? Sarah said she'd undertake it in a spirit of curiosity – and, anyway, she'd have done a lot of messy jobs at the oysterage.

There's a lot about the music hall in the book, and I thought I would find some good songs for Nan and Kitty to sing, but none of them seemed quite right. I was looking for playful, transgressive double entendre, and I realized it would be easier to write the songs myself. I'd written all the lyrics for *Fearless Frank*, and it was fun to get back into songwriting. (One of my unfulfilled ambitions has always been to write a hit pop song.)

Rehearsals went well. Rachael Stirling led by example with her bold and uninhibited performance. Keeley Hawes was lovely, as always, as the music-hall star who captures Nan's heart. And Anna Chancellor was mesmerizing as posh and dominant Diana. My vote for best kisser was Sally Hawkins as the maid, who had a wonderful way of saying "Oh, miss! Oh, miss!" at the peak of sexual pleasure. We even had Benedict Cumberbatch, long before he was famous, as Freddy, Nan's spurned boyfriend.

When it aired, the reaction was lively. Some viewers were delighted – others were appalled. Newspapers had great fun with headlines about "Victorian Lesbians on the BBC". But what I remember most clearly is how many people wrote in to say how refreshing it felt to see that world depicted openly rather than coyly hinted at. For the BBC it was something of a gamble, but it paid off. The series drew a large audience, travelled well internationally and, perhaps more importantly, opened the door for a different sort of historical drama. Period television had often treated sexuality as something to be tidied discreetly away. *Tipping the Velvet* suggested that the past might have been rather more complicated and considerably more interesting – which, of course, it always was.

I'd felt something similar years earlier reading Alan Hollinghurst. I'm a great admirer of his work, particularly *The Swimming-Pool Library*, which I read with a mixture of fascination and unease. It's set in early-1980s London, in a languid, slightly doomed pre-AIDS summer when everything feels possible and faintly dangerous. The narrator, William Beckwith, drifts between country houses and West London gyms, cruising and collecting experiences, until he becomes entangled with an elderly aristocrat who keeps secret diaries of his own colonial past. The novel moves between desire and repression, privilege and moral blindness. It's about class and empire as much as it is about sex, and it's unsparing. I met Alan at a party once, and told him how much I'd loved the book and how, reading some of its more explicit passages, I'd found myself simply transposing the boys into girls. I wondered aloud whether he minded such imaginative liberties. He laughed. "Fine by me," he said. "How do you think I've spent my whole life? Transposing all those heroines into boys." That, really, is the bargain. We borrow each other's bodies and stories in order to understand them. We change the pronouns and keep the feelings. And if you do it honestly, the emotion survives the crossing.

Going on holiday with very little to do has also presented the opportunity to discover compelling reads that have turned into productions. It was 2000 or 2001. Diana and I had rented a sprawling villa in Corsica with our dear friends Jim and Sarah. There was a lively assortment of children and young adults – ours and theirs, and their partners – spilling in and out of rooms. Someone proposed we form a holiday book group, which sounded very ambitious given the quantity of rosé being consumed. But we did. We played a lot of cricket too. And also Bop It – anyone remember Bop It? Addictive, anyway.

The runaway book-club favourite that summer was *Falling* by Elizabeth Jane Howard. I read it in a kind of fever, and had that familiar internal lurch: "I must do this." Almost immediately I knew I wanted to do it with my daughter Anna. By then she was working at Yorkshire Television. It seemed right, professionally and personally, to join forces. Anna's boss at YTV, Keith Richardson, was the kind of executive one dreams of. He trusted writers. "We'll bring in a producer to realize the script exactly as you want it," he said. "If they do anything else, we'll tell them to do it again." It was music to my ears.

Meeting Elizabeth Jane Howard – famous for *The Cazalet Chronicles*, her love affairs, the memoirs, her marriage to Kingsley Amis – was a great honour. *Falling* drew from her own experience of becoming enthralled by a charming older man, brilliant in bed, appalling in morals, whose attentions were directed more at her bank account than at her heart. In real life, after falling deeply in love, she was rescued by a vigilant friend. But Robert McKee's maxim was ringing in my ears: "Never let the resolution slip out of the hands of the protagonist." Dramatically, if the rescue comes from outside, it weakens the structure of the story. So, in our version, she saves herself.

We were fortunate in the production. Tristram Powell directed with a sure touch, and Chris Parr, the producer… well, he was a bit shambolic, but he got there in the end. Penelope Wilton brought extraordinary emotional precision to the role, every flicker of doubt and desire visible. Michael Kitchen, whom I had known from much earlier days, played the seductive predator with unsettling subtlety. I was fascinated by his pauses and hesitations – very Pinteresque (unless he was struggling to remember his lines…). Anyway, it worked. It was one of those experiences where everything aligned: the right book at the right moment, the right collaborators, the right trust. And lovely to be working with my daughter Anna for once.

Dickens and Me

The BBC I grew up with, and then worked with, felt like a sort of extended family. I remember going to see Louis Marks and Rosie Hill, and before any serious business was conducted, we'd invariably trundle off to the bar. There would be producers leaning against radiators, directors mid-rant, somebody enthusing about a medical drama set in the A&E department of a large hospital. That show turned out to be *Casualty*. You could feel things beginning in those corridors.

Later, there was a golden stretch, when it felt as though the BBC was my natural habitat. One classic serial after another. Jane Tranter was then at the helm. Before I embarked on *Bleak House* in 2004 – my second brush with Dickens, but my first adaptation into a series drama – she more or less threw down the gauntlet.

"I want you and Nigel to come up with a new concept. I don't know what, exactly, but do something new."

The challenge was both inspiring and terrifying. The idea that producer Nigel Stafford-Clark and I landed on was radical at the time: half-hour episodes spread across the week, immediately after *EastEnders*. Thirty minutes of Dickens in the nation's living rooms between tea and bedtime. To our surprise and relief, people loved it. In truth, *Bleak House* and *EastEnders* have much in common. One revolves around Lincoln's Inn, the other around Albert Square. Both are crowded urban ecosystems. Characters brush past one another without realizing how their destinies are interrelated. Secrets ferment, old grievances resurface, plots weave and tangle. Dickens, in his way, invented the long-running serial form that television soaps depend upon. And he did so, originally, not in leather-bound volumes, but in weekly and monthly instalments. Dickens was a master of the periodical. His novels appeared chapter by chapter in magazines, sold cheaply for a shilling or two. Readers would queue for the next episode. He wrote to the rhythm of anticipation and gave us cliffhangers before we even had a word for them. Recasting *Bleak House* as a series of thirty-minute episodes felt less like heresy and more like restoration. We were returning it to its bloodstream: fragmentary, urgent, communal.

I hadn't adapted any of his major works before, but Dickens had been with me since childhood. I'd read heavily abridged children's editions of his novels before I was eleven, then tackled his full oeuvre as an adult. I had even taught *Bleak House* at college, so I knew what awaited me: a sprawling dual narrative, one strand told in the present tense by an omniscient voice and the other by Esther Summerson in the first person. Fog everywhere, lawsuits without end, whole families damaged by the inertia of the Court of Chancery.

It's a book riddled with narrative problems, and therefore irresistible to me. Dickens's own life, if you look closely, was full of concealed disorder: debt, guilt, complicated loves. He tried to tidy it up in public, but it leaks through his novels. Dickens's childhood was not the genteel, hearth-warmed prelude to genius that later admirers liked to imagine: it was erratic, financially unstable. One moment the family was living in something resembling middle-class respectability – the next, his father John was hauled off to the Marshalsea debtors' prison. The young Charles, at twelve, was sent to work in a blacking factory pasting labels on bottles – a humiliation he never entirely recovered from. That sense that the floor could give way at any moment stayed with him all his life. Out of that precariousness came his great gift: the ability to observe every rung of society without sentimentalism. He'd known clerks and criminals, debtors and dreamers, respectable ladies and drunken ne'er-do-wells. He carried them all with him. You can feel them – the clerks, the con men, the hopelessly optimistic fathers – striding through his novels in barely disguised form. But alongside the talent ran a profound insecurity. Even when he was rich and lionized, fêted in America and applauded in packed halls on his public-reading tours, he feared slipping back to the bottom. Success didn't soothe him: it drove him harder. Work was both necessity and an opiate.

His father was a hopeless model for stability, and Dickens in turn was hardly exemplary at home. He married Catherine Hogarth, who bore him ten children, which would test the equilibrium of any household. Time and repeated pregnancies took their toll on her body, and Dickens, who could be terrifyingly exacting, became critical of her changed shape and then estranged from her completely. He publicly attributed difficulties to her "unsuitability" and ridiculed her loss of figure. Into this domestic discontent stepped Ellen Ternan, who was eighteen when she met the forty-five-year-old Dickens. A young actress and bright, loyal, discreet. By this point, Dickens was not merely a novelist: he was a national institution, the man who had practically codified Christmas: snow, redemption, plum pudding, second chances. Respectability was his brand. Unlike his friend Wilkie Collins, who made no secret of his relationship with his mistress and shrugged at scandal, Dickens could not afford such openness. Nor did he have George Eliot's stubborn defiance: she lived with a married man, George Henry Lewes, in plain view and let society grumble. Dickens required the admiration of the public. He fed on it – he needed it. Ellen became a secret. There is a persistent story that she became pregnant, that they went to France and returned without a baby. Did the child die? Was it adopted? The paper trail is thin.

Dickens's health faltered in his later years. He drove himself mercilessly on reading tours, exhausting his body in packed theatres where audiences wept and roared on cue as he acted out his characters before them. It was an extraordinary performance – part theatre, part sermon, part literary seance – and he repeated it night after night until his body began to give way. He suffered a series of strokes – though, characteristically, he refused to slow down. In 1870, at his house in Kent, he collapsed after dinner and never regained consciousness. Gad's Hill was a comfortable red-brick house just outside Rochester, the home he had long dreamt of owning. As a child, he'd walked past it and been told that if he worked hard enough one day it might be his. Years later, at the height of his success, he bought it and installed himself there as a kind of literary country gentleman, with views over the Kent countryside and the road along which coaches once travelled between London and the coast.

Earlier that day, he'd nearly died at Ellen's house in London. When he collapsed there, propriety intervened with astonishing speed. Victorian reputation management operated with remarkable efficiency when required. He was bundled into a carriage, maids sworn to secrecy, and transported back to his official family home, so that he might expire respectably. No whiff of impropriety – no suggestion of another address. He died surrounded by his children, the narrative neatly closed. It is all deeply Victorian and tragic. A man who wrote so penetratingly about hypocrisy and social injustice unable to live fully in the truth of his own arrangements. A man who understood human frailty intimately yet could be blind to his own.

Complicated? Certainly. But complexity is often the dynamo of literature. The very insecurities, humiliations and concealed passions that dogged him gave his writing its electricity. Without the Marshalsea, without the blacking factory, without the secret life and the relentless need to perform goodness in public, we might not have had *Bleak House* or *Great Expectations*, or the furious tenderness of his satire. He built Christmas for the nation and smuggled his own contradictions into it.

That was the real challenge: not just to modernize Dickens, but to reveal the rot beneath the Victorian veneer, to let the human mess breathe. And to slip it into the broadcast schedule after *EastEnders* without anyone noticing that they were, in fact, being offered high nineteenth-century satire with their evening cuppa. Easier said than done. Austen and Dickens generally know exactly what they're doing. They are formidable dramatists. The task is not to improve upon them – God forbid – but to enter a kind of collaboration across time. And if you *do* feel something needs reimagining, you must be brave enough to own it.

Dickens was a master storyteller – perhaps the greatest – but he was also a man writing for weekly or monthly instalments.

Bleak House, like most of his novels, was originally published in serial form, each chapter designed to sustain interest, sharpen suspense and ensure that readers handed over their next shilling. The structure reflects that. He'll give you twenty pages introducing a set of characters, then break off and begin another strand altogether – a different social class, a contrasting tone, sometimes even a new narrative voice – before knitting them together later. It works beautifully on the page, especially when read in instalments. On television, however, beginning over and over again is not always a mercy.

Let's take that extraordinary opening.

> London. Michaelmas Term lately over, and the Lord Chancellor sitting in Lincoln's Inn Hall. Implacable November weather. As much mud in the streets as if the waters had but newly retired from the face of the earth [...].
>
> Fog everywhere. Fog up the river [...], fog down the river [...]. Fog creeping into the cabooses of collier brigs [...], fog lying out on the yards and hovering in the rigging of great ships.

It is atmospheric, yes, magnificent, incantatory, but it is also thematic. The fog is not merely meteorological. It is moral fog – legal fog. The great Chancery case of "Jarndyce and Jarndyce" – dragging on for generations, devouring inheritances, lives, sanity – is the fog. And everything and everyone in the novel breathes it in. I wrote a lot of fog into my first draft – a real London pea-souper. Something thick enough to taste. The fog would seep through Lincoln's Inn and into the court, into Tulkinghorn's chambers, into Lady Dedlock's drawing room. It was my homage to Dickens, and also my thematic signpost. But fog, in television terms, has a will of its own. The production team pumped in gallons of artificial mist, and it obligingly drifted for perhaps nine seconds before disappearing in a gust of studio air. I could control what I wrote. Technology, however, controlled the studio weather. The fog, largely, had to go.

Structurally, I felt we needed to begin differently. Not a sequential, but a multi-stranded, simultaneous beginning. Instead of Dickens's wave-like introductions of this cluster, then that one, I wanted Esther, Ada and Richard at the heart of the story from the outset – the three young innocents stepping unknowingly into the machinery of Chancery. And from their orbit we could glimpse the others: Nemo, the copy writer, already broken and drifting through opium fumes; Jo, the crossing-sweeper, perpetual witness and victim; Guppy with his unsettling earnestness. A single tapestry woven before the viewer's eyes. One of the greatest structural problems, and therefore opportunities, was Esther herself. Half the novel is narrated in her modest, self-effacing voice:

> I have a great deal of difficulty in beginning to write my portion of these pages…

To my ear, it can sound painfully disingenuous. "Oh, I am but a humble young lady, scarcely worthy of note." Which is all very well, but she provides the emotional backbone to the story. If she's coy, sentimentalized or slightly inauthentic, then the whole thing collapses. We needed to feel her intelligence, her courage, her practicality. Not simpering virtue, but moral stamina. Dickens can be a bit sentimental with women. He can gild them. Lady Dedlock, though, is an exception. She strides in from pure Gothic melodrama, and somehow becomes tragically real: a woman undone by secrecy, shame and repression. With Gillian Anderson in the role, there could be nothing phoney about her. She was icy, poised and trembling underneath.

So we went ahead with the bold move of writing thirty-minute episodes to sit after *EastEnders* – *Bleak House* as soap opera… and why not? I set myself the mad task of delivering a half-hour script every two weeks – shorter scenes than I was used to. Hard cuts. In retrospect, I sometimes wonder whether an hour format would have allowed the story more breathing space. But, at the time, the velocity was exhilarating.

And suddenly it was the day of the read-through – all sixteen episodes in one day. There were actors, eighty or so of them, coming and going, a horseshoe of tables in a huge room in a big gloomy old church off Shaftesbury Avenue – scripts clutched, coffee cups everywhere, Mr Davies in a state of high excitement, Mr Stafford-Clark (the producer) a bundle of nerves. Charles Dance couldn't make the morning session, so I read Tulkinghorn opposite Gillian Anderson's Lady Dedlock. What a thrill. I learnt long ago that I am no actor, but I can read pretty well, and reading Tulkinghorn with Gillian.... Wow. She fixed me with that cold, appraising stare, then let me have it. I genuinely felt the hairs on the back of my neck rise. Burn Gorman, as Guppy, was a complete revelation. No one quite knew where he'd come from, and suddenly he was funny and weird and unsettling and entirely right. You could feel the room tighten: "Oh. We'd better all be good." I always had a soft spot for William Guppy of Messrs Kenge and Carboy, and I longed for him to win Esther's heart, instead of that grumpy young Welsh doctor who was always moaning about something.

Dickens was always standing behind me, while I was working on *Bleak House*, as a kind of noisy, extravagant, avuncular ghost. You begin to feel the muscularity of his storytelling, the confidence with which he creates entire microcosms of people and then lets them collide. At first glance, the novel has something of a fairy tale about it. Richard and Ada are introduced with that almost storybook simplicity: cousins, young, affectionate, instantly drawn together. There is sweetness there. They are the radiant pair who believe in love and possibility and a future unclouded by fog. If Dickens had stopped there, it would have been charming, but superficial. Of course he doesn't stop there. The real cleverness is what he does with Richard. He allows us to love him: he makes him impulsive, warm-hearted, impressionable, one of those young men who mean well and believe they will sort it all out once they've found the right path. And then he feeds him slowly to the mastiffs of Chancery. Dickens's genius lies in the way he portrays Richard's delusion. He convinces himself, and tries to convince Ada, that

Jarndyce and Jarndyce is not about money, not really: it's about justice, it's about clearing a name, it's about principle. That is how addiction works. Dickens understood that perfectly. Richard is not merely greedy: he is seduced by the idea of righteousness. And that, of course, is a far more dangerous weakness. We watch him deteriorate physically and morally while still loving him. It's merciless and humane at the same time.

It's never difficult to glimpse Dickens in his own creations. There's a generous scattering of himself in his novels. In *Bleak House*, if I had to place a bet, I'd put my money on John Jarndyce as one of Dickens's self-portraits: the benevolent patriarch, the rescuer, the man who gathers damaged souls under his wing. Dickens adored being the benefactor. He rescued women from the streets. He involved himself energetically, sometimes intrusively, in the lives of the distressed. He created circles of dependence around him. It's admirable and slightly histrionic all at once.

Jarndyce, with his hearth and his "east wind" jokes and his determined kindness, feels like Dickens imagining himself at his most generous and composed. Then there's Harold Skimpole, the man-child of whimsy and irresponsibility. Dickens based him unmistakably on Leigh Hunt, the poet and essayist, who had once been his friend. Hunt was not amused. He recognized himself in Skimpole's evasions and financial fecklessness, and protested bitterly. But Dickens, like all writers, was a thievish magpie: he plundered, he borrowed faces and mannerisms and weaknesses. Friendship doesn't render anyone safe from literary appropriation.

It was imperative – given the speed at which I was churning the scripts out – that I use tried-and-tested collaborators. You simply cannot deliver an episode every fortnight while constantly renegotiating taste, tone and temperament. Familiarity wasn't just comforting: it was structurally necessary. Ellie Wood was our script editor, and we'd already crossed stormy seas together. She had that rare gift of being both rigorously intelligent and cheerfully encouraging. She would gently steer an awkward moment into clarity without ever making you feel that you'd driven into a ditch. When you are racing through sixteen episodes, that spirit matters enormously. A raised eyebrow can derail you – a well-timed "This is working" carries you through another hundred pages. Jane Tranter was brilliant with notes – surgical, precise. When too many voices joined the chorus, gangs of executive producers, each with their bit of wisdom or baloney, I developed the habit of saying, "I only want Jane's notes."

We'd originally planned twenty episodes, which felt deliciously expansive. We pruned them down to eighteen, then to sixteen. It meant the ending had to stand as firmly as the beginning. No flabbiness. Dickens could afford to digress – we couldn't. Nigel Stafford-Clark, the producer, was deeply invested, sometimes too invested for his own well-being. He wanted me to revisit certain sequences, particularly the meeting between Lady Dedlock and Esther, when the great secret is revealed. It reads, on the page, as pure Victorian confession.

"I am your wicked and unhappy mother."

There's nothing ironic about the line. It is naked, melodramatic, bold. You either retreat from it or you lean into it. I felt one had to go with it. I replaced "wicked" with "wretched", a word that appears later in the dialogue. Gillian delivered the line without tremor or falsity. No sentimentality, no hand-wringing, just restraint and devastation. It landed. The room held its breath.

Nigel is retired now, which astonishes me. Producing was oxygen to him, although he would work himself into such a state about budgets, schedules, editorial notes and creative disputes that he would declare, more than once, that he was stepping down. I am sure he didn't mean it. Each time, after suitable tea and persuasion, he returned. Producers are supposed to be the calm centre, the diplomatic oil in the machinery. Nigel was more combustible. But he was passionately on the side of the work, first with the writing and then, once shooting began, wholly supportive of the director. That kind of total investment is exhausting. I suspect it cost him more than he would ever admit.

Justin Chadwick came in as director. At the time he hadn't done any period drama, and had just come off *Spooks*, the BBC's fast-moving espionage series about MI5 – all urgent plotting, surveillance rooms, shadowy briefings and people striding purposefully through corridors while national security hung in the balance. It was shot in a deliberately contemporary style: hand-held cameras, quick edits, scenes unfolding with the nervous energy of a thriller rather than the stately composure of traditional television drama. Justin brought that same bold, restless energy with him, as well as his modern camera technique. This gave us constant movement, and scenes that felt immediate rather than staged. He often began a take without announcing it, allowing actors to drift naturally into the moment before anyone quite realized the camera was rolling. That rather unsettled some of our more experienced actors, who had spent decades carefully calibrating angles, light and posture before a director called "Action". Justin preferred to ambush them slightly – which, as it turned out, produced something rather alive on-screen. Certain performers would very politely ask which side of the face was being favoured, and whether this was technically a close-up. They wanted to marshal their craft. The younger actors, meanwhile, adored the spontaneity. They thrived on it. In retrospect, Justin's approach suited the compressed structure beautifully. The short scenes allowed for swift editing, moments flickering across one another, giving you a fuller sense of Dickens's London without anchoring it too long in any single room. It felt modern without feeling gimmicky – which is always the trick. And it did work. Magnificently.

I remember watching Carey Mulligan as Ada on set: radiant, romantic, entirely open. In the early days she was nervous, almost breathless, and lines would occasionally run away from her before she'd quite caught them. But that fragility fitted Ada perfectly: a teenager in love overwhelmed by hope. Sometimes an actor's nerves are an asset.

When *Bleak House* aired, it was greeted with a level of enthusiasm that slightly surprised us. Dickens adaptations had often been treated as worthy but rather stately affairs, admired more than devoured, yet this one seemed to catch people off guard. Critics immediately noticed the pace, how Dickens's sprawling world had been turned into something urgent and alive, helped by the half-hour serial format, which allowed the story to unfold with the momentum of a thriller while still retaining the author's vast array of characters and his moral fury. Anna Maxwell Martin's Esther Summerson, who could easily have been played as a dutiful and rather dull Victorian heroine, but instead emerged intelligent, humorous and emotionally resilient, was the still, humane centre around which the whole story turned. Gillian Anderson's Lady Dedlock possessed an extraordinary composure, a kind of frozen dignity suggesting strong undercurrents of feeling held just beneath the surface, while Charles Dance's Tulkinghorn was magnificently implacable: the lawyer as a granite monolith, conveying menace through stillness and patience rather than bluster. Between them, Lady Dedlock and Tulkinghorn created a kind of glacial duet of secrecy and power at the heart of the drama. The result was that rare thing: a Dickens adaptation that felt both faithful and startlingly modern, with and without fog. There were some other stunning performances. Denis Lawson was very moving as John Jarndyce, who comes to love Esther and is generous enough to let her go; Johnny Vegas, in his first acting part, was sensational as the self-combusting Krook. Phil Davis's Smallweed was a hit – for a time you could get his "Shake me up, Judy!" as a ringtone for your phone.

Bleak House went on to win multiple awards, including a BAFTA for Best Drama Serial. Carey and I found ourselves seated together at the ceremony. I said, "You must be feeling wonderful. We're such a success..."

"I'm just going along with what's happening," she said. "Lots of calls. Lots of auditions. I keep getting down to the last two... and Keira Knightley gets the part." Of course that didn't last long. Discerning directors spotted her. She chose wisely. And the nervous breathlessness became control and power. But I'm rather fond of remembering her that way – half running through lines on a Dickens set, absorbing everything, slightly puffed out, on the rise in her remarkable trajectory. Which is one of the huge pleasures of long-form television: you are not simply adapting a novel – you are watching careers bloom.

*

Everything seemed to accelerate for me after that, with hardly any time to draw breath myself: *The Line of Beauty*, *Northanger Abbey*, *The Diary of a Nobody*, *Fanny Hill* and *Sense and Sensibility* were broadcast in quick succession between 2006 and 2008. After *Bleak House*, however, I was keen to return to Dickens. His novels were written in instalments, after all, and he understood something television executives later rediscovered with great enthusiasm: audiences quite like a story that keeps them coming back the following week.

Not long after *Bleak House*, we began talking about which Dickens might come next. The conversation happened, as these things often did with Jane, over dinner rather than in a formal commissioning meeting. I suggested a couple of possibilities: *Dombey and Son* and *Little Dorrit*. Jane thought about it briefly, and said she rather liked the sound of the latter. That was essentially that. Looking back, I think it may have been the last substantial drama we developed together before she left for America. At the time it simply felt like the continuation of a productive partnership and another Dickens adventure. It turned out to be a rather good one.

Little Dorrit is, on the surface, a story about debt and imprisonment. Amy Dorrit grows up inside the Marshalsea prison because her father has been incarcerated there for years. The Marshalsea, located in Southwark, not far from the Thames, was where those unable to pay their debts were confined, sometimes indefinitely. Dickens's own father had been imprisoned there, and it left a scar on his life. Families often lived alongside the convicts, creating a peculiar, semi-domestic world behind the walls. The prison becomes the strange epicentre of the Dorrit family's life, at once constraining and oddly familiar. Around that small domestic story, Dickens builds something much larger: a satire about bureaucracy, financial speculation, social pretence and the peculiar British talent for avoiding responsibility. The Circumlocution Office, Dickens's glorious parody of government inefficiency, feels, if anything, even more topical now than it did when he wrote it.

At the emotional centre of the story is Amy herself, one of Dickens's most heroic characters. She is patient, observant and morally steady in a world where almost everyone else is compromised by vanity, ambition or money. When adapting Dickens, I try to locate that core of emotion first and allow everything else to move around it. Otherwise, the sheer number of characters can overwhelm the story. And there are a great many characters in *Little Dorrit*.

We were lucky to get Tom Courtenay for the part of Amy's father, and he revelled in it. For Amy we had Claire Foy, straight from drama school. I thought she might be almost too fragile and waif-like, but that was before I met her. Claire is very robust in real life, with a raucous sense of humour. And for Arthur Clennam we got Matthew Macfadyen, one of my favourite actors and a most lovely person too. Around them were actors of tremendous range – Judy Parfitt, Alun Armstrong, Andy Serkis, Russell Tovey and many others – the sort of ensemble Dickens always deserves. Our read-through was held in a large hall near Shaftesbury Avenue, because it was the only place big enough to hold everyone: a Dickens adaptation can easily involve seventy or eighty speaking parts. Actors tend to approach read-throughs with understandable nerves. They are exposing themselves before the characters have quite settled into their bones. I, on the other hand, love them. For a brief moment, the entire story unfolds in front of you – the rhythm of the dialogue, the shape of the scenes, the emotional pulse of the narrative. I usually read the stage directions myself, partly so I can indicate pace and tone. It is also the last moment in which the writer feels completely in charge. After that, the story belongs to everyone else – directors, actors, editors, designers. Which is entirely as it should be.

We had three different directors, and there was no clear directing style, unlike *Bleak House*. Anne Pivcevic, whom I'd known since the days of *House of Cards*, was executive producer and a big (and benign) influence on the style of the piece. Dickens's world is heightened, certainly, but it must also feel real and inhabited. When *Little Dorrit* was broadcast in 2008, it was received with great enthusiasm, both in Britain and internationally. Viewers seemed to take Amy Dorrit very much to heart, which is the best outcome one can hope for with Dickens. The series went on to win seven Primetime Emmy Awards, including Outstanding Miniseries, Writing and Directing, as well as receiving numerous BAFTA nominations across the craft categories. It was an unexpectedly triumphant afterlife for a story about debtors' prisons and bureaucratic incompetence.

But the real satisfaction lies elsewhere. What Dickens understood, and what television occasionally manages to rediscover, is that large social stories work best when tethered to intimate human lives. A quiet young woman in a prison. A father clinging to dignity. A man returning home to discover that the past has not finished with him. Once those elements are in place, the rest of the machinery can begin to turn beautifully. And Dickens provides cogs of the most elaborate kind.

A Difficult Year

2008 slid nicely into 2009. It was a busy back-to-back time – everything was rolling along, and my schedule was that of a man very much in demand: LA in January, Texas soon after, assorted lunches at the Ivy, the Connaught and the Dorch. I wasn't someone who felt unwell often – and, when I did, I tended to ignore it. There had been signs, though, that something was wrong with me. One episode in particular: lunch in London with Gareth Neame. We'd worked together on *Tipping the Velvet*, and he would later go on to shepherd *Downton Abbey* into the world. We were discussing one of those projects that didn't get made – there are many – when I started to feel distinctly off. I couldn't eat, and I drank more than usual, which didn't help. The train journey home was miserable. But the feeling passed, and I soon forgot about it.

The kitchen renovation consumed that summer. Daisy, our half-sized Alsatian rescue who was terrified of other dogs and wary of most humans, inexplicably adored the kitchen fitters, and the months of upheaval didn't bother her as much as it did us. Then, almost as soon as the builders left, I felt a severe abdominal pang – nine out of ten on the pain scale. I couldn't go to the toilet or puke. My stomach swelled alarmingly, and there was a weekend dash to A&E, as I've previously mentioned. The first doctor prescribed laxatives for what he diagnosed as constipation. The pain intensified, and so did the certainty that something was badly wrong. I went back.

"I think it's a growth. It looks like a mass. Let's get you an X-ray."

Those three sentences saved my life.

I was X-rayed and put into a bed. A senior doctor arrived.

"The bad news is that you've got a very big, aggressive cancer in your bowel. But the good news is that you're in hospital and we're going to do something about it."

Morphine relieved the pain, and I felt, oddly, vindicated. I'm not prone to histrionics, but I'd known something was not right. Now the invisible thing had a name.

"You could have died. And you're not out of the woods yet."

The strangest aspect of it all was that I didn't feel frightened. I felt energized, as though we were all engaged in a joint enterprise. Saving my life was the shared objective. It felt collaborative.

"I've just got to try and stay alive," I remember thinking.

The doctors explained the scale of the operation.

"It's a rather major one, Mr Davies. It'll take a lot out of you."

Doctor Franklin, the stent specialist, had the assured calm of an action hero.

"You're doing great. Really great. Hold on."

Someone held my hand. The anaesthetist murmured, "Surgeons think they're the main ones. I'm the one keeping you alive."

And then it was done.

There was a sense of collective triumph, as if we had all just won something together. I spent a week in hospital. Diana, and our children Bill and Anna, visited daily, trying to make me laugh – but laughter and abdominal stitches are not natural allies. Home, then recovery. The weeks passed without London lunches or script meetings. My full-time job was simply to stay alive. Slow walks in the woods were permitted. High-calorie drinks were prescribed. Two and a half stone had vanished almost overnight. The body, confused, consumes itself before deciding it's safe not to. The days were quiet, and I secretly enjoyed the fact that no one expected anything of me for at least five weeks. The district nurse dressed the wound daily. She gazed at my substantial scar.

"My, you've been through it."

"Does it have to be that big?"

"Oh yes," she said. "They have to take everything out and put it on your chest."

I winced.

After a bit I could manage to sit up long enough to watch *Midsomer Murders*. It matched my intellectual bandwidth perfectly.

Nigel Stafford-Clark came round for lunch, really to assess whether I could work on the Marlene project we were both engaged on. Jane Tranter, producer extraordinaire, had rung me and asked if I'd like to write a biopic of Marlene Dietrich. I said yes before she'd finished the sentence. It was to be a co-production with HBO, based on the book by Marlene's daughter. On paper it had everything: Weimar Berlin in the late 1920s, smoky cabarets, *The Blue Angel*, Hollywood reinvention, war work, lovers strewn across continents, and then that extraordinary final act as a recluse in Paris, living behind drawn curtains, the glamour waned but still potent. I made it clear to Nigel that I would cling on by my teeth and fingernails. I was thinner, probably greyer, but determined not to look fragile. The idea that Marlene Dietrich might slip away from me was unthinkable. So I hung on and wrote what I still think was an extremely good first draft.

Someone, I can't remember who, suggested that Gwyneth Paltrow would be a great fit for the title role. German extraction, a classic blue-eyed blonde. Could she sing? Nobody knew. Would she be happy playing this larger-than-life character? Let's go and ask her. So Nigel, Jane and I went round to Gwyneth's Belsize Park mansion, which she shared with Chris Martin, Apple and Moses, and, as it turned out, a live-in chef and several assistants. It was quite hard to get in: there was a scary electric gate and an intercom, and then it turned out we had gone to the wrong entrance. Finally we were in, and one of the assistants told us to take our shoes off, which we did. And we were shown into a huge living room – and there she was, sitting in the middle of an enormous sofa, looking alarmingly thin, but pleased to see us, very giggly in fact, in flesh-coloured leggings. And she was a jolly good sport about everything, assuring us that however raunchy the scene, she would be up for it. At one point she kicked her legs high in the air to demonstrate her flexibility, briefly reminding me of my mother-in-law, who was fond of doing the same.

The room we were in had one of those fake coal fires blazing away at each end. The chef came in with some snacks, and then Apple appeared. She was as friendly as her mum, and seemed to take a fancy to me. "Would you like to see my rumpus room?" she said, and I said I would, never having seen a "rumpus room" before. It turned out to be a sort of home gym with nice soft surfaces to land on. Apple showed me a few of her moves, then we went back to the meeting, which continued to go very well.

Jane, Nigel and I left feeling pretty good about our Marlene Dietrich film, which of course never happened in the end. I tried to buy my script back from HBO, but they wouldn't let me. Still, we did get to meet Gwyneth. And I saw Apple's rumpus room.

*

Just as I was beginning to feel stronger, Daisy, our lovely Alsatian lookalike, got run over. Diana was walking her in the woods when it happened. It wasn't anyone's fault, not really. There was an elderly man who regularly walked three large dogs that belonged to his daughter. He struggled to control them. They spotted Daisy and gave chase. They meant no harm, but Daisy didn't know that. She bolted. Straight out of the woods and onto the road. A car came along at speed. We took her to the veterinary hospital. It was our neighbour who drove us – I had not been not cleared for driving yet. We were there for hours. Then they came out and said, "Look, she's crashed five times – we think we should let her go." Diana took it hardest. She felt somehow responsible, though she wasn't. But poor Daisy. She'd had such a hard life – a stray in Coventry, scared and lonely, then safe with us, but never quite feeling it, then run over by some guy who wanted me to pay for the damage to his car...

2009 was also the year when Jane Tranter abandoned me (well, it felt like that at the time) to go and work for the BBC in the States. It was *certainly* not a good year.

Guillermo del Toro, the Beast That Got Away and Baryshnikov

How it came about: Disney wanted to do a live-action *Beauty and the Beast*. Someone at Disney thought Guillermo del Toro would be the ideal director. And, to my astonishment, he wanted me to write the script because he was a fan of *Bleak House*. I was somewhat in awe of the great eccentric. *Pan's Labyrinth* was an extraordinary film, and I was excited to meet the man who had created it. I got on a plane to Toronto, where Guillermo was filming. The city was covered in snow. There were two lady producers, and we met Guillermo in an upmarket steakhouse.

He was physically immense, weighing nearly four hundred pounds at the time. He had a tiny, slender wife who had been his childhood sweetheart – they had sat side by side in class when they were eight years old. (I thought of my old classmate Sheila Bateman and warmed to them both instantly.) There was something tremendously boyish about Guillermo – an exuberant enthusiasm.

"You want to know why I am so big? I wanted to beat my brother. I wanted to dominate him. And he wanted to dominate me."

He was eating a T-bone steak about a foot square. The lady producers and I had dainty filet mignons. Guillermo liked me, and our version of the *Beauty and the Beast* was a go project. Emma Watson was attached from the start. The next time we met was in New York. He was staying in a strange hotel that had its reception on the thirtieth floor, which was a bit disconcerting. I soon realized that he had a Continental approach to developing a script: he would do the *scenario* and I would handle the *dialogues*. Fine by me. He set the story in 1805, at the onset of the Napoleonic Wars. He introduced a new villain: a rogue French officer bent on destruction. Unsurprisingly, the Beast would not only win Beauty's heart, but he would also remain a beast. And Beauty preferred him that way. I loved this notion. But I did wonder whether Disney would. Or indeed Emma Watson. Sexual congress with a great slavering wolf-man? Why not? And anyway, I was just the *dialogues* guy.

Guillermo draws all of his films. Not thumbnails: whole worlds. Leather-bound sketchbooks filled with images that sit somewhere between nineteenth-century illustration and graphic novel. You could see the influence of Doré, Rackham – those shadowed, haunted line drawings – but infused with comic-book dynamism. And he adored fountain pens – serious ones: heavy, beautiful, expensive. Watching him draw with one reminded me of my own childhood attachment to a Conway Stewart pen – as if the instrument itself conferred artistic legitimacy. I've grown less fussy. He hadn't.

"Disney want us to meet with Emma Watson," he said.

"OK," I said.

I wanted to ask him if he thought she was good enough to be in his wild transgressive masterpiece, but there was no point. She was attached, and that was that. She came to the hotel, and we ate dinner in a private room. We must have looked a pretty funny trio. Huge Guillermo, tiny Emma Watson and me. Guillermo was by now on a strict diet, living on steamed cabbage. Emma didn't eat much more than that. I ate quite a lot, and drank a great deal, as usual. The conversation was excruciating. Emma was very keen that the message of the film should be positive. Guillermo said it would be. I was thinking: "This girl has not really had a childhood or an adolescence: she's been chaperoned and swaddled all through the Harry Potter years, and here she is telling us what to do." I wish I could remember any of the specific things she said, but it was all just lovely and correct. Then it was over: Guillermo went off to his room, and Emma and I went thirty floors down in the lift to street level, where her driver was to pick her up.

Street level was not reassuring: quite dark, with a sort of back-entrance feel to it, and there was no sign of her driver. Various randoms wandered past, but fortunately no one recognized her. I started to get very worried, but Emma showed no indication that she might be in any danger. (I had once crossed Leicester Square on foot at midnight with Joanna Lumley and a guy in a wheelchair, and a gang of drunks had surrounded us – not pleasant, but Joanna dealt with them brilliantly.) I was acutely aware that I was in charge of this extremely valuable bit of property. I managed to make small talk for a while, then her driver eventually turned up.

I went home to Kenilworth and wrote the script. Guillermo liked it. Disney didn't. Our *Beauty and the Beast* would have been something feral, not cosy, not merchandisable. But cinema is never only art: it is finance too. And somewhere along the way the project evaporated. Disney, with its infinite resources and brand sensitivities, eventually gave the world a much gentler Beast. That's the nature of the work. Nobody told me, of course, and I only found out once the film had wrapped, with a different writer and director. Emma Watson was in it, though.

The Guillermo moments, or indeed any moment when a stranger whose work you respect says "I love what you did", are always very special. It's that sensation of being understood, of someone looking at a thing you've made and seeing exactly what you hoped they would see – or even, more intriguingly, seeing something you didn't realize you'd put there.

And sometimes it can all go wrong.

Many years earlier, I had written the screenplay for one of the worst films ever made. It was called *Consuming Passions*, and it was based on a TV play from 1973 called *Secrets* by Michael Palin and Terry Jones. The premise: three men working in a chocolate factory fall into the vat, and far from ruining the product, it improves the flavour. Merriment ensues. Mildly amusing as a one-liner, unendurable if stretched to over ninety minutes. I can't remember how I got involved. Giles Foster was directing, so maybe Louis Marks recommended me. Giles was one of Louis's favourite directors. Anyway, we were working for Sam Goldwyn Jr Some terrific actors were in it – Vanessa Redgrave, Freddie Jones – but the problem, I'm afraid, was the script, and, to a lesser extent, the direction. 24% on Rotten Tomatoes, and best forgotten.

*

But Sam was made of sterner stuff. He wanted more of me.

He was witty, cultured, educated in the way his father most definitely was not. The original Sam Goldwyn was all instinct – a man who couldn't write a grammatical sentence but could smell what audiences wanted. Junior, on the other hand, had read everything. He could talk about Chekhov and Willem de Kooning. The problem was not his intelligence: it was his decision-making. He knew all about art, but he didn't know what he really liked. Nor did he have a clear idea about what the audiences would like.

"What if," he would say, "we reworked one of my father's pictures?"

He still owned the rights to most of them, and was always thinking about revivals – not remakes exactly, but reinterpretations. One in particular involved a ghost. It had a slightly melancholy romantic premise. He suddenly decided it would be perfect for Mikhail Baryshnikov. He'd seen Mikhail in a film, playing a dancer of course, and concluded that he was not only a world-famous dancer, but also a serious actor – which was true enough. There was no dancing required in this new script, fortunately, as Mikhail was by then in his early forties and running his own company in Los Angeles.

So I'm sitting in the Russian Tea Room in Midtown Manhattan with Sam Goldwyn Jr to discuss a script, and within twenty minutes we're talking about his father's back catalogue, then about Baryshnikov, and then he says, quite casually:

"Would you mind flying to LA?"

I'd been in New York for the better part of a week. A flight to Los Angeles seemed hardly inconvenient. Why not go and meet one of the greatest dancers of the twentieth century?

"I'll make sure you have a car in LA," he said. "Take you wherever you'd like. Please, just do it."

I walked out of LAX to find a uniformed driver holding a placard with my name. Behind him, a stretch limousine for my personal use. I remember thinking, with some amusement, that my father, champion of steady pensions and incremental pay rises, would have regarded this with both fascination and suspicion. A David Hockney exhibition was on in town, so I instructed my driver, who turned out to be an aspiring songwriter and screen-writer (of course he was) to take me there before dinner. Only in Los Angeles does your chauffeur play you his demo tapes and ask you to promise to read his script. I did both. That evening he deposited me outside a restaurant fringed with red ropes and queues of hopeful diners. I stepped out of my limo and was immediately ushered past them as if I belonged. Inside, in the corner of a large room at a table yards apart from the rest, was Mikhail Baryshnikov. Compact, alert, charming. He rose, smiled and immediately dissolved any anxiety I might have had. I had assumed that dinner would be restrained – a dancer approaching middle age with battle-worn knees, perhaps nibbling lettuce. I was entirely wrong. We ate well. We drank even better. We talked and talked – about ballet, about defection, about exile, about women. He was curious and intense, with that famously dry Russian humour. At one point, leaning across the table, he said, "Andrew, I am so glad you are European. I hate Americans – except, of course, the women I have loved. But they do not understand life. You and I, we understand." That felt good. Me and Mikhail. We're European. We understand life.

At the end of the meal he asked, "Shall we have a small brandy?"

"Why not?" I said.

"Maybe medium?"

Medium it was. The evening lengthened.

Mikhail – I was calling him Misha by then – invited me to the ballet the following afternoon.

"Come," he said. "I am not dancing. But I will be there."

The next day, fully recovered, I went. After the performance, he suggested a drink with a friend. That friend turned out to be Dennis Hopper, who didn't radiate warmth. He was perfectly courteous, but with a palpable magnetic field about him and an air of danger. It was thrilling to sit there – the dancer, the actor and the writer. Then Joe Pesci turned up as well. I'd just seen his terrifying performance in *Goodfellas*. The real guy turned out to be very nice, not scary at all. Someone should have taken a picture.

The ghost film never happened, of course. It would probably have been terrible. I never saw Sam again, or Misha.

*

Unreal. Russian Tea Room, limousines, Baryshnikov, Hopper. And then, I'm back home in Kenilworth: dining-room table, new script, dog at my feet. Getting on with the next thing.

As I mentioned before, one of the most curious things about writing, and perhaps storytelling more broadly, is that we make up entire worlds and then populate them with aspects of ourselves. Fragmented versions. Exaggerated qualities. The man who is too weak to act, the woman who is braver than we've ever been, the romantic hero who dares to say what we never could. We write versions of ourselves and versions of people we've known. And then they cast beautiful actors to embody these projections. Then those actors fall in love with each other and go at it like rabbits. Well, not always. But more often than you might suppose. They don't fall for the writer. Why would they? There's a very old joke about the actress who was so dumb she slept with the writer.

A man told me once that great stars reach out directly to the audience. Ignore the script, ignore the co-star, it's just you and me. "Love me. Save me. I'll shine back at you." One damaged soul reaching out to another. Writers do something similar, though without the cheekbones. We write, in one form or another, "See me. Save me. Make it make sense." Not in a literal way – most of us would deny it, if confronted – but the impulse lies there underneath it all. There's always a bruise somewhere. For me, that probably goes back to Wales. I was loved. I know that rationally and emotionally. I am loved now. But love doesn't always land in the shape we need at the time. Perhaps that's what writing is: an attempt to retune the world. You're not conscious of doing it, but that's what's happening. Maybe. And if someone else gets it, that feels great. And keeps you going.

Changes

For a very long time Diana and I had very little – not disastrously little: we were never destitute, but modest. Academic salaries. Cheap holidays. Cheap clothes. Careful budgeting. It didn't feel like deprivation: it felt normal. And then, little by little, particularly after I was fifty, our financial situation improved. Writing began to pay properly – not overnight, but increasingly so. It didn't feel, however, as though our lives altered dramatically. We were already content. We had friends, a house that held us, routines that anchored us. I carried on living like a university professor who happened to write scripts, except that I was writing more, earning more and spending, really, about the same. Our domestic life hardly changed at all: same kitchen, same dog walks, same food on the table. There were, however, some changes.

Paul was one of my closest friends, at university and for years after. Fiercely intelligent, slightly intimidating in the way great brains can be. I admired him. He left what could have been a brilliant academic career to become a psychotherapist, working with troubled young men. Hard work, necessary work, but not well rewarded. One evening, at one of our parties, he told me that he couldn't remain friends. His wife was in love with another man, and because they couldn't afford to divorce, they continued to share the house, Paul upstairs, his wife and her new bloke downstairs. Daily humiliation. He saw me as a success and himself as a failure, and he couldn't bear that. I'd never felt I was competing with him. If anything, I felt inferior. I didn't want to lose him. Diana and I were both very fond of him. But he'd made up his mind. Losing his friendship hurt far more than any professional slight ever has. I went to his funeral in London about ten years ago, with John Cumming, the nun-fancier, who had come all the way from France. His wife was there, and spoke fondly of him. Various young men got up and spoke about how Paul had changed their lives for the better. I wanted to say how he had changed mine, but I didn't.

*

I'm quite well-off now. I never expected that, nor did Diana. "I never thought you'd turn out to be such a good little earner," she said, more than once. She believed that we would always be all right because we were sensible. I remember my father saying, "It's a nice thing to have a steady job. You get a little bit more each year, and when you retire you've got a decent pension, enough to live on." I remember thinking, yes, who would want more than that? For years I thought of the writing income as pocket money, an agreeable extra to a teaching career to be spent on treats, and later paintings. It was only when I stopped teaching that the balance shifted and the "extra" became the basic. Perhaps because it arrived later in life, it never defined me. It didn't feel transformational: it felt incidental. And yet it altered how others saw me. Sometimes that is the change one doesn't anticipate. It's a curious thing to discover that your luck can become someone else's pain.

A surprising amount of what people politely call "success" happened once the real work of life had already shifted to its next chapter. Bill and Anna were firmly established in their own worlds, and suddenly Diana and I found ourselves promoted from parents to grandparents. It's an odd graduation. Young children are in your lives once again, but without the responsibility. Bill's son Ben arrived first. Bill and Jane would bring him to Kenilworth and decamp for the weekend, looking faintly apologetic, but also delighted at their freedom. We grew used more and more to having Ben in the house.

When Ben was four, Max was born, a little philosopher with a penetrating gaze. By this point, we'd bought the house next door, which meant Diana could annexe it entirely for art projects. It became, in effect, the boys' studio. She organized "private views" of their work. Invitations were issued, drinks and nibbles served through the little hatch between the kitchen and dining room as if

The biter bitten: (left) the front jacket of my novel *B. Monkey* (1992) and (right) a detail from the poster of its film adaptation (1998), starring Asia Argento and Rupert Everett.

Marketing card for a 1992 feature-length spin-off of *A Very Peculiar Practice*, set in Warsaw and starring Joanna Kanska.

The beginning of a great season of adaptations: (top) *Middlemarch* (1994); (middle) *Circle of Friends* (1995); (bottom left) *Pride and Prejudice* (1995); (bottom right) *Wilderness* (1996) and *Emma* (1996).

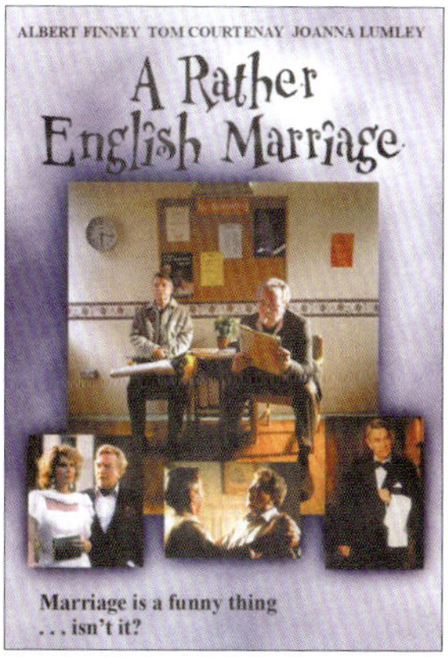

More book adaptations: (top left) *Moll Flanders* (1996); (top right) *A Rather English Marriage* (1998); (middle) my own 1989 novel *Getting Hurt* getting the treatment in a 1998 BBC adaptation; (bottom left) *Vanity Fair* (1998); (bottom right) *Wives and Daughters* (1999).

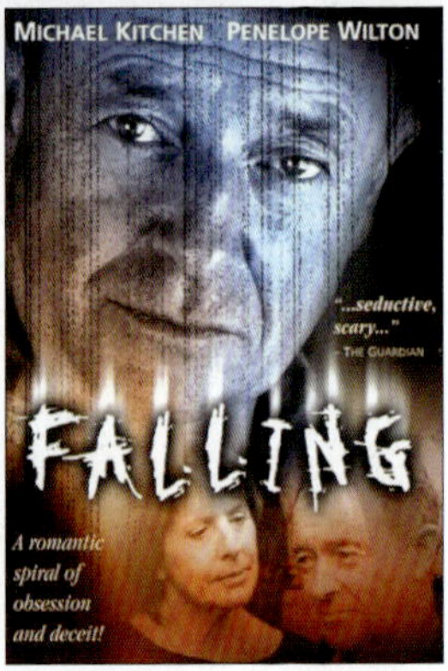

On a roll: (top) on the set of *Doctor Zhivago* (2002) with seventeen-year-old Keira Knightley; (middle left) *Tipping the Velvet* (2002); (middle right) *Falling* (2005); (bottom left) *Bleak House* (2005); (bottom right) *The Line of Beauty* (2006) and *A Room with a View* (2007).

Three more classics adaptations: (top) a Pooter for the ages: Hugh Bonneville in *Diary of a Nobody* (2007); (middle) *Fanny Hill* (2007); (bottom) Carey Mulligan in *Northanger Abbey* (2007).

Bringing more stories to the screen: (top left) *Little Dorrit* (2008); (top right) *Sense and Sensibility* (2008); (middle) *Mr Selfridge* (2013–16); (bottom) *A Poet in New York* (2014).

Some of my latest adaptation work: (top left) *War and Peace* (2016), which I celebrated at Cannes, on the occasion of my eightieth birthday, with my agent Stephen Durbridge (top right); (middle left) *Les Misérables* (2018–19); (middle right) *Sanditon* (2019); (bottom) with Vikram Seth (left) and the lead actors from *A Suitable Boy* (2020).

Some of my drawings: (left) a charcoal self-portrait from last year; (right) two watercolour drawings from recent travels in Europe.

My four BAFTAs, which I won for *Anglo-Saxon Attitudes* (1993), *A Rather English Marriage* (1999), *The Way We Live Now* (2002) and *Bleak House* (2006).

we were opening the Tate Kenilworth. The boys would stand beside their crayon-and-glitter masterpieces, gravely accepting praise. There were often shows as well: recitals, short theatrical pieces – which invariably concluded with Max flashing his bottom at some strategic moment. Art, as they say, must take risks. We took them to galleries. The Herbert Museum in Coventry was a favourite. (Lots of bare ladies.) Then their sister Sophie came too. She had a passion for Peppa Pig, and would programme our TV to show nothing else.

Warwick Castle was also a favourite, as was the Ghost Walk, which genuinely unsettled Ben, though he endured it with grim determination. The Butterfly Farm in Stratford-upon-Avon was another frequent destination. Vast tropical butterflies floated about like confetti with wings and seemed particularly attracted to my white hair. I'd stand there while they landed on me, looking as though I'd commissioned an unusually flamboyant milliner. The giant spiders in their glass cases were less welcome, though Ben faced them bravely before insisting we retreat. The day would usually conclude with a pub lunch, where snacks were served on a lazy Susan – a name which has always struck me as unfair on Susans and mystifying in general. One afternoon, Diana gave the lazy Susan a more enthusiastic spin than intended, and the entire contraption leapt off the table and clattered onto the floor. I instinctively said "Oh, Diana" in a tone usually reserved for her when addressing me. The children collapsed with laughter. They still remember it. Diana was not a woman who courted foolishness. I, on the other hand, have never been shy of it. Max and I developed an allegiance around silliness. He had that instinct for comic timing and an ability to leave people in stitches with the right facial expression. His younger sister Sophie and her friends dubbed him "Mr Silly", which he wore as a title of honour. I've never minded being that chap either. He was, like me, a bookish child. He would arrive clutching a novel of some sort, and I'd ask, "May I have a look?" He'd hand it over solemnly and warn me: "There's nothing really rude in it." Which meant there was nothing sufficiently filthy to interest me. We had rituals too – the local Italian restaurant, Zizzi, among them.

Diana once announced to the waiter, "I'd like to start with a nice glass of prosciutto." The children still recount it.

Anna and Will's children, Tom and Katie, often came to stay too, at first with their parents, later on their own, when they were old enough to travel independently. Katie has inherited something of the performance gene. She sings in a band and is wholly at ease before a crowd. I recognize something there. It is a slightly unnerving and rather profound experience to see parts of yourself walking about in later generations. Bill, for instance, shares my voice almost exactly. When he was a young adult living at home, people would ring the house and launch into conversation assuming they were speaking to me. He would gently interrupt. "I'm afraid you need to talk to my dad." Only Louis Marks seemed able to tell the difference without hesitation. When Ben and Max were born, I felt too young for "Grandpa". They called us "Andrew" and "Diana". It suited us. It still does. Anna was more traditional with Tom and Katie. All four of their grandparents were alive then, and titles had to be assigned with care. So we became "Grandad Andrew" and "Grandma Diana". By that point we were ready for it.

Mr Selfridge and a Walk Down Downing Street

Mr Selfridge sat somewhere between adaptation and invention. Selfridges, that vast flagship store on Oxford Street, stands as grandly now as it did in 1909 when Harry Gordon Selfridge, an American showman from Chicago, opened its doors and revolutionized British shopping. He flooded the place with electric light before most London homes had it. He placed the goods where customers could touch them. He turned windows into theatre sets and browsing into pleasure. He encouraged women to enter alone and stay. Whether or not he truly coined the dictum "the customer is always right", his establishment embodied the sentiment.

Kate Lewis, whom I'd first met as a junior script editor at the BBC, was now an executive producer at ITV. She'd optioned a biography of Harry Selfridge by Lindy Woodhead and took me for lunch at Julie's to talk about it. Her script editor Siobhan Finnigan came too. It was the first time I'd met Sib, and I liked her straight away. It was a lovely day, and we sat outside at Julie's. The location is unbeatable: it's on Clarendon Cross, an elegant and traffic-free patch near Holland Park. We started with a bottle of white wine, and were toasting the project when a priest came past on a bike, stopped and looked at us. Sib blushed scarlet. It was her parish priest, and she'd been caught drinking at lunchtime. It was like being in a Maeve Binchy novel. When she had recovered, they told me about the idea. It would be a big returning series. There was plenty of scope for creation. The book had lots about Selfridge himself: his family, his love life, his triumphs and his downfall. What it didn't have was the detail: the people who worked in the store, Harry's work family. The upstairs-downstairs of it, so to speak, just as we see it in

Downton Abbey for a stately home and in *Titanic* for a ship. Heaven on wheels, right? And, in truth, I didn't have a lot on, with my erstwhile patron Jane Tranter now firmly established in the States. I said let's do it.

*

Over the next few weeks, I spent time with Sib putting together an ensemble of key characters: Harry Selfridge, the ebullient showman; his shy sweet wife, who finds London difficult; Frank Edwards, man about town, who helps our hero infiltrate society, Lady Mae Loxley, ditto, and the key shop characters: Mr Crabb, the accountant, Mr Grove, Head of Personnel, Miss Mardle, dragon of the shop floor, and Agnes Towler, the youngest and lowliest of shop assistants. We had a vague plan that Agnes would rise and rise and ultimately take over the whole enterprise.

It all came to life one day when Sib said to me: "I bet you didn't know this: Miss Mardle and Mr Grove are having an affair. It's gone on for years. She's followed him from store to store."

"Wow," I said. "Maybe he goes round to her flat every Tuesday, when he can leave his sick wife – and they have a bath together. She has a firm hand with the loofah."

That little exchange generated so many good scenes. I wrote the first couple of scripts. Peter Fincham, boss at the time, liked them, and we set off to raise some money – or, rather, get some co-producers on board. We pitched it at Cannes, telling them if they got in now they'd be much better off than if they had to buy in later, after it was made. Then we went and pitched it in the States.

The money people liked it, which is always encouraging. One problem was that we didn't have any casting yet. We all thought we needed a real American for Harry, and we settled on Jeremy Piven, who had been a great success in *Entourage* as the charming but ruthless agent. "Let's hug it out, bitch!" was his most memorable line. Jeremy came over, and we went to Le Caprice. We talked about the show, and he was interested. When we said goodnight on the pavement outside, I said "Let's hug it out, bitch!" and took him in my arms. He gave me a very funny look.

We had a writing team, mostly made up of Kates. I found out I could make Kate O'Riordan helpless with laughter, so I regret to say I spent a lot of time in meetings fooling about. Kate Brooke would get very cross with me, which only made me more mischievous. I was reverting to my twelve-year-old self. Someone should have given me the cane or expelled me, but as I was the creator and show-runner, no one could. But somehow the scripts got written. The show did four seasons, forty episodes altogether, and that felt like enough. By the time it was halfway through, I was well into *War and Peace*.

*

When *Mr Selfridge* aired, it was met with that mixture of admiration and mild condescension glossy period dramas often attract. Some critics enjoyed the scale and sweep, the bustle of the shop floor, the unapologetic melodrama. Others treated it as slightly indulgent entertainment. One described it as "endearingly daft". I didn't mind that. Department stores are theatrical by design. To dramatize one without flair would have been perverse. The audience tuned in, which is what ultimately matters. In television, success is frequently proportional to confidence. And timing is everything: the slot it goes on, the day of the week, what else is going on. We got lucky. We had a cracking cast too: Amanda Abbington as Miss Mardle, Tom Goodman-Hill as Mr Grove, lovely Frances O'Connor as Harry's wife Rose and Aisling Loftus as Agnes Towler. Aisling can play naive integrity like no one else. A few years later she would be heartbreaking as Sonya in *War and Peace*. Then we had Ron Cook for Mr Crabb. There's always a nice comforting feeling having Ron in the cast. He is a show's ballast: he makes it all feel real. And then there were Katherine Kelly as Lady Mae Loxley, Zoë Wanamaker as Princess Marie Wiasemsky de Bolotoff and Samuel West as the journalist Frank Edwards. Sam is one of those actors who engages fully with his character's moral and political life. At read-throughs he'd sidle up and propose what Edwards might be investigating next. I always enjoyed that. Years earlier, his father Timothy West had played Sir Leicester Dedlock for me in *Bleak House*, and before that he'd appeared in *A Very Peculiar Practice*. That continuity is one of the pleasures of working long enough.

Around the time *Mr Selfridge* was being aired, Sam and I both found ourselves participating in a festive *University Challenge* special – Writers vs. Actors. It was all filmed in a day. Our teammate Iain Banks, ferociously clever, was the main player – or, perhaps I should say, the only one that played properly. The rest of us were somewhat less focused, partly because we were more interested in the wine than in pressing our buzzers. It was supposed to be saved until the end of the show, but no one intervened when we carried on regardless. Afterwards, Sam and I were chatting about the idea that actors are all terribly "dahling, dahling".

"We're rational human beings," he insisted.

At that exact moment, another actor bounded into the room crying "Darling!" and enveloped him in an embrace. Sam looked at me over her shoulder and said, "That never happens."

*

For every series that makes it to the screen, there are half a dozen that don't. "Downing Street" was one of those original ideas that very nearly made it and then didn't – a familiar pattern by now. It got further than many others. We had a writers' room – four of us around a table: me, James Hawes, Caroline Henry and Edward Docx. Ed was, and is, one of those fizzing-brain people I'm instinctively drawn to. A novelist, politically astute, impatient with cliché and gloriously quick. If I gently batted an idea away with an "I don't think so", he'd immediately fire another across the net. No sulking, no clinging – just momentum. It was invigorating. He later joined the writers' room on *Slow Horses*, which tells you something. That show has bite, intelligence and a taste for institutional dysfunction, all of which Ed has in abundance.

The "Downing Street" project began when producer Carl Beverly approached me. He'd seen the appetite there was for political drama. *House of Cards* had proved that audiences enjoy watching power being exercised and stealthily abused. Political drama has a particular pull: it combines high stakes with intimate rooms. The future of a country can hinge on a conversation in a corridor. It is theatre with consequences. Decisions about war, law, public morality are made by human beings who are simultaneously worrying about their marriages, their children, their image in tomorrow's papers. That interplay between the public and the private spheres is irresistible.

Carl wanted something set in the domestic heart of government. At the time the Conservatives were in government with Boris Johnson at the helm, all theatrical bluster and collapsing deckchairs. I said, "We've got to make it about a new Labour government." If you're going to invent, you might as well invent boldly. And so I created a charismatic Labour prime minister, newly elected, full of idealism and bruising intelligence, with a mixed-race wife and two teenage children. Immediately you have generational tension, media scrutiny, a modern Britain pressing in at the windows. The premise was simple and strong: a new government arrives in office buoyed by hope and is instantly flooded with crises, economic shocks, foreign-policy embarrassments, internal party rebellions, while simultaneously grappling with domestic upheaval. Power changes everything, especially at home. We began weaving strands together: cabinet rivalries, backbench mischief, special advisers with wandering loyalties, journalists sniffing blood. It would have been full of scandal, secrets and the transactional compromises that keep democracies staggering onwards. Ed, being deeply steeped in political journalism, brought texture I would never have been able to create on my own. He knew people, he knew tone – he knew how things were actually phrased when the microphones were off. Through the process I met several figures who'd been in Tony Blair's administration. At one point someone introduced me to Yvette Cooper, and I listened carefully, mining detail – not gossip exactly, but atmosphere. How does it feel at 7 a.m. when the overnight brief has gone wrong? Who really holds the pen on the speech? Where does doubt sit in the room? It became, for me, a sort of informal political education. We crafted the whole first season and sketched possible trajectories for later ones. I wrote the opening episode, the election win still echoing, boxes barely unpacked, a crisis erupting before the leftover champagne had gone flat. It had urgency. It felt real enough to be uncomfortable. We were forever hatching ridiculous ideas. One of my favourites, though it never made it past the speculative stage, was something we called "Nappygate". A very senior front-bench politician, the sort of man who publicly radiates granite certainty, secretly dealt with the pressures of high office by visiting a discreet establishment somewhere in London where a number of similarly burdened elderly gentlemen gathered to sit around in nappies and revert, temporarily, to babyhood. It was not, in our minds, salacious so much as psychologically intriguing: a private display of vulnerability among men whose public lives required the permanent performance of authority. The more dignified the politician, the funnier the image became – a room full of grand old lions surrendering to infancy. It struck us as a rather elegant metaphor for politics. Alas, the idea never quite made it off the ground. Perhaps the nation was not ready. Or perhaps the lawyers weren't. Still, we had a great deal of fun along the way.

Carl Beverly, the producer, would schedule regular conference calls so that we – or rather he – could discuss the various schemes that might or might not become television. These calls had a very particular rhythm. Carl would begin enthusiastically and then continue in that vein for the next ninety minutes without noticeable interruption. It was a performance of stamina as much as creativity. Ideas cascaded from him in a continuous stream – sub-plots, reversals, entire new series – while the rest of us listened in respectful silence, occasionally wondering if oxygen might become an issue. There was another executive producer on the calls who spoke very little. Technology being what it is, we could see her on-screen while Carl continued his extended monologue. Gradually, over the course of the call, she'd begin to move through her day: first glancing at her phone, then standing up, then putting on her coat and getting into a car. The call continued normally. At one point, she appeared to arrive at a rather smart restaurant somewhere, greeting people and sitting down at a table. Carl, meanwhile, was still in full rhetorical swing as he outlined the narrative possibilities of Act Three. Eventually her screen would go dark. The call would go on. It was, in a way, a perfect illustration of the modern development process: an abundance of ideas, heroic quantities of talking and the occasional suspicion that the most sensible participants had quietly gone out for dinner. In the end, Carl couldn't sell it.

These things happen. A script can be good, even very good, and still not find a home. But you can't spend your life grieving about unmade shows. If anything, there's a strange consolation in it. I'd have had to write the rest of the series, after all, and that would have been a massive undertaking. Work and relief often arrive together. In this case, the real gift was my friendship with Ed Docx.

James Hawes and James Hawes

A few years ago, I was invited to do a gig in Cardiff about adapting novels for the screen. The interviewer was the novelist James Hawes. I met him for a drink beforehand at the St David's Hotel on the bay, a short walk from the venue. I hadn't met Jim before, but I had read a couple of his books and found them very funny and very clever. And when I met him, I took to him even more. The event was to feature Niall Griffiths as well, who had a novel he was adapting for the screen. I think the Arts Council were worried that the audience would be vanishingly small, so they had invited two writers who appealed to very different audiences. When we got to the venue, Niall and his entourage were already there, drinking pints. Jim and I were sipping claret. By the time we got on the stage, we had all drunk a fair amount of our respective tipples. Niall, I think it is fair to say, had a rather grand opinion of himself, buoyed by the adulation of his acolytes, and he had a lot to say about his "raw and lyrical" novels.

The one he was adapting was called *Kelly + Victor*, "an intense and doomed love story". That's putting it mildly. It has a climax in which Kelly fists Victor to death. When I was able to get a word in, I said that I thought one of the tricky bits of the adaptation process was going to be how to handle the fisting scene. Niall said that he had thought of leaving it out of the movie.

"No! No!" I cried. "You can't leave it out! It's the beating heart of the book!"

Unfortunately, I had got the giggles. Very childish, but it was the only way I could deal with the hero's tragic death. Also, unfortunately, I found it impossible to say "fisting" without involuntarily making the appropriate pumping movement. This did not go down well with Niall, though the audience found it quite funny. I am sorry to say the chairman had the giggles too. Somehow, we got to the end of the evening and parted ways. It was the beginning of a beautiful friendship – not with Niall, sadly, but with Jim Hawes. *Kelly + Victor* did get made into a film, and Google says it won a BAFTA. I didn't see it, but from what I read on Wikipedia it looks like the fisting scene was in the end replaced by a more genteel choking one.

*

Around this time, another James Hawes was one of the leading directors of *Doctor Who* in its first (and best) Russell T. Davies era. He did the one where the little zombie in the gas mask says, "Are you my mummy?" So he was miffed, to say the least, when he was not invited to the big launch event. The invitation had gone, of course, to the wrong James Hawes. Not as bad as some other BBC blunders, I suppose, but right up there. The cock-up was compounded by the BBC's withdrawal of the original invitation to the novelist James Hawes.

I was in a unique position to heal the wounds, as I knew and liked them both. I arranged a slap-up lunch in a French place in (I think) Pontcanna, and the great meeting of the Haweses duly took place. Physically, no one would confuse them. James the director is small but perfectly formed – dark hair, cool and suave. James the novelist (and historian) is six foot three, bald-headed and excitable. We all got on very well and hatched a plan to adapt James the novelist's *Speak for England*. The other James was to direct it.

Speak for England is a very funny novel about a planeload of kids and teachers who crash on a remote island. One difference from *Lord of the Flies* is that there are girls – another is that the headmaster and some of the teachers survive. The Head is a mad old sod, reminiscent of my first headmaster at St Clement Danes. By the time they are all rescued, they have formed a new society, right wing and authoritarian in many respects, curiously liberal in others, such as sexual matters. When they get back to the UK, the Head sweeps to power, ousting Labour, and establishes a patriotic Nationalist government. Julie Gardner was encouraging, even though *Speak for England* was an odd title for a BBC Wales production – but then, as happens so often, there was regime change at the Beeb, and the new person in charge was uninspired by our screenplay.

So that's another show that never happened, though the three-way friendship still survives. James the director now makes Hollywood movies, while James the novelist writes brilliant books about Germany and is happily married to his third (and German) wife. I got him onto the writing team for "Downing Street", but for some unfathomable reason he was fired. But we had some jolly times before that happened.

A Poet in New York

Professional associations can blur into friendships over time, and Faith Penhale and I go back a long way. She was instrumental in getting *A Poet in New York* onto the screen, and she was the one who, a couple of years later, got the BBC to do *War and Peace*.

Dylan Thomas had been an early inspiration to me – not because I wanted to write poetry like his (though I did, from sixteen to twenty-one, and pretty bad it was), but because I felt he was a writer with a background very much like mine. Black writers and other creatives say, "You have to see one to be one" – and it can be the same for little Welsh boys too. There were no writers in my family: all teachers, miners and grocers. Writers were posh, and came in books like Palgrave's *Golden Treasury*. Then I read *Portrait of the Artist as a Young Dog*, a book of stories about growing up in Swansea and Carmarthen, and found that Dylan's childhood was not too dissimilar from mine. His dad was a teacher too. He'd been for picnics on Rhossili beach, as I had. If a boy like that could be a writer, then I could too. It has always interested me that in accounts of Dylan's life, the father dominates the story: the schoolmaster, the frustrated academic, the literary influence – while his mother indulged him, let him eat sweets in the bath and gave him unconditional love. And that was what he sought from all the women in his life.

When Griff Rhys Jones approached me about writing a drama centred on the death of Dylan Thomas, I replied enthusiastically. Of course I was the man for the job! Why had it not been done before? Griff is another one of those fizzing minds, always juggling a thousand projects, loving the stage most of all, but wanting to do a lot more. He had the instinct that Dylan's final days in New York – the drinking, the collapse, the mythology – would make for gripping television. The question floated in the air: who killed Dylan

Thomas? There were a number of suspects: doctors, enablers, even the poet himself. It could be a most intriguing whodunit.

Great idea, but I didn't want to write that. I said there are people who don't even know who Dylan Thomas was, let alone care who killed him! I thought that was a great chance to show how wonderful a writer he was, how irresistible he was, and how self-destructive and obnoxious he could be... But those great poems! We absolutely needed to showcase the poetry!

Griff was very nice about it. He laughed and said, "All right. Of course, you must write whatever works for you." His development executive was Sarah Broughton (a novelist and filmmaker in her own right, who has subsequently become a dear friend), and she and I started working together. I remember driving to Laugharne with her, and clambering over the rocks in a pair of cowboy boots I'd acquired on a trip to Texas. (Not recommended, that.)

If we were going to make good television, we couldn't simply unpick the death. We had to celebrate the life, the brilliance, the voice, the profound musicality of his readings, the chaotic love story with Caitlin, the combination of charm and ruin. I proposed framing it around the final forty-eight hours, intercut with flashbacks to his Swansea childhood and his life in Laugharne. That gave us psychological context: not just the spectacle of decline, but its roots. Laugharne mattered enormously. It's a town that seems almost designed for introspection: an estuary where the tide recedes, exposing boats resting awkwardly in mud. Dylan's writing boathouse, perched above the water, was bare and simple. He wrote *Under Milk Wood* there. He seemed, for stretches at least, comparatively settled. The rhythm of his writing mornings. The landscape doing some of the holding. There is something about that landscape that is enclosing, protective, steadying. The counterpoint to New York's glare.

The budget for *A Poet in New York* was modest. We didn't spend any time in New York at all. Cardiff was our stand-in Manhattan – yellow taxis, sections of Eighth Avenue, the Chelsea Hotel, all recreated in the backstreets of the Welsh capital. Television is very good at illusion. We did film in Laugharne, though, which Thomas described as "the strangest town in Wales" – and that felt essential. I'd written a scene with Dylan and Caitlin on a boat in the estuary – a fragile, intimate exchange. Production baulked at the perceived cost and safety issues. Frogmen were mentioned, which seemed excessive, given the water depth. Faith calmly intervened: "The boats are here already. People go out in them all the time." Her point was well made. And, without booking frogmen, we shot it. The weather wasn't friendly. It rained that soft, persistent Welsh rain that seeps into everything. We pretended not to notice. Tom Hollander played Dylan and surrendered himself to the role. He put on weight, abandoned vanity and captured that mixture of mercurial brilliance and insecurity. We had a lovely little boy to play the child Dylan, and used him while Tom read 'Fern Hill': "Now as I was young and easy under the apple boughs..." And we follow little Dylan running through an orchard, down through fields to the wide shimmering estuary.

Dylan was not a man overflowing with confidence. He had agreed to write an opera with Stravinsky, and was terrified of failing. "What do they want me for? I can't do this." That is not unfamiliar territory for any writer. As I've grown older, I still feel the nerves, though they've become companionable rather than paralysing. Dylan seemed never to reach that equilibrium. The charm that drew people to him also concealed a deep self-doubt and a dependence on intoxication to numb it. The film, directed by Aisling Walsh and produced by Ruth Caleb with Faith's steady drive behind it, became one of those smaller pieces that feel perfectly in proportion.

Dylan died in New York in November 1953 at thirty-nine, after collapsing during an American tour. There were medical complications: pneumonia, asthma, injections administered by a New York doctor attempting to revive him after yet another drinking spree. His famous final words, "I've had eighteen straight whiskies. I think that's the record", may or may not have been embroidered, but the truth was sobering enough. He was physically fragile, emotionally exhausted, creatively burdened. More important to me was the childhood, the countryside and seaside that inspired his finest poetry, his cantankerous dad and very indulgent mother, his quiet working mornings, in glaring contrast to his boisterous nights in London and New York. And I find myself wondering whether what undid him was not only drink or ambition, but distance from that anchoring presence – from place, from the quieter version of himself that Wales allowed.

Debbie Wiseman composed the music, with a beautifully simple piano riff that evokes calm, home, happiness. One of the irritations of being the writer is that I'm the first one on a project and the composer is usually the last, so often you never meet. I did meet Debbie, though, at a special screening in Laugharne with an audience Q&A, and I was able to tell her how much I admire her work and thank her for making such a potent contribution to our film. In the Q&A, one man got up and said, "You've totally destroyed Dylan Thomas for me. I never knew he was such a dishonest, lecherous drunkard. I can never read his poems again." I said, "Well, the poems are still there, still as wonderful as ever." I don't think I convinced him, though.

To quite a few people's surprise, we were nominated for a BAFTA. We didn't win, but it was great to be there. When they say "And the winner is..." I am always sure it's going to be us, and my thigh muscles tense up, ready to stand up – and then it's someone else, and I try not to growl or shout "Oh, damn!" But it remains one of the projects I care about most. And we did do a fantastic job, though perhaps I shouldn't say it.

War and Peace

We were in J. Sheekey, the fish restaurant, off St Martin's Lane – Faith Penhale, Laura Lankester and me. Suddenly Laura said: "Andrew, shall we do *War and Peace*?"

"For BBC Wales?" I said.

"Yes. Why not?"

The cheek of it appealed to me – the tail wagging the BBC dog. And I fancied a big project with Faith and Laura. Years ago, Laura had wanted to be my assistant, and I'd recommended her to Faith at Kudos. Now they were together at BBC Wales.

"Can you swing it?"

"Danny Cohen's a mad Tolstoy fan." (He was running BBC One at the time.)

"OK, then," I said. 'I'll have to read it first, mind."

*

Before there were close-ups, Tolstoy was already writing them. Before cinema learnt how to pan across battlefields and then rest, trembling, on a single human face, *War and Peace* had done it in ink. It's less a novel than a literary continent – snowbound plains, candlelit salons, cannon smoke drifting across history. Three young people – Prince Andrei, Natasha and Pierre – stand blinking in the blast of events, trying to understand who they are and how to love in a world in a state of flux. Tolstoy gives us thunder and intimacy in the same breath. The camera pulls back to show Europe on fire, then cuts abruptly to a young girl singing in a drawing room. And somehow, impossibly, both matter equally.

Meetings were arranged at the Beeb. I remember us all going up in the lift. Faith turned to me and said, "How many episodes do you reckon it will be?" Thinking about the minimum number of hours in which the story could be told, I said, "Six." Six hours for Russia, Napoleon, philosophy, snow, duels, dances, despair, fate. Quite modest, really. The meeting went well. Timing was on our side. It felt like one of those fortuitous industry moments when ambition aligns with opportunity.

*

The Penguin edition of *War and Peace* was too big and unwieldy. Feeling like a vandal, I took the kitchen scissors and hacked it in half. Now I could carry it around in two coat pockets. A Kindle version accompanied me to Antigua, where I lay under a Caribbean sun reading about Russian winters: snowstorms and sleigh bells against turquoise sea – not quite the intended climate, but surprisingly effective. Back home, I loaded the audiobook into the car and played it on a continuous loop until Bolkonsky, Rostov and Bezukhov felt as familiar as my own family. I spent hours on the sofa mapping names. There are so many. Tolstoy digresses shamelessly into philosophy, historical theory, into lengthy arguments about why Napoleon was not steering history but being carried along by it. Tolstoy had fought in the Crimean War; he understood the confusion and chaos of battle. He distrusts tidy explanations. He favoured the Mike Tyson explanation: everyone has a plan until they get punched in the mouth. But beneath the sweep of war and the dismantling of the "Great Man" theory, the novel is intensely human. At heart, it is about three young people trying to discover how to live. And the subordinate characters are fascinating too. Dolokhov, fearless fighter, passionate friend with a compulsion to betray. Sonya, the Rostovs' poor relation, hopelessly in love with Nikolai. Boris, the engaging social climber. Anatole and Hélène, the beautiful and decadent brother and sister who are the cause of so much strife and unhappiness. Laura had been rereading the novel too, and pointed out to me something I had missed: as young teenagers, Anatole and Hélène had been "too close" and had been kept apart for a while. And when you know that, something clicks.

They're still very close. TV is a visual medium. If you can't see it, it doesn't register. So I wrote a scene, very early on, where Anatole comes back from a ride and finds Hélène still in bed. "What a lazy sister I have got," he says. So far, typical brother-and-sister teasing. Then he gets into bed with her. She protests, but mildly. And gives in. Various self-styled Tolstoy experts were outraged. They, like me, had not read the book closely enough.

*

I knew the adaptation had to feel youthful and immediate. The emotional engine had to be urgent. What are these characters doing if not trying to work out who to love, what to believe and how to survive catastrophe? That is modern enough. I wrote the first draft in six months. That kind of immersion is intoxicating. To live inside Tolstoy's world without actually freezing, starving or being in a battlefield is a privilege. The book invades the study, the kitchen table, the car. Characters accompany me on walks. They sit with me when I wake in the night. If I'm doing it properly, they're not constructs, but presences. And living among them is not a neutral act. All writing is draining. You can't inhabit these lives day after day without their emotional weather seeping into your own. I cried more than once while writing *War and Peace*. There's a moment when Andrei speaks to Pierre about seeing some young girls in an abandoned orchard. He starts trying to express their innocence to Pierre, then breaks off to talk about Natasha: "It was her soul I loved!" It's such a simple line. And yet it caught me off guard. I was sitting at the kitchen table in Kenilworth, pages everywhere, a mug of tea going cold at my elbow. Outside, nothing particularly Russian was happening. But suddenly I wasn't in Warwickshire at all. I was in that orchard. Then in the dugout with Pierre. Feeling Andrei's loss.

*

Tolstoy's greatness lies partly in his refusal to protect his characters from feeling. Beneath the sweep of battles and the arguments about history, he keeps returning to emotional vulnerability – to people who barely understand themselves, yet feel everything acutely. To adapt him honestly, you have to allow yourself to feel it too. There were knotty script meetings in Kenilworth and long lunches at Poms. George Ormond, our executive producer alongside Faith, could be analytically relentless. He was particularly so around the inheritance plot. Pierre's social ascent depends on disputed wills being concealed by certain family members for tactical reasons. "The audience won't understand it," George would insist. "It has to be clearer." There were moments when I had to sit on my hands and not say, "Oh, stop it, George." We smoothed it out eventually. Laura Lankester was brilliant at safeguarding tone and spirit, Will Johnston forensic about detail.

*

In the early stages of the process, I had to go to California, to attend an event at a university in Orange County and talk to students at Chapman University. I'd been to Los Angeles before, but never to Orange County. What I hadn't anticipated was that one of the world's most respected Tolstoy scholars taught there and that *War and Peace* was his principal text and the book to which he had dedicated his life. A meeting was arranged. He turned out to be lovely. Soft-spoken, precise, with that faintly amused air that serious scholars often have when confronted with people like me. He was fluent in Russian. He'd read all of Tolstoy in the original and could move effortlessly between text, context and subtext. He spoke about Tolstoy not as a sacred monument, but as a living mind – contradictory, idealistic, moral, restless – which was immensely helpful to me. I asked him what he thought was the most important quality in Tolstoy – what he would want a dramatization to bring out.

"It's impossible to do a television series," he said, and then: "But if you are going to do such a mad thing, you must capture Tolstoy's childlike quality – his purity of perception."

That was the word. Purity. Childlike purity. The young girls in the orchard have it. Natasha has it. Pierre too, in his own way. The world is large and chaotic, and historical forces may be vast, but experience is always immediate, felt through the body and the heart. That stayed with me.

We talked about the battles too. Tolstoy had been there – in the confusion, the smoke, the incompetence and terror. That's why his battle scenes feel so real: they are not choreographed triumphs, but experiences of uncertainty. All of this fed my thinking. Once I'd finished the first draft, buoyed and slightly exhausted, I sent it to the distinguished scholar, and then waited. Nothing. I guess he must have hated it. In the unlikely event that he ever reads this, thanks for the insights, and sorry I wasn't able to please you.

*

One problem I wrestled with was: how can we make this feel Russian when it's an English-language version? I thought the music would be important. Russian bass voices, Slavic harmonies. The Rostovs sang a lot, and the songs would be Russian folk songs. There's a scene in the book after the wolf hunt, where the aristocratic Rostovs mingle happily with peasants in a big, shambolic hunting lodge. Music, drinking, wild dancing – and Natasha gets up and dances on her own, as if in a trance, and she is magnificent. "How does she know the steps?" someone asks. "It's in the blood," says an old hunter.

*

Tom Harper was chosen to direct. I was a bit taken aback when I met him, because he looked about fifteen years old. No doubt he thought I was ready for the scrapheap. He had plenty of ideas for rewrites, but kept his directorial vision close to his chest. I had seen this often enough before not to be too disappointed. Casting was crucial. For Pierre we chose Paul Dano, who was thoughtful, morally searching and capable of visible introspection. He thinks on-screen, which is invaluable for Pierre. Harvey Weinstein had either suggested Paul or been instrumental in bringing him into the conversation. Harvey was passionately keen to be involved, an autodidact with an appetite for literary prestige. For Prince Andrei, we had a bit of an argument. Andrew Scott sent in a self-tape I thought was utterly brilliant: edgy, complicated, heartbreakingly moving. Tom Harper agreed. "A great reading. He's shown us how it should be done," he said.

"Well, cast him then."

"No – he's not Andrei. He has a receding hairline. And he's too old."

"You mean he's older than you? But *everybody* is older than you!"

I didn't actually say that, of course. In the end, we cast James Norton, who was excellent. Lily James also sent in a brilliant self-tape. I was blown away. She was so fragile, so childlike, so… Russian. "Who is this girl?" I said. "Where has she been? She's wonderful!"

"Didn't you see her in *Downton*?"

Then I realized… yes, of course I had. She'd been playing a sweet silly girl. But more profound material had brought out something extraordinary. Luckily this time everybody agreed. There was a surreal conversation with Disney about her hair colour because of *Cinderella*, which she was booked to do directly after. We compromised on dirty blonde. Around the central three, Jack Lowden, Gillian Anderson, Brian Cox, Greta Scacchi, Jim Broadbent, Rebecca Front, Callum Turner, Tuppence Middleton, Stephen Rea, Tom Burke and Adrian Edmondson. What a bunch. The read-through felt like conducting an orchestra for the first and last time. Filming took place in St Petersburg and Lithuania, which was vast, beautiful and convincingly Russian.

*

We had a bit of a problem with the ending of the series. If you've read the book, you'll know how disappointing the ending is. There's a focus on young Nikolai Bolkonsky, Andrei's son, whom we've never met, and we need to be with the people we've got to know and love throughout the story: Natasha, Pierre, Nikolai, Marya and Sonya, the survivors of the war. So I wrote a scene of a family get-together *en plein air*, a lot of eating and drinking, lots of babies and toddlers, Natasha and Marya both blooming young mothers, Nikolai and Pierre both very relaxed and informal in peasant shirts. Just talk of food and babies, saying (without words): life goes on, here's a new generation, what will their story be? But Harvey Weinstein said there had to be more. Someone should say something to sum up what it's all been about. And if I didn't want to write it, he would get Tom Stoppard to. Well, I wasn't having that. I had another look at the book. Tolstoy added an Epilogue in which he reflects on free will, chance, dumb luck and destiny. And I thought that Pierre might reflect in a voiceover about all the events that brought him to this point, a happy young father married to the girl of his dreams.

And I wrote this for him: "They say that suffering is always a misfortune, but if I were asked would I stay as I was before I was a prisoner or go through it all again, I would say: 'For God's sake, let me be a prisoner again.' When we are knocked off course, we imagine everything is lost, but it's only the start of something good and new. As long as there is life, there is happiness. There is a great deal still to come."

I was glad that Harvey pushed me into doing it. He was an awful man, but he did give great notes.

After the series was broadcast, I travelled to Russia. The Russians, as one might expect, had opinions. Older viewers felt there was too much gaiety and not enough suffering. Putin was reported as saying we had captured something of the Russian soul. Not sure how I feel about that.

Les Misérables

There is, I've discovered, a curious moment that comes after you've spent several years wrestling with one literary giant. You don't retire to something modest and manageable. Quite the opposite. You look up, dust yourself off and think: "Well, then… who's next?" I don't approach "the greats" with any sense of conquest, though. It isn't about planting a flag: it's more like entering into a long conversation – sometimes a respectful one, sometimes argumentative. After a while, you find yourself debating with Tolstoy while making tea – arguing with Dickens in your head about a structural decision. You begin to feel that, if they could see what you've done, they might raise an eyebrow, but perhaps concede the point.

There is something intoxicating about scale. The most enduring novels display the whole gamut of human experience – politics, sex, faith, shame, hunger, injustice, love, grief, ambition – all of it colliding in the lives of ordinary people. They offer not merely plot, but atmosphere – not just characters, but emotional turmoil. And once you've inhabited one vast fictional continent, you rather crave another.

Victor Hugo had been prodding at me for years. *Les Misérables* is not so much a novel as a tidal surge of revolution and redemption, sewers and saints, barricades and betrayal. It dares you to attempt it. Hugo writes as if he has a camera in his hand. He pulls back to show the machinery of society grinding lives down, then pushes in close enough for you to see a tear form but not quite fall. And this, for me, is irresistible.

Having survived Russia and Napoleon, I found myself stepping towards France and revolution. Actually, it was a step back, as the whole *Les Mis* adventure had begun before *War and Peace* and then was halted by the Tolstoy project taking over.

*

When I was a little boy – about seven, I think – I had a book called *Gems from the Classics*, or something equally edifying. It was one of those anthologies designed to give children exposure to greatness. Among its treasures was the story of the bishop's candlesticks. In it, a kindly old bishop befriends a fearsome bearded ruffian, who repays the kindness by stealing his silver candlesticks in the night. When the thief is caught and dragged back by the police, the bishop calmly insists the candlesticks were a gift. I was completely transfixed by the illustration. The ruffian loomed over the sleeping bishop, torn between theft and murder, beard bristling with criminal indecision. I felt the delicious terror of it and entirely missed Victor Hugo's message. I was far more interested in whether the bishop would survive the night. And I would have been utterly astonished if anyone had told me that the bearded baddie would turn out to be the hero of the entire story.

*

Seventy-odd years later, Simon Vaughan of Lookout Point took me to lunch at Quo Vadis in Soho, now a trendy place, but at the time still preserving some of its movie-restaurant glamour.

"Great to meet you, Andrew," he said, slightly louder than necessary. "*Les Misérables*. Great idea. I could sell that in forty countries." That was Simon's gift. He sees scale immediately. Big story, out of copyright. Big recognition, big market – what's not to like?

"I'd have to read it first," I said. So I did. Structurally, it's all over the place. But I thought that could be sorted. Just after the battle of Waterloo, a rogue called Thénardier is robbing corpses on the battlefield. Meanwhile, our hero Jean Valjean is in prison under the authority of his nemesis, Javert, and in Paris a sweet young seamstress called Fantine is having a lovely time with her pals and her rich student boyfriend. I loved that last bit, which is not in the musical version of the novel.

I sorted the rest of it out with Simon's script editor of the time. Her name now escapes me, but she was great and I'd work with her again any time. We wrestled the story into a five-episode structure. Then suddenly it was all about *War and Peace* and I put *Les Mis* on the back burner.

*

When *War and Peace* became a major success, we found ourselves launching it at Cannes, in a mild state of euphoria. I remember saying casually to Tim Davie, "*Les Mis* next?" "Brilliant idea," he replied. Harvey Weinstein wanted in as well. And that was that. As with most television projects, the personnel changed. Faith Penhale, no longer at BBC Wales, had joined Simon's company Lookout Point and brought Laura Lankester and Will Johnston with her. Chris Carey joined the team as producer. All that led to more meetings in Kenilworth and more jolly lunches at Poms.

Then something odd happened. I was at home when the phone rang. It was Harvey Weinstein. He wanted to talk about *War and Peace* and the upcoming *Les Mis*.

"What do you think of the BBC, Andrew?"

"I've done so many things there – broadly speaking, I think they're great."

"I'm not a fan of the BBC," he said. "What about Faith Penhale?"

"I love working with Faith," I said.

"I don't think we need Faith. Or Simon Vaughan. Not a fan of either of them. I think it ought to be just you, me and Idris Elba as Jean Valjean. Oh, and Julia Stannard." (She had been the boots-on-the-ground producer of *War and Peace*.)

I said: "Yes to Idris Elba and Julia Stannard, no to the rest of it."

"Think about it, Andrew. You and me, we could have a great time. Make a great show. OK. I'll let you go now."

I put the phone down and phoned Faith. Next day Harvey's office phoned with fervent apologies – apparently Harvey had been having trouble with low blood-sugar levels.

*

What moved me most in the story was Valjean's relationship with Cosette. He learns to love her selflessly. It's his first genuine act of emotional generosity. And then he must accept that she will leave him. That rang deeply true. Every father who has loved his daughter understands the necessary ache of letting go. It was how I felt about my own daughter, Anna. (I was able to bring to life another tender father–daughter relationship in *Wives and Daughters*, with Bill Paterson as Justine Waddell's dad. Bill was for years the go-to man for dad parts. He seems to have played everyone's dad, including Fleabag's.)

It took nearly a year to write the scripts. It was difficult compressing Hugo into six episodes without diluting its power (and we'd thought we could do it in five!). Every draft underwent questioning. Producers and script editors came to Kenilworth for meetings. Chris Carey was an incredibly supportive producer, which is always a tonic when you are waist-deep in Hugo and doubting almost everything. He was hands-on in the best way: he was organized without being suffocating, practical without being over-anxious. He seemed to operate on a different metabolic system from the rest of us. He got up before everyone else, answered emails at a rate that suggested either superhuman efficiency or insomnia, and still had the energy to suggest a drink at the end of the day. The only small charge I level against him concerns sweet-potato fries. After Kenilworth meetings, we'd head out for lunch, and most of us tended to order the same thing: a three-cheese toasted sandwich with onion jam and sweet-potato fries. Chris, however, treated other people's fries as his demesne – or, at the very least, as communal property. He would devour his own in record time and then start tucking into everyone else's, especially mine. Apart from that, he was an excellent producer and a congenial colleague.

*

Tom Shankland was signed up to direct. I took to him straight away: he's one of those directors who is very open, and we had some great conversations. He had an inspiring vision for the look of the piece, the sweep of it, the archetypal feel of the struggle between Valjean and Javert. And, on the shoot, Tom was always calm, despite the long, long days and the flurry of questions, problems and setbacks. He would take time at the start of every day to meditate, and no one dared to get in the way of that. And he was so modest with it, too. Not your typical director at all.

The casting felt like a gift. Dominic West was great as Valjean. David Oyelowo gave Javert terrifying intellectual conviction. Lily Collins's Fantine was touching and shockingly intense, and was widely described by critics as "shattering". Adeel Akhtar's Thénardier avoided stereotype. When the series aired, the response was huge. More importantly, the show was taken seriously. Critics praised the decision to return to Hugo rather than attempt to rival the musical. Many remarked on its timely denunciation of inequality and institutional cruelty, something that resonated uncomfortably with contemporary politics.

There used to be a comfortable piece of industry wisdom that anyone over forty-five had lost their ear for the present. In my case, the opposite seemed to have happened. *War and Peace* was broadcast when I was eighty, and *Les Misérables* followed when I was eighty-two. I thought it might be all over for me when in 2009 Jane Tranter left the BBC, but the work kept turning up, sometimes in surprising forms, which is how I found myself in 2018 embarking on a new project involving Jane Austen.

Sanditon

I'd read *Sanditon* years before, but had never seriously considered adapting it. It was, after all, an unfinished novel, and there were several perfectly good, finished ones still requiring attention. But when my *Mr Selfridge* pal Sib Finnigan, now working at Red Planet, suggested developing it, I thought, "Why not? Let's have a few lunch meetings and see what we can do."

Belinda Campbell, Sib's boss, tends to favour a refined cuisine, so we went to the Cross, Kenilworth's only Michelin-starred restaurant, where we had to endure the waiters telling us what we'd just ordered in excruciating detail.

There isn't much of *Sanditon*, because Jane Austen died before she could really get going on the story, but what she managed to write is intriguing: three brothers – one an entrepreneur, one a hypochondriac, one a smouldering sexy enigma. The one who interested me most was Tom Parker, the entrepreneur, a new kind of Jane Austen man – a man who wants to change his world, not preserve it. His ambition is to turn a sleepy fishing village into a bells-and-whistles seaside resort, risking all his money on the project. A Mr Selfridge type, with a *Boardwalk Empire* project. I thought: "Wow." Maybe she was sending him up – but I wanted to take him seriously.

There was a no-nonsense girl, eldest of nine or ten children: no money, lots of go, clearly the heroine. But the most interesting of the other characters was Miss Lambe, a West Indian heiress sent to England to finish her education. What did Jane mean to do with her? There was only enough story material for half of the first episode, and Red Planet wanted a returning series, so lots of work to do. Sib and I started talking and building the world.

Our heroine is Charlotte Heywood, a spirited young woman, played in the series by Rose Williams. She arrives in Sanditon after a carriage accident brings Tom Parker into her orbit. She is instantly infected by his enthusiasm and wants to be part of his project. Also, she sees the chance to get away. Early seaside resorts were a little like Bath, places where social rules relaxed: strangers could meet, reputations could be reinvented, fortunes could be made or lost, and a certain amount of flirtation could occur.

Sanditon also contains a splendid Austen archetype in Lady Denham, played magnificently by Anne Reid, a wealthy matriarch surrounded by a number of anxious relatives hoping to inherit. Among them are Sir Edward Denham, his stepsister Esther and their impoverished relation Clara. Austen sketches them with delicious ambiguity. Something is clearly afoot among this trio: secrets, schemes and emotional cross-currents, which provided fertile ground for invention.

A few quarrels, intrigues and misunderstandings, a couple of balls, some romantic misdirection and a generous amount of sea bathing, and suddenly the unfinished manuscript began to look like a treasure chest.

The excellent Justin Young joined the writing team for the middle of the series. Georgina Lowe, with whom I had previously worked on *Tipping the Velvet*, came aboard as producer, Olly Blackburn directed and Grant Montgomery created the elegant visual world of the town. And suddenly we were off.

While the production team filmed, I was busy writing the next scripts, which meant I was acutely aware of what I'd inflicted on the actors. I'd written a lot of sea-bathing scenes, and these were filmed early in the year, when the English Channel can best be described as "invigorating". A one-minute dip on-screen might require an hour of filming in water that felt determined to freeze the cast solid. The actors endured it heroically. They even managed to look as though they were enjoying themselves. What pleased me most about *Sanditon* was that we managed to create something that felt recognizably Austen but also slightly different: a period drama with youth and energy in it that was bright, a little mischievous, perhaps even modern – Jane Austen, but not quite as you remembered her. The series ran for three seasons in total, and found a loyal audience both in Britain and internationally, the "*Sanditon* Sisterhood". The people who liked *Sanditon* liked it very much indeed. There were just never quite enough of them.

It's All Archive

I've got an archive now, at De Montfort University in Leicester. They are quite strong in Adaptation Studies there, and I've been there many times to give talks and run Q&A sessions, so it seemed fitting to let them have my archive.

In reality, it's nothing but a collection of boxes – a great many boxes of drafts, letters, notebooks, annotated scripts with crossings-out that I can't recall making – or even why I made them. Early versions of scenes that later shed half their dialogue. Old laptops. Old notebooks.

When the material was first gathered and catalogued, it was done with care and patience by the archivist, Katharine Short, whose professional aplomb lent an air of gravitas to stacks of paper that had once lived in carrier bags and box files and were becoming part of the furniture of our house. Justin Smith, professor of Cinema Television History at the university, has taken a scholarly interest in the collection too, and the thought that my work may have influence upon new generations of storytellers is a heart-warming one.

It's slightly unsettling to watch one's chaos being organized by other people: seeing it properly assembled produces a curious sense of alienation each time I visit it. Posterity doesn't come into my thinking when I write. Writing keeps me in the present. An archive gives the illusion of inevitability. But the papers tell a different story. They reveal the mess: scripts rewritten under pressure; letters dashed off in annoyance; pieces that stalled; adaptations that nearly collapsed under negotiation. There are memos that record tactical retreat, handwritten notes correcting what was, at the time, thought to be definitive. Researchers now request access. I'm often tempted to hover and point out which passages I later came to dislike. If the archive does anything useful, I hope it demystifies craft.

The archive suggests completion, which isn't a feeling that I inhabit at all. I remain very much incomplete. Still, there is something moving in the notion that one's working life has been considered worth preserving. It's a peculiar experience to encounter your own past as research material. But perhaps that is the final irony: we are all being archived daily, whether we give our consent or not. Memory does it haphazardly. I'm doing it right now by pulling thoughts from my internal filing system.

The Davies Archive holds eighty-four produced scripts and forty-three projects that were written but never made – forty-three! There's something sobering about that number. Success creates a public narrative. The unmade work creates a truer one. Laid side by side in archival boxes are titles that travelled the world and titles that stalled at development. Both form a kind of accidental autobiography. In some ways, the abandoned pieces reveal more. They were written without certainty of reward. They contain preoccupations that perhaps felt too strange, too personal, too unfashionable at the time. Recurring patterns emerge, and I recognize that I've been wrestling with the same emotional questions for decades. And, looking at it as a whole, I have come to realize that, whether produced or not, each script marked where I stood at that particular moment in my life: what I believed in, what I was worried about, what I hoped might still be true. Looking through the archive, I was struck less by the successes than by the themes that refused to go away. Certain emotional questions kept resurfacing – sometimes disguised, sometimes almost embarrassingly naked.

Patterns reveal themselves over time: the tension between law and mercy; fathers and daughters; love complicated by pride; the possibility or impossibility of change. One of the clearest examples lives in a piece that was never produced.

Idea for a Thirty-Minute Film
"Workings of the Heart"
by Andrew Davies

Edgar, a middle-aged doctor, finds himself continually haunted by memories of a girl he loved, but never made love with, in university twenty years ago. The memories of the girl come to him unbidden, at strange times: while examining a patient in his surgery, changing at the squash club, at home in the kitchen. Edgar is an easygoing, well-balanced man, moderately happily married, more than moderately successful, but the obsession grows. This could have been the real intense love affair of his life if he had pursued it, he feels – the great love of which he feels his heart could have been capable. He must, now, before it's too late, do something about it.

Eventually he advertises for her in *The Times*, and, amazingly, she replies. Feeling absurd, certain that it will be a let-down, he goes to meet her. And again amazingly, she is as beautiful as he remembers her: the girl is still there inside the forty-three-year-old woman. The same wonderful smile.

They go to a bar. She doesn't say much. Yes, she was married, but it didn't work out; she's alone now. Yes, she understands why he felt he had to see her. Yes, she knows he loved her then. And yes, she could have loved him too.

Then… couldn't we?

Perhaps, she says. It's too soon to say. She excuses herself and gets up. Lost in his dreams, he just manages to see out of the corner of his eye that instead of coming back to their table she's gone outside. He rushes out, just catches sight of her going into a big shop. (All those years ago he used to wander through Heal's with her.) Now he desperately pursues her through those acres of sofas, all that equipment for all those thousands of middle-class lives that were not theirs…

(At intervals, from the time when we first see them together, there are quick flashes – like momentary memories – of Edgar in his surgery, the counterpart of the memory flashes he has of the girl earlier on.)

Now he follows her again. A few doors down the street she turns up an alley. He follows. His path is barred by strange, grotesque-looking men. He tries to explain – he's a doctor, it's important – he tries to bribe… suddenly, they seem to understand and relent and let him in.

It's some sort of tiny theatre. He sits down among the silent audience. The curtains swish back silently. It's her! She is in some sort of weird surrealist sex show. The audience, fat Japanese mostly, love it. Edgar is terribly upset. There must be some terrible mistake. He must save her, stop the show, protect her somehow. He finds he has leapt onto the stage: he's shouting at the vile men. People are trying to drag him off.

The stage now seems huge. With a mighty effort he throws off his assailants. Now he is lying alone in some vast empty space. She leans over him: she smiles. And kisses him deeply.

Quick flash to the surgery. Edgar is lying on the floor. A nurse is giving him mouth-to-mouth resuscitation.

Lying in the huge empty space, Edgar looks up as she draws back from the kiss. She looks down at him, gives him a sweet, regretful smile, produces a knife from her bag, raises it…

In the surgery the nurse whacks him really hard on the chest several times with both fists…

Edgar's face as he lies in the big empty space.

Mingled images, Japanese blurring into Heal's sofas… the woman's face getting smaller and smaller…

The screen floods red.

The nurse: Doctor Harvey. Can you hear me? Can you hear me?

Fades away. The bangs on the chest fade.

Titles.

There are so many echoes of me in this – me, yet not me. Elizabeth Savage. Heal's. Japan. Edgar. University. It still reads like a piece I'd like to write up properly one day, and perhaps I will.

There's another title in that stack of unmade shows that always makes me smile. Seeing it typed out on an A4 list in a brown archive box transported me instantly back to the late 1970s, when Diana and I had just moved to Kenilworth and life felt bracingly new and full of possibility. Kenilworth itself struck us as a solid, respectable, mildly aspirational place. There was a supermarket two minutes away from our little house. In those days, you could leave a baby asleep in a pram outside a shop without provoking national headlines. The pavement became a nursery annex. I squeezed through the wheels and chrome and pastel blankets, and said to the manager, who was gazing out of the window, "Lot of babies today." He nodded.

"Yeah. Sexiest village in the Midlands, this is." That got me thinking. Perhaps Kenilworth was throbbing with sexual desire. So I wrote a radio play called *The Sexiest Village in the Midlands*. No one would put it on. Lost now. Good title, though. Maybe I'll write another with the same title. One day.

Getting Adapted: The Biter Bitten

Getting Hurt, and later *B. Monkey*, took me into more dangerous territory: obsession, violence, erotic charge, risk. The seeds were always there. I wrote *Getting Hurt* at a time when I was increasingly interested in what lies beneath apparent decency. The polite surfaces of English life – respectable jobs, sensible marriages, the neat hedges, as it were – had begun to intrigue me less than the fault-lines running underneath them, which were much closer to the sort of writing I instinctively wanted to do. *B. Monkey* grew partly out of something I'd read by Ruth Rendell – a novel about a woman who had once lived a criminal life but was now attempting to go straight. The premise fascinated me. What interested me was not the redemption itself, but the residue from the past. If you've lived dangerously – if you've robbed banks, carried guns – then, to my mind, that thrill can't simply vanish because you have resolved to behave better: it must linger somewhere in the bloodstream. The question, dramatically speaking, is whether that makes its presence felt when life grows dull or difficult. That struck me as fertile territory.

Beatrice, in *B. Monkey*, is trying to leave a criminal life behind, but can't forget the thrill of being bad. I wanted to explore that tension within a love story between two people who are almost comically ill-matched. Alan is cautious, thoughtful, essentially decent. Beatrice is passionate and impulsive. Put them together and you've got the ingredients for both romance and disaster. I also wanted to set the story in and around West London, which was territory that I knew well. And, of course, there was a real love affair behind it too.

Writing a novel feels very different from writing for television. For a start, with a novel you are entirely in charge. There are no producers, no commissioning editors. You're pleasing yourself.

The story pulls you along, rather than being carefully engineered in advance. I try to preserve a little of that looseness when I'm working on screenplays, but it's never quite the same. And the voice, inevitably, is not wholly yours. The novels were different.

Both *Getting Hurt* and *B. Monkey* are written in the first person. That closeness can be intoxicating. Being Beatrice in particular felt wonderful and scary – not knowing what crazy thing I was going to do or say next. When I wrote them, I'd only the roughest sense of where the stories were heading. Decades ago, I was doing a creative writing course on the Greek island of Skyros. The institute was high up in Skyros town. In the evenings, we'd go down into the town to the restaurants and bars nearer the harbour. And I found I could only get back up that tangle of alleys to my bed if I was drunk. My legs would just take me there. Magic. And writing can feel like that, sometimes.

Getting Hurt opens not with romance, but with danger: a young woman living at the edge of violence, and a man drawn to her against every instinct of self-preservation. No one in it is entirely safe from themselves. That was very deliberate. On the surface, it appears to be a crime novel, and in many ways it is, but what I was really exploring was obsession. It surprised some readers that I had gone there. Up to that point I was known for the satirical sharpness of *A Very Peculiar Practice* and the political ruthlessness of *House of Cards*. Irony, structure, language – that was the perception. The pigeon-hole they had placed me in did not include sexual obsession and moral collapse.

But it felt right to me. I'd just left teaching and there was suddenly space – mental space as well as physical time – to write with greater urgency. I'd become interested in what I privately thought of as "the bloke" as a new kind of hero. In the 1980s we weren't especially fluent in male vulnerability. I thought: "It's time to hear from him too." Out of that came Charlie Cross. Charlie has an almost naive desire to be wholly transformed by love. He longs for absolute acceptance and absolute passion – no half measures, but total immersion. What begins for him as a yearning slips into self-destruction. Blokes get their hearts broken as much as anyone else – though at that time they tended not to narrate it.

Gareth Neame, who liked dark stories about the male psyche, asked me to write a version of it for BBC Television. I had to put a bit more story into it, with the result that the film and the book are two very distinct things. Viola became a waitress and singer in an after-hours club. I wrote a song for her. Amanda Ooms played the part brilliantly, and Ciarán Hinds was Charlie, a big bloke blundering into chaos. In this version, he's still married, with a young teenage daughter and a Diana-like wife played by Miranda Richardson. At one point, she calls Charlie a "cunt-struck moron" – a line she delivered with beautiful precision, as you would expect. We used a lot of Harry Holland paintings in the film, as in the book, and that feeling you get of brooding uneasiness in some of Harry's paintings pervaded both book and film.

The screen adaptation of *Getting Hurt* had a mixed reception. *Time Out* (still influential then) called it "sexist rubbish" – but I loved it. It was never produced as a DVD, and you can't get it on iPlayer. I'm in the process of trying to get a copy from the BBC archives, just because I long to see it again.

*

B. Monkey fared even worse, despite its promising beginnings. A producer called Colin Vaines read it and liked it so much that he had someone do what's known in film circles as "coverage" – which is a brisk one- or two-page summary evaluating how it might work as a film. Apparently, the coverage was lively and persuasive. After that, things moved with surprising speed. Colin got the money for me to write the script, and Michael Caton-Jones was brought in at an early stage as director. He had directed my comedy drama *Lucky Sunil*, which had done well. Michael was establishing a strong reputation: he was sharp, instinctive, independent-minded. We got on very well. He loved my script, and had a lot of good ideas for making it even stronger.

Then, as I mentioned before, Harvey Weinstein got involved. Harvey had a famously brutal method of operation: he liked control and applied pressure. Directors generally yielded to him. Michael did not. Eventually, he was removed, and so was I. Another writer was brought in to rewrite the script. I couldn't see why the film shouldn't stay very close to the book – but I didn't have the rights: Harvey did. And he could do what he wanted – which, in the end, he did. The project was rewritten again. Another director was dismissed. Rupert Everett was brought in as Paul, the posh drug dealer, and that character seemed to take over the entire film. Jared Harris played Alan. The young Italian actress Asia Argento played Beatrice, so rather than the girl having an Italian mother, she simply became Italian, which complicated things rather unnecessarily. What emerged was not, I felt, a good film.

I know what you're thinking: Davies can hand it out, but he can't take it. All over *Sanditon* like a cheap suit, and when someone does it to him, he's whining like a little bitch.

Fair enough. But it hurts, all the same.

A Suitable Boy

I first read *A Suitable Boy* about twenty years ago, when someone asked, rather tentatively, whether I might consider adapting it. I remember reading it and thinking that it was perfect as it stood – that perhaps nobody should meddle with it. But then, in 2019, Laura Lankester asked me to do it, and since it was Laura, I said why not. By that point, I'd already tackled a Russian masterpiece and a French one, and I thought it might be time to turn to an Indian one. And it turned out that Charlotte Moore at the BBC thought this was just right for the time. First, we had to convince Vikram Seth to entrust his novel to me, then we had to convince the BBC. It wasn't so hard, as it turned out. Vikram had seen *War and Peace* and loved it. We took him for lunch at the Ivy. Vikram is a man of formidable intelligence and cultural range, and on this occasion he appeared to feel that we should be cross-examined for evidence of our own knowledge. The conversation drifted towards Shakespeare, and it wasn't long before he was quoting lines and inviting us to complete them or identify the play. It became, rather quickly, a sort of literary quiz. Now, there are people who would become visibly anxious under these circumstances – the faint terror of appearing insufficiently educated in front of a celebrated novelist. I was worried about Stella Merz, our new junior script editor, but she couldn't have looked less troubled. Poor Will Johnston, the executive producer, a very handsome chap, had to wear a rose between his teeth for Vikram's delectation. He did that with style and charm, and what with Faith's expert schmoozing, a lavish lunch and a few bottles of champagne, we sealed the deal. Vikram approved of us – and we all warmed to Vikram, this diminutive, supremely gifted guy who had been struggling to write the sequel to *A Suitable Boy* for years and carried the manuscript with him wherever he went. I thought if he could only submit himself to

Laura and Faith, they'd solve his problems, whatever they were, in no time.

Mira Nair, the distinguished Indian director, joined us, and her contribution was crucial. Firstly, she cast Indian actors from the subcontinent – no one familiar to the British or American audiences, although Ishaan Khatter and Tabu were huge Bollywood names. This created some co-production problems: no one wanted to put their money into the show, since there were no recognizable stars. We had originally planned eight episodes, but budget restraints meant that we had to cram the material into six, losing some of our favourite sub-plots. The other decision Mira made was to put more of the dialogue into Urdu. (Vikram had written his novel in English, with English dialogue.) Mira's decision here was a good one, as the Indian actors were of course more comfortable and fluent in the language they knew best. And everyone can read subtitles.

At the heart of this deceptively simple story is a girl called Lata Mehra, played in our adaptation by Tanya Maniktala, and the eternal, irresistible question: whom will she marry, if anyone? Around that personal dilemma swirls the wider turbulence of an emerging nation: India in 1951, still absorbing the shock of Partition a few years before – political tensions, religious divisions, economic fragility. But Vikram does something extraordinary: he places enormous historical weight around what is, at its core, a domestic question. I made an early decision to concentrate primarily on Lata and the male protagonist, Maan, allowing their trajectories to serve as the emotional backbone of the story.

Working with Vikram Seth was a great privilege. There is something slightly daunting about adapting the work of a living author of such brilliance. But from the outset he was generous. Another great experience was going to India to watch the shooting.

A Suitable Boy aired in 2020, when the world rather abruptly came to a standstill because of the global pandemic. Streets were empty, productions had halted, audiences were confined to their homes – anxious, isolated. There was something almost surreal about releasing a sweeping, sensuous drama crowded with weddings, music, political rallies at a moment when human proximity itself had become suspect. Perhaps that was partly why it resonated. Critics were, by and large, generous. There was praise for the scale and ambition of the film, for Mira's direction, for the performances – particularly Ishaan's restless Maan and Tanya's poised Lata. Some regretted the necessary compressions – that was inevitable. Others admired the way the series balanced intimate romance with the tremor of a new nation finding its shape. For many viewers, both in Britain and India, it offered immersion at a time when escape was not frivolous, but curative.

Looping Back

I've been thinking about my mother more lately. I'm not sure why. Possibly because I know I'm going to die soon. Not this week, I hope. But it's there, floating about, hovering just behind the clink of the coffee cup or the rattle of the post. I've got things I still want to do: a life class or two, some ideas to wrestle into shape, the usual dramas waiting to be written. But still, there's this unresolved situation. Her. Hilda, my mother.

She had a strange hold over me, an almost psychic power – or so it seemed. She died after a stroke – a long time after. I remember going to see her, in our house in Rhiwbina, the house I grew up in, the three-panel mirror in the bedroom still intact. The bed, the floral carpet, that half-sour smell of antiseptic and talcum powder. I sat next to her on the bed, something I hadn't done since I was a child. And she was changed: her body swollen, her eyes wild – not with emotion, but with the broken circuits of her mind. It was hard to look directly at her, so I looked in the mirror instead. But even that was unbearable: that mad stare, her face multiplied by hundreds, receding into infinity, smaller and clearer, ugly, inescapable. That woman wasn't my mother – except, she was. And that mad gaze was saying: "Look what you did to me." How do we find forgiveness when it's all already gone too far? How do you make peace when the other person can no longer understand the conversation? How do you make peace when you're still full of rage? In the end, I didn't say anything. I didn't take her hand. I couldn't.

*

At her funeral, I was consumed with anger. All these nice old Welsh blokes coming up to me: "Oh, God – you look so much like Hilda! You could almost be her... you're the spitting image of her!" Sod off! You think that makes me happy? You think I *enjoy* looking like her?

There was no dramatic reconciliation, just the silent work of understanding. Ha ha ha… as if… I try to offer Hilda the same empathy I offer the characters I write. But I can't. Anger always takes over. Why couldn't you just simply love me? What the *hell* was the matter with you? I try to make space for her, for the girl that she was, and the woman that she never got to be. Try to like her. Can't do it. Wish I could. Hilda Davies, née Jones. She made me, in more ways than she knew. And I carry her with me still. In my voice, for example. And I see her every time I look in the mirror. Wide shoulders. Hooded eyes. White hair. Sagging body.

"God, boy! I thought you was her for a moment! Spitting image!"

She died before most of the big stuff happened – before the adaptations, the BAFTAs, the reputation. How would she have felt about it all? Who knows? She might have been proud. She might have taken credit for it. I was her boy after all, and she was the one who pushed and encouraged me to sing the songs, go in for competitions, not to shy away.

My mother died in her early sixties – far too young, really – and left my father utterly adrift. He was stunned, hollowed out. He had nursed her for two years, taking early retirement from the job he loved to do, and yet he managed to write a book about language and structuralism to pass the time. For months after her death, he drifted around the house like a bewildered ghost. I'd visit, and he'd try to be brave about it, but you could see the confusion and anger in his face: "Where has everyone gone? Why do the neighbours suddenly cross the road?" Why, when death is the most natural and inevitable thing in the world, do people behave as if it's the most awkward? He was lonely. And wounded. Then he went a bit crazy. He went off to America, leaving the back door open, to look up long-lost relatives. When he came back, he was a different man – or, rather, the man he had always had it in him to be. He started to go out, see exhibitions, meet people. And he met Tessa, a young widow in her thirties. She worked for the Welsh

Arts Council, and all her friends were in the art world. He became something of a man about Cardiff and developed a friendship with Harry Holland, the painter. He asked Tessa to come to Paris with him, and she said yes, and they had a ball. And she was with him until he died, at ninety-six.

And this new Wynford was much more extrovert, was much more the life and soul of the party. It was as if my mother had stopped him from blossoming, or something. She always had to be the centre of attention, and now it was his turn. And he was never embarrassing, and you never had to worry about him: he could flourish in any group. Through Tessa he became much more political, went on marches in his best dark overcoat. Tessa, of course, never met my mother, but she heard a lot about her from my dad. And the Hilda she heard about was not exactly the one I knew. Tessa told me, after Wynford died, that they had talked about Hilda – how she might be up there in heaven looking down on them, happy about their happiness with each other and their fulfilled lives. "Oh, no," I thought. If she could see them, she'd have been bloody furious. Or maybe not. What do I know? What do any of us really know about each other?

*

And so, if I were to loop back anywhere, it wouldn't be to Soho or Bloomsbury. It would be to Wales – to Rhiwbina Garden Village, with its clipped verges and white-rendered houses standing in reasonable formation, to Lon-y-dail, to the small, contained world in which everything appeared manageable if the hedge was trimmed and the blackout curtain drawn properly. It begins there, with Hilda, whether I like it or not. I think my mother believed, quite sincerely, that she was special – not extravagantly gifted, but marked out in some essential way. She carried herself with that assumption, and she passed that on to me. Maybe we all feel special, to ourselves. In fairness to her, she was good at teaching, for the short while she did it. She had clarity, authority, a sharpness that kept children alert. I can imagine her in a classroom being brisk, organized, not easily trifled with. But at home I cannot recall her being curious – I don't remember her reading widely. It was as though she believed that being herself, being Hilda, was enough.

I spent years resisting her. And yet the impulse began with her. It began with watching a woman who felt thwarted, with sensing, long before I had language for it, that lives could narrow without anyone noticing. If I've spent my working life writing about women deciding how to live, it is not accidental. Hilda was the source of that. She made me, in more ways than either of us understood.

*

And now what? I feel as energetic, writing-wise, as I have ever done. I want to write a novel set in the Fifties, a first-person narrative by a girl like Diana, from a working-class background in Yorkshire, the first of her family to go to university. At my age, the desire to write about her feels less like ambition and more like unfinished business – not because I imagine it would cause a revolution, but because beginning something, inventing a new consciousness, remains the most reliable rebuttal I know to endings. People speak solemnly about legacy. I find myself more interested in appetite: the appetite to observe, to question, to prise open the corsetry of an era and see what was wriggling underneath. If I am approaching a final chapter – and who isn't? – I would rather it be written with forward momentum.

Diana is waiting, and it would be rude to keep her standing there indefinitely. And yet I do. She sits there. An eternal challenge. A quiet insistence that I look again, properly this time, at that period – at the world as it appeared through her eyes rather than my own. It is all in my mind's eye. Students pouring into Foster Hall for the first lecture of the new term. I'd begin there, where I first saw Diana. I was sitting behind her. She turned, glanced at me – not dramatically, not knowingly: simply looked. And in that look there was curiosity, appraisal, the faintest hint of challenge.

That is where the story would begin. Who knows how far I'd manage to go with it – retrieving all those feelings of that time, hers and mine entangled. It might be uncomfortable. Memory often is. But it would be bracing to attempt it – to see those early days not through nostalgia, not through male recollection, but through the sharper, more precarious lens of a young woman negotiating a world that was simultaneously expanding and constricting. It might be painful, but it would probably be worth doing before too long.

But there are other projects to be completed first: *Mansfield Park*, which now might become a stage show at the Belgrade Theatre as well as a TV series; a celebration of Guy Burgess, the most outrageous of the Cambridge spies; an adaptation of Jane Austen's *The Watsons*, with Stella Merz. I want to see a six-part drama about Dickens to the screen, as well as my twelve-hour "Rabbit" saga from Updike's novels.

Once those are finished, I say, I will turn to Diana. Then I'll begin. The thought process is painfully familiar. The project not yet undertaken always gleams more attractively than the ones in progress. The unwritten book glows with possibility; the written one reveals its compromises. I know perfectly well that once I begin Diana's story, something else will sidle up beside me, whispering seductively about its own urgency. And whether I write Diana's story or not, the argument with Hilda, about how to live, how to love, how not to shrink, is the one that started it all.

Make no mistake. I'm not finished yet.

*

In the process of sharing my story, I have become even more convinced that writing, like life itself, always involves a certain amount of wrestling with uncertainty. The trick is not to panic. Fear is the most efficient way of blocking the process, and I've learnt, over a long apprenticeship, that the best response is simply to keep going. The mind, after all, is still there. It belongs to me. The work may take a little longer some days, but the instincts remain intact. So far, at least. I keep an eye out for slips. If they appear, I'll notice. Sometimes I dream that I'm in the early stages of Alzheimer's and can't locate myself – unable to remember what I'm doing even as I'm doing it. Oddly, I'm never frightened. I assume, even inside the dream, that things will be all right in the end. That's generally been my working philosophy. Most things, in the end, sort themselves out, or else become irrelevant. I steady myself. There may come a day when I decide I've done enough. I can imagine enjoying a quieter life: reading more, watching television without professional analysis intruding every five minutes. At the moment, though, those things feel slightly illicit – guilty pleasures rather than retirement plans. Even now, if I find myself idling in front of the television for too long, a small internal voice eventually pipes up:

"Stop doing that. You ought to be writing!"

WORKS

Key to the abbreviations: (B) fiction work or novelization of a TV film or series; (CB) children's book; (EP) educational programme; (F) feature film; (M) musical; (P) stage play; (PAN) pantomime; (POE) poetry; (RP) radio play; (SIT) sitcom; (TVF) TV film; (TVP) TV play (what would later be called "TV film"); (TVS) TV series; (TVSP) TV school programme.

Works in Progress

The Rabbit Novels of John Updike (TVS)
Mansfield Park (TVS), adapted from a novel by Jane Austen
The Mystery of Charles Dickens (TVS)
The Watsons (with Stella Merz) (TVS), adapted from a fragment by Jane Austen
Our Guy in Washington (F)

Produced Titles

The School (RP), 1960
Student Teacher (RP), 1964
The Hospitalization of Samuel Pellet (RP), 1964
A Day in Bed (RP), 1967
Getting the Smell of It (RP), 1967
Who's Going to Take Me On? (TVP, RP), 1967, 1969
Is That Your Body, Boy? (TVP), 1970
Come on Then, Astonish Me! (RP), 1970

Filthy Fryer and the Woman of Maturer Years (RP, P), 1970, 1979
The Innocent Eye (RP), 1971
Steph and the Man of Some Distinction (RP), 1971
The Fantastic Feats of Doctor Boox (CB), 1972
The Short-Sighted Bear (P, RP), 1972, 1978
Steph and the Simple Life (RP), 1972
No Good Unless It Hurts (TVP), 1973
The Water Maiden (TVP), 1974
Grace (TVP), 1975
Can You Smell Gas? (P), 1975
The Imp of the Perverse (TVP), 1975, adapted from a story by Edgar Allan Poe
Over to You (with George Moore) (EP), 1975
Rohan and Julie (P), 1975
A Martyr to the System (TVP), 1976
Randy Robinson's Unsuitable Relationship (P), 1976
Steph and the Zero-Structured Lifestyle (RP), 1976
The Signalman (TVP), 1976, adapted from a story by Charles Dickens
Eleanor Marx (TVS), 1977
Going Bust (P), 1977
Happy in War (TVP), 1977
Teachers Gone Mad (P), 1977
Conrad's War (CB), 1978, winner of the Guardian Children's Fiction Prize
Brainstorming with the Boys (P), 1978
Fearless Frank (P, M), 1978
Renoir, My Father (TVP), 1978
Stabs at the Simple Life (P), 1978
Battery (P), 1979
Diary of a Desperate Woman (P), 1979
The Legend of King Arthur (TVS, B), 1979
Marmalade and Rufus (CB), 1979 (repr. in 1982 as Marmalade Atkins' Dreadful Deeds)

Accentuate the Positive (RP), 1980
After the Gold Rush (TVP), 1980
Babes in the Wood (PAN), 1980
Rose (P), 1980
To Serve Them All My Days (TVS), 1980–81, adapted from a novel by R.F. Delderfield
Bavarian Night (TVP), 1981
Marmalade Atkins in Space (CB), 1981
Dark Towers (TVSP), 1981
Educating Marmalade (TVS, CB), 1983
Heartattack Hotel (TVP), 1983
Diana (TVS), 1984, adapted from a novel by R.F. Delderfield
Badger Girl (TVSP), 1984
Campus Blues (RP), 1984
Danger: Marmalade at Work (CB), 1984
Marmalade Hits the Big Time (CB), 1984
Baby I Love You (TVP), 1985
Pythons on the Mountain (TVP), 1985
Alfonso Bonzo (CB, TVS), 1986, 1990
A Very Peculiar Practice (TVS), 1986–88
Time after Time (TVS), 1986
Inappropriate Behaviour (TVP), 1987
Thermal Underwear (P), 1987
Consuming Passions (F), 1988
Lucky Sunil (TVF), 1988
A Private Life (TVF), 1988
Ball-Trap on the Côte Sauvage (TVF), 1989
Mother Love (TVS), adapted from a novel by Domini Taylor (Roger Longrigg), 1989
Getting Hurt (B, TVF), 1989, 1998
Dirty Faxes and Other Stories (B), 1990
House of Cards (TVS), adapted from a novel by Michael Dobbs, 1990
Poonam's Pets (with Diana Davies) (CB), 1990
Prin (P), 1990

Filipina Dreamgirls (TVF), 1991
Anglo-Saxon Attitudes (TVS), 1992, winner of a BAFTA TV Award for "Best Drama Serial", adapted from a novel by Angus Wilson
B. Monkey (B, F), 1992, 1998
A Very Polish Practice (TVF), 1992
The Old Devils (TVS), 1992, adapted from a novel by Kingsley Amis
Anna Lee: Headcase (TVM), 1993, adapted from a novel by Liza Cody
To Play the King (TVS), 1993
The Boot Street Band (TVS), 1993–94
Harnessing Peacocks (TVF), 1993, adapted from a novel by Mary Wesley
A Few Short Journeys of the Heart (TVF), 1994
Middlemarch (TVS), 1994, adapted from a novel by George Eliot
Raj in Charge (with Diana Davies) (CB), 1994
Circle of Friends (F), 1995, adapted from a novel by Maeve Binchy
Game On (with Bernadette Davis) (SIT), 1995–98
Pride and Prejudice (TVS), 1995, adapted from a novel by Jane Austen
The Final Cut (TVS), 1995
Emma (TVF), 1996, adapted from a novel by Jane Austen
The Fortunes and Misfortunes of Moll Flanders (TVS), 1996, adapted from a novel by Daniel Defoe
Wilderness (with Bernadette Davis) (TVS), 1996, adapted from a novel by Dennis Danvers
Bill's New Frock (TVF), 1997, adapted from a novel by Anne Fine
A Rather English Marriage (TVF), 1998, winner of a BAFTA TV Award for "Best Single Drama", adapted from a novel by Angela Lambert
Vanity Fair (TVS), 1998, adapted from a novel by William Makepeace Thackeray
Wives and Daughters (TVS), 1999, adapted from a novel by Elizabeth Gaskell

Take a Girl Like You (TVS), 2000, adapted from a novel by Kingsley Amis

Bridget Jones's Diary (F), 2001, adapted from a novel by Helen Fielding

Othello (TVF), 2001, adapted from a play by William Shakespeare

The Tailor of Panama (F), 2001, adapted from a novel by John Le Carré

The Way We Live Now (TVS), 2001, winner of a BAFTA TV Award for "Best Drama Serial", adapted from a novel by Anthony Trollope

Daniel Deronda (TVS), 2002, adapted from a novel by George Eliot

Doctor Zhivago (TVF), 2002, adapted from a novel by Boris Pasternak

Tipping the Velvet (TVS), 2002, adapted from a novel by Sarah Waters

Boudica (TVF), 2003

He Knew He Was Right (TVS), 2004, adapted from a novel by Anthony Trollope

Bridget Jones: The Edge of Reason (F), 2004, adapted from a novel by Helen Fielding

Bleak House (TVS), 2005, winner of a BAFTA TV Award for "Best Drama Serial", adapted from a novel by Charles Dickens

Falling (TVF), 2005, adapted from a novel by Elizabeth Jane Howard

The Chatterley Affair (TVF), 2006

The Line of Beauty (TVS), 2006, adapted from a novel by Alan Hollinghurst

The Diary of a Nobody (TVS), 2007, adapted from a novel by the Grossmith brothers

A Room with a View (TVF), 2007, adapted from a novel by E.M. Forster

Fanny Hill (TVS), 2007, adapted from a novel by John Cleland

Northanger Abbey (TVF), 2007, adapted from a novel by Jane Austen
Affinity (TVF), 2008, adapted from a novel by Sarah Waters
Brideshead Revisited (F), 2008, adapted from a novel by Evelyn Waugh
Little Dorrit (TVS), 2008, adapted from a novel by Charles Dickens
Sense and Sensibility (TVS), 2008, adapted from a novel by Jane Austen
Sleep with Me (TVF), 2009, adapted from a novel by Joanna Briscoe
South Riding (TVS), 2011, adapted from a novel by Winifred Holtby
The Purple Land (RP), 2011, adapted from a novel by William Henry Hudson
The Three Musketeers (F), 2011, adapted from a novel by Alexandre Dumas
Mr Selfridge (TVS), 2013–16
A Poet in New York (TVF), 2014
Quirke (TVS), 2014, adapted from the novels by Benjamin Black
War and Peace (TVS), 2016, adapted from a novel by Leo Tolstoy
Les Misérables (TVS), 2018–19, adapted from a novel by Victor Hugo
Sanditon (TVS), 2019, adapted from an unfinished novel by Jane Austen
A Suitable Boy (TVS), 2020, adapted from a novel by Vikram Seth
Pride and Prejudice (P), 2021, adapted from a novel by Jane Austen
Emma (P), 2023, adapted from a novel by Jane Austen
Persuasion (P), 2026, adapted from a novel by Jane Austen

Selected Unproduced Titles

The Accident Man (RP)
The Boleyn Inheritance (F), adapted from a novel by Philippa Gregory
The Book Group (F)
Charlie (Chaplin in America) (TVS)
The Child in Time (F), adapted from a novel by Ian McEwan
The Count of Monte Cristo (F), adapted from a novel by Alexandre Dumas
Donna Joanna (TVS)
Feeling All Right (RP)
Foreign Languages (F)
From a View to a Death (TVF), adapted from a novel by Anthony Powell
Hope I Never Go in One of Those (RP)
Just Friends/My Time With Prue (TVF)
Keep Me Company (TVF)
London Belongs to Me (TVS)
Marlene (TVF)
Mayakovski (F)
The Misogynist (F), adapted from a novel by Piers Paul Reed
The Monk (F), adapted from a novel by Matthew Gregory Lewis
The Moon Is Down (F), adapted from a novel by John Steinbeck
My German Summer (F), adapted from a novel David Lodge
A Nation's Health (TVF)
Norah Docker (TVF)
The Perfect Mile (F), adapted from a novel by Neal Bascomb
Phineas Finn (TVS), adapted from a novel by Anthony Trollope
The Pigs Who Went to See the World (with Diana Davies) (CB), 1991
Poems (POE)
Pope Joan (TVF), 1997–98
The Robber Bride (TVS), 2003–04, adapted from a novel by Margaret Atwood

Rossini! Rossini! (F), 1989
The Russian Girl (TVS), 1996, adapted from a novel by Kingsley Amis
Season of the Witch (F), 2009
The Sexiest Village in the Midlands (RP)
The Slaves of Solitude (TVF), 2009, adapted from a novel by Patrick Hamilton
Speak for England (TVF), adapted from a novel by James Hawes
The Spoils of Poynton (P), adapted from a novel by Henry James
The Tortoise and the Hare (F), 1995–98, adapted from a novel by Elizabeth Jenkins
Working Well (RP)